Winning
with the
American Quarter
Horse

DON BURT

DOUBLEDAY
NEW YORK LONDON TORONTO SYDNEY AUCKLAND

PUBLISHED BY DOUBLEDAY
a division of Bantam Doubleday Dell Publishing Group, Inc.
1540 Broadway, New York, New York 10036

DOUBLEDAY and the portrayal of an anchor with a dolphin are trademarks
of Doubleday, a division of Bantam Doubleday Dell Publishing Group, Inc.

All rules and excerpts from the American Quarter Horse
Association rule book are reprinted with permission.

Book Design by Beverley Vawter Gallegos

Library of Congress Cataloging-in-Publication Data
Burt, Don.
Winning with the American quarter horse /
Don Burt. — 1st ed.
p.   cm.
Includes index.
1. Quarter horse—Showing.
2. Quarter horse—Exhibitions.
I. Title.
SF293.Q3B87   1996
798.2'4—dc20   95-45235
CIP
ISBN 0-385-46813-X

Without the "Lady" that keeps this cowboy
on the straight and narrow,
this book would not be a reality.
Her encouragement, dedication, and tenacity
kept it focused and on track,
and should rightfully bear her name as coauthor.
The "Lady" is my best friend and partner,
my wife, Ardys.

ॐ

Acknowledgments

Deepest thanks to the American Quarter Horse Association and staff, and the *Quarter Horse Journal* and staff for all their help in the preparation of this book.

Thanks also to the many people who contributed to various chapters through their lectures, teachings, and published articles.

Dr. G. F. "Andy" Anderson
Dr. G. Marvin Beeman
Dr. Milton Kingsbury
Dr. Deb Bennett
Bob Loomis
Clay MacLeod
Pete Kyle
Chip Knost
Bruce Beckman
Judy Richter
Patty Boxell
Shannon McCullough

ILLUSTRATIONS

BY

NANSE C. BROWNE

RENOWNED ARTIST

AND SCULPTRESS

Contents

Introduction

UNDERSTANDING THE HORSE

UNTIL the invention of the automobile, the horse was an essential component in the life of almost every American family. Today the power of the horse is no longer essential, but the animal still remains an intrinsic vehicle in the lives of countless individuals. The old saying that "the outside of a horse is good for the inside of a man" was never more true. While we no longer rely on them to get us from Point A to Point B, horses today provide a rewarding counterbalance to the stresses of our high-tech world. From the pleasure of relaxing on a trail ride or competing on a cutting horse to the rigors of steer roping, equestrian activity is a welcome way to reestablish our sense of physical well-being while honoring the tradition of interdependency that has long sustained both man and beast.

Before we begin a discussion of Quarter Horses in particular, there are a few things you need to be aware of to thoroughly enjoy and appreciate the merits of any horse. The first prerequisite is to understand how a horse thinks. We can do this by comparing horses to computers. Horses already come programmed with an operating system that we cannot change—those fundamental aspects of how the horse behaves. The software that we will add must be compatible with that operating system. If the two don't jibe, no amount of earnestness on our part will ever get that animal to perform the tasks we have set for it. The result will be endless frustration, since if you don't program a computer or a horse for the correct response, it will not perform to your command.

Horses do not have the ability to reason. You must realize that a horse's will is governed by feelings of pleasure or discomfort. Its mind is capable only of direct association of ideas—cause and effect. Horses have excellent memories; thus, for example, if they are punished repeatedly, they will associate the misconduct and the maltreatment. The horse's relationship to humans is ultimately one of trust or mistrust.

There is no magic formula to train a horse effectively. The handling and training of horses are limited only by lack of knowledge, time, and desire. To be a successful trainer, you need to understand a horse's three basic instincts: fear, mating, and hunger. Even though the instinct of fear determines the approach for training the horse, you will not be successful if the horse is afraid of you. Trust must be established between horse and trainer.

1

The horse is not a naturally aggressive or combative creature. In other species, the mating instinct or even hunger may be dominant. But in horses the dominant instinct seems to be fear. This fear isn't a pathological, permanent state, which would be abnormal, but rather a fear of some danger the horse has perceived through its sense of sight, smell, hearing, touch, or intuition.

When its basic fear of predators is stimulated, for example, the horse's instinctive reaction is to hide or run away. Only if it is blocked or cornered, unable to escape, will it fight back. On the other hand, horses are constantly seeking security and comfort in some safe place. Once you've given the horse this safety, and once you've earned its trust, it will overcome its fear and come to you. But there's no way you can get a horse to work with you effectively if it hasn't first gotten rid of its fear and established its trust in you.

The horse's trust can be destroyed by training methods that give conflicting signals, such as when a rider's position and pressure ask it to stop and go at the same time. Horses are very confused by being called to the trainer, responding, and then being punished for some disobedience they have already forgotten.

As a matter of fact, punishment can cause more problems than it solves. Horses don't have the same ideas we do about right and wrong. But they do have some simple sense of justice and know when they're being deceived or abused. You can take a horse right off the range, a newborn foal or an unspoiled horse of any age, and it will respond naturally to basic commands transmitted through the rider's position and pressure. Horses that don't respond have probably been badly handled.

Always remember the three "Golden Rules" of horse training:

1. *Never* punish a horse. In order to be effective, punishment has to come immediately after the misbehavior for the horse to associate them properly, and this is seldom possible. Horses interpret our actions with them as cues, and punishment is a cue they don't understand. So whenever you get angry while you're working with a horse, stop at once and walk away. If you're in an irritable or angry mood, don't even start a training session.

2. Never forget that the horse's eyesight is different from ours. Try to imagine how things look to horses. Their eyes are placed differently from ours, on the sides of their heads. Since the eyes don't move in their sockets, horses cannot focus as quickly as we can. Their eyes are trifocal, which means they need a lot of time and positioning in order to see things far away or close up. Horses' eyesight is particularly limited when they are facing the light, because their pupils close down. If you are aware of these things, you'll understand why a horse has to jerk its head to focus on you when you're working close in front of it, for example. And you'll

be able to avoid many misunderstandings that are simply due to the peculiar kind of eyesight all horses have.

3. Realize the horse can only think in one place at a time. Always keep in mind the basic instincts that influence a horse's behavior: fear (trust), mating (companionship), and hunger (food). I've put the strongest instinct first because a hungry horse will leave its food to pursue an interesting mate, but will forget all about sex and run away or hide if something frightens it. However, it will put up a fight if forced to do so.

Remember, the most important thing in judging Quarter Horses and showing them successfully is to understand how they function in mind as well as in body.

EVOLUTION OF THE QUARTER HORSE

The Quarter Horse was originally bred to run on the short tracks of colonial America. Quarter-mile races, known as quarter races, were invented by the English and Irish colonists who settled on the Atlantic seaboard from North Carolina north. Because this area was densely wooded, the British manner of racing, around oval courses, was difficult if not impossible. Since colonists literally had to chop their courses out of the forest, they reduced the three- or four-mile tracks, so prevalent in England, to a quarter of a mile on parallel paths. The races were matches between two horses, frequently started by the jockeys themselves with a code of signals.

To supply stock for these quarter races, the colonists (mainly Virginians) propagated during the seventeenth and eighteenth centuries a breed of horses founded on stallions and mares brought from England and Ireland. Colonial requirements called for a saddle horse that would be comfortable to ride and a horse that was fast enough for warfare and a bit of sport-racing. The Hobby, a strain of horse, common in Ireland, met these needs. It was the fastest runner in the world with an intermediate gait that was not a trot but the far more comfortable (for the rider) lateral gaits, the amble and rack. The breeding stock was selected with great care—shipping horses across the Atlantic was expensive. The first horses and their offspring were imported into Virginia in 1611. While probably few of these importations included racehorses as such, the imported colonial stallions and mares provided the very best foundation stock on which to build a breed of racehorses.

The lateral gaits of the seventeenth-century Quarter Horse were passed down in the horses of the Southern planters and helped to found the present-day Tennessee Walking Horse and the American Saddlebred of Kentucky. Both the Virginia Quarter Horse and its New England cousin, the

Narragansett Pacer, helped to create the harness racehorse, known as the Standardbred.

As these horses moved west with the trailblazers and pioneers, the amble and rack slowly disappeared as Quarter Horse stallions were bred to diagonally gaited (trotting) mares of Spanish origin; in Mississippi and east Tennessee to mares of the Chicksaw Indian strain; and in the Southwest to the mares of the ranches established by descendants of the Conquistadors. The melding of these strains west of the Mississippi River during the nineteenth century produced not only fast Quarter Race Horses for the primitive tracks of frontier settlements but also the cowman's partner for the western range cattle industry. A quick burst of speed became the trademark of this unique equine.

At the beginning of this century, the true origins of the breed had nearly been forgotten. A handful of pioneer horsemen recognized the value of the sprinters and cow horses, commonly called Steeldusts, that had been perpetuated for so long without the benefit of a formal registry. By 1939 a number of horsemen had come to believe that the Quarter Horse deserved to be acknowledged as an animal of a distinct physical type. After much research into bloodlines and listening to people who had spent their lives on and around Quarter Horses, threads of a common ancestry came to light. In Fort Worth, Texas, on March 14, 1940, the American Quarter Horse Association (AQHA) was born. When the first stud book was issued the following year, it listed 537 horses that had been inspected and approved to be of Quarter Horse type and ancestry. Today over 3 million horses have been registered and the membership stands at over 300,000.

Besides quarter racing, the AQHA provided halter shows and performance contests that gave breeders and exhibitors the opportunity to compete for awards. These public events also demonstrated progress in breeding for type, quality, and the ability to perform. No other horses in the world are used by so many people for so many things as are Quarter Horses.

The Quarter Horse is not only one of the world's oldest breed of racehorses, it is also one of America's oldest breed of horses.

CHAPTER I

Reading the Judge's Mind

WHEN it comes to using Quarter Horses in competition, we've come a long way from the colonists who set two animals on parallel tracks to run for the finish line. As we all know, even a flat-out race, if it is close, requires a third party to help determine the winner. Tests of beauty or competence, of course, are quite a bit more subjective than races, so it wouldn't do to have the contestants, however pure of heart, deciding the outcome themselves. When you consider the myriad competitive activities at which we now ask Quarter Horses to perform, it is no wonder that the judge has become such an important personage in the show arena.

If you're going to compete before this arbiter—as anyone riding in a sanctioned event of any kind will need to do—then understanding how the judge reaches his or her conclusions will give you an immense advantage. Any competitor who can get inside the judge's head and truly empathize with his or her plight has an opportunity to perform in a way that will make it easy for the judge to rule in that competitor's favor. We'll talk a lot about the rules for different events in this book. But more important than rules will be how the judge interprets them. Once you understand that, then you can concentrate on meeting the judge's criteria to be a winner.

The first thing you must realize is that any judge has a difficult job. Unless you've ever been a judge, you may have a really hard time understanding this. A lot of pressure is placed on judges, not only from the outside but from within, and every judge has to learn to deal with it. Oftentimes judging is physically tiring. On average, most judges can work a ten-hour day, but much over that sets a person up to make mistakes. Those exhibitors who show late get a tired judge. Judges recognize this problem, which adds to the pressure on them.

For many years lack of uniformity of judging in the show ring was a major concern among Quarter Horse breeders and exhibitors. Horses winning under one judge might not even place under another a short time later or in a different part of the country.

One of the Quarter Horse's major attributes, its very versatility, is in large part responsible for this lack of uniformity in judging. Whether it is reining, cutting, jumping, racing, pleasure classes, or just riding the trails at home, the uses to which we put Quarter Horses substantiate their claim to being America's most versatile breed.

While we all can be proud of this moniker, as judges we must realize that with diversity—particularly when one breeds for a specific function—comes a lack of uniformity of type, conformation, and way of going.

Judging is the art of establishing a fixed image of the ideal for each class and then being able to select the horse that comes closest to that ideal for that particular event. Judging is comparison: comparing one horse or rider with another either individually or collectively. Judging is opinion and only opinion. Opinion, even though one judge's may differ from that of others, must be based on fact.

Today exhibitors and owners are making major investments of money and time in pursuit of the elusive blue ribbon. As a result, they are becoming more aware of the rules for judging and quickly note when judges do not adhere to them. A judge's conduct should be above reproach and integrity one of his or her primary attributes.

Judging is an honor and a privilege, and judges should put forth their best effort in every step of the process, from their appearance to the decisions they render. Judges carry a heavy weight on their shoulders when they enter the horse show arena. Their decisions are final and very important; in fact, through these decisions judges channel and control the horse show industry.

Judging is hard work, mentally as well as physically. Judges must make a minimum of 300 to 500 split-second decisions each day while walking, standing, sitting, and writing endless hours. Judges must be able to calculate numbers quickly, take shorthand so they can transcribe it afterward, know enough psychology to keep their feet out of their mouths, and be polite while doing all of these things.

Judging is rewarding, not just for the remuneration at the end of the show but for the achievement itself: knowing when the show's over that you've done a good job.

There is also a lighter side to all of this. Judging can be fun, especially if you're judging with others. The camaraderie in this show biz of ours generates moments of laughter along with a few practical jokes thrown in for good measure. So, another strong prerequisite for the job is a good sense of humor. It relieves the tension and helps to lift your spirits, especially if the weather is bad, your feet and back ache, or you're still trying to find a winner.

Judging is a challenge. Judges must keep up with new ideas, new innovations, and the times. Young, up-and-coming horsemen should be encouraged to stick their necks out and not be afraid of making a mistake, and to be honest enough to correct a mistake if it can be corrected.

Not everyone makes a good judge. Judges need to learn from experienced ones and then add their own fresh ideas in hopes of coming up with something workable. Senior judges should not be afraid to let the learner judges in on their stored-up know-how, for they are the best teachers. Apprentices can sort out and use what works best for them—if they have something to sort out.

Judging all over the country, as I have, enables you to see all kinds of horses, good and bad. I have witnessed all the outside pressures and subtle techniques such as merchandising, local champions, popular trainers, and undefeated horses that are used subliminally to sway the staunchest of judges. However, when the gate opens and each class enters the arena, I become just as anxious as the spectators to see who will win.

WHO SHOULD JUDGE?

When the question concerning who should judge arises, it refers not only to the person but also to his or her qualifications. The judge should be an experienced horseman or horsewoman. The pseudohorseman who talks a big game but has not done any actual showing, preparing, or schooling of horses is simply not qualified. Judges have to understand the mechanics and the psychology of the horse in order to make a proper evaluation. They have to have worked their way into and out of trouble to appreciate the way the horse responds.

Some people who show try to take shortcuts by cheating and using forbidden aids or gimmicks. If judges don't know what these things are, how they affect the horse or even where to look for them, then they should not hold a pencil. Actual service in the field is one of the most important requirements for judges.

If you're sick, why call the plumber? If your plumbing stops up, why call the grocer? To judge horse shows, why not call a horseman? What more qualified person is there than one who knows horses, their habits and ways, as well as every trick in the business and how to relate to them?

The next prerequisite is temperament. Not everyone has the personality to judge. Many people, even those who can do wonders with a horse, can't get up before an audience and give a speech, and judging is much like that. You have to roll with the punches, continually adjust to situations, and never get flustered. If you have a short fuse, you're definitely handicapped. Another trait in the same category is bullheadedness. The judge must be opinionated but open minded. Decision makers must be analytical by nature, inquisitive, and firm in personality.

Physical fitness enters into all of this because judging is tiring. Your mind as well as your body is under a great deal of pressure. If you tire easily, judging is not for you.

Last, but certainly not last in order of qualifications, is the ingredient only the individual knows for sure, and that is integrity or honesty—in other words, ethics. At what point (if at all) will an individual compromise him- or herself? "To thine ownself be true," the saying goes. Only those who can give an honest, open opinion of what they see in front of them at a given time and place without yielding to pressure, either self-induced or by others, should be standing in the arena.

Where will the judges of the future come from? At first they will come from the ranks of the known horsemen and women who are winning in the show ring. But this doesn't always mean that those who line their tack rooms with blue ribbons will become the best judges. Some amateur competitors make excellent judges, as do some horsemen or women in noncompetitive fields. There are also those who have risen through the ranks by way of youth programs, especially youth judging team exposure.

Tomorrow is bright for those who are on the verge of moving up the ladder of decision making. Being prepared when opportunity knocks is most important today. Judging is truly an honor and must be taken seriously. How you walk, talk, dress, what you do after hours, and how you conduct yourself in everyday life will be among the deciding factors of how you'll perform in the judging business.

Politics or pressures on judges come in many forms: some intended, many not really meant to be taken into account. One such instance that I recall happened when I was asked to judge a Tennessee walking horse class early in my career. I felt I was not qualified as I did not have a strong background in that division; but this was only one class at a small open show, and the management prevailed upon me to go ahead.

About eight walking horses came nodding into the ring. As they made their pass by me, I started to categorize them in the proper order according to my own opinion.

Then I overheard the photographer talking to the ring secretary. "Look at horse number 270, isn't he something? They paid $10,000"—a lot in those days—"for him and he hasn't been beaten yet."

Well, naturally, my head jerked up and I looked at 270 and then at my notes. Oh, great! On my sheet I had the horse third. The conversation between the two kept going and so did the class. I went through the whole routine both ways of the ring, and in my mind the horse was still third. I even called for a work-off of the top three to see if by chance I had overlooked something—all the while the pressure was building. The rider was showing to the hilt while the owner applauded wildly on the rail.

I lined up the horses, looked them over again quickly, walked to the announcer, and turned in my card. The sweat was dripping off my brow as I walked back to where the photographer and secretary were and said, "This will probably be the last time I ever judge a walking horse class because I just tied the unbeatable for third."

Well, after the awards and pictures, the photographer came over and said, "You know, I was mistaken about that horse. They left the good one at home and brought this one to school."

Politics, pressures, you bet. But integrity will always win out!

ETHICS AS THEY RELATE TO JUDGES

It is difficult to think of a field in which the acceptance and use of an ethical and/or moral standard plays a more crucial role than it does in judging horses.

Ethics, or moral philosophy, is the systematic study of the nature of value concepts—good, bad, right, wrong—and of the general principles that justify us in applying them to anything. Organized society exists with the aid of formal law, supplemented by moral or ethical standards. Many of the laws or rules by which a society, profession, or group conducts itself cannot be formally recorded because the written rule cannot anticipate or cover all situations.

Consider the following examples: A trial judge will disqualify himself from hearing a case in which he has a personal interest; a physician, although she may legally treat a member of her family, will usually not treat one with a serious illness for fear that her personal feelings and emotions may prejudice or influence her medical judgment.

Compare those two relatively simple situations, where members of a profession exclude themselves because of personal interest or emotions, to the dilemma that faces a horse show judge with almost every class he adjudicates. There are twenty to thirty horses in the class, one or two by his own stallion (the foundation of the family's breeding program for the past ten years); one or two horses that the judge trained and sold from his breeding program (including that three-year-old bay filly out of a favorite show mare that the judge expected would be the next champion, but Uncle Sam said this was the year to make a profit); two kids are now showing whom the judge had as equitation riders for about five years; there's good old Charlie Professional, who taught the judge almost everything he knows riding his great new show horse; there's Tom Trainer, who has a red-hot prospect for that $25,000 horse he wants to sell; and there's Joe Manager, who manages that prestigious horse show he's always wanted to judge. By the time I list all the possible conflicts of interest, the class will be out of the arena.

There simply is no substitute for a judge's integrity. There is no way we can pass rules to govern all the above conditions. Nor can we exclude all horsemen and women, trainers, veterinarians, from judging our horses. The horse show world is a small segment of our society, and we must rely on those who know horses to judge them. Broad guidelines as to how a class is to be judged can be established, but the main criterion we must rely on is the integrity and ethical standards of our judges.

Foremost, judges must be able to live with themselves; to know that in their opinion, their placings are inherently right. To accomplish this, they must be knowledgeable of the rules and standards for the breed and the classes they will be judging. Otherwise, they cannot approach judging the class with confidence, nor can they turn in their cards and be able to live with themselves.

While on the show grounds, the judge is bound to meet friends and associates who are also exhibitors. Certainly he or she should greet them, but long conversations in public are a no-no. Remember, there are more losers than winners, and they all assume the judge is talking about the exhibitors' horses even though he really is discussing the cuisine from the restaurant he ate at last night. There will always be that one exhibitor who is a tabloid-talker, but the judge who follows a few simple guidelines will find himself above reproach. As a judge, when in doubt, use logic, think of how a situation may look to someone else who doesn't know the inside information.

Good judges also must understand the mechanics of running a show and the guidelines for each class. They should develop a step-by-step method for marking each class: a simple, quick shorthand record of their observations. Judges must have total confidence in their own ability and show no sign of uncertainty or panic if they are suddenly confronted with hundreds of horses or have several hundreds of thousands of dollars riding on their judgment.

Exhibiting horses is a very emotional undertaking. By preparing themselves properly and maintaining the highest personal ethical and professional standards, judges can make the showing of horses an exciting, stimulating, and rewarding experience for all involved.

TO ERR IS HUMAN

No one likes to make a mistake. Human error is something we hate to 'fess up to and hope no one notices. When the poles do come down in jumping, when barrels are knocked over or calves and steers missed along with leads, most just shrug it off and look forward to the next contest. Naturally, the bigger the mistake, the less easily it is shrugged off, but mistakes are expected.

Yet certain people are not supposed to make mistakes, not even tiny ones. These include clergy, doctors, pilots, those in high office, parents, referees, umpires, and horse show judges. When judges step into the ring, they are supposed to know every rule and variation thereof, and to see every horse in every class at every angle.

Realistically, we know this is not possible; but that ideal keeps dangling in front of us. One such incident illustrates my point: Awhile back, at a reining competition, three judges independently scored a horse 72, 73, 73½, which subsequently became the high-scoring performance. The awards were presented and the winning rider rode into the arena, supposedly to pick up her trophy and blue ribbon. But when she got to the ringmaster, standing alongside the ribbon handler, she stopped and said, "I can't accept this. I was off course."

The ringmaster's mouth unhinged and he stood for a minute dumbfounded. The announcer's monologue of "next bests" abruptly halted while the ringmaster, seeking advice, approached the judges and informed them of the dilemma. They all consulted their scorecards. No, they agreed, she was not off course and should accept the prizes.

Upon returning to the woman on horseback, the ringmaster assured her that she was not off course and to please accept the awards. To his chagrin, she refused once more, explaining that her husband said she was off course, so she must have been, and therefore she couldn't accept the award.

By now the show manager had been summoned. Either the three judges had made a mistake or the lady's husband had; a no-win situation. The manager talked to the judges, who still held firm, and then finally convinced the woman to take the trophy and discuss it outside so the show could resume. Thinking it was all settled, everyone went back to work. The woman rode out to a rousing applause, trophy and blue ribbon in hand, shaking her head "no" all the way.

She put her horse away and returned later to the horse show office, asking if there was some kind of a protest she could file, as she wanted to file it against herself—or, more accurately, against the three judges for not calling her off course. And to this day, the judges, as well as many watching the class, felt that the rider was *not* off course!

When judges make mistakes, whether real or perceived, they become the topic of conversation for days, sometimes months and years, whereas exhibitors rarely are cited for their mistakes. Forgiveness of mistakes appears to be directly related to those who make them.

While spectators see many mistakes, such as wrong leads and even lameness, judges may not see them because of their angle or viewing point. Some mistakes are dealt with by filing a letter of protest, others by persecution and gossip. When judges find out they've made an error, they experience that empty feeling deep in their stomachs and the memory of it lasts forever.

At times judges are forced to accept the mistakes of others. One such incident comes to mind. In a futurity, the judge may give the ringmaster a list of the horses to return for the finals. The ringmaster then sees to it that the horses are asked to return via the announcer. However, often the judge is escorted out before the numbers are read.

One time a substitute ringmaster stepped in during one of the go-rounds and informed the judge simply to list the culls and everyone else could come back. When it came time for the finals, the judge stepped into the arena and was greeted by all the horses he had excused. It seems the announcer mistook his "cull" list for his "keep" list. All his good horses had gotten the gate, loaded up mad, and gone home. That judge will have to endure the mistake— not even his—over the years, even when trying to explain the mix-up. The only consolation is that judges can always learn from their mistakes.

We used to judge horse shows mostly on the mistakes of horses and riders, but today fewer are made. Needless to say, that fact presents more of a challenge than ever for horse show judges, since their decisions now rely much more on subjectivity. As a competitor, it's important to keep perspective and to remember that mistakes will still be made by everyone, and judges are no exception. The seriousness with which they generally approach their task is more important than any specific result. And, in any case, as we develop more casebooks and educational materials and the what-if situations are explained and discussed, the risk of error should diminish—particularly if those who live through the experience of making a mistake share it with other judges.

READING THE RULES

"There's a right way, a wrong way, and the navy way" was the motto we lived by in the service. After attending many conventions and judges' seminars, I've come to the conclusion that this statement is more convincing than ever, especially when interpreting rules.

I've narrowed it down to two choices: If the rule book doesn't say you can, you can't; if it doesn't say you can't, you can. The discovery, which really shouldn't be surprising, is that each individual always interprets the meaning that best suits his or her particular needs. I've found that all rule books, regardless of the association, fall prey to this kind of thinking.

There is no possible way to write rules to cover all situations. I remember one case in point, and I quote from the Quarter Horse rule book: "A five-second penalty will be assessed if the hat or helmet is not on the exhibitor's person for the entire time the exhibitor is in the arena in Barrel Racing." Seems like a simple enough rule ... intended to get rid of the common practice of riding into the arena and tossing off the hat before proceeding on course. At one of the first shows after this rule was enacted, it was put to the test.

The rider entered the arena, hat on head as specified; around first barrel, hat still in place; second barrel, hat still on but loosened; third barrel, hat still on but obviously not for long; heading for home, hat starts to fall; rider reaches up to grab it; hat falls but catches on spur as rider crosses finish line; hat still on spur as rider leaves the arena. Judge's dilemma: Was the hat on "the exhibitor's person" when she left the arena as specified in the rule book? I'll let you be the judge.

Over the years, judges have resolved many quandaries. Years ago, I was judging a trail class held in a big field, and the first obstacle was the gate, followed by a ditch, logs, bridge, back through, and so on. Wanting to make it all quite simple, I said, "Go through the gate any way you want without losing control [as it was placed in a difficult position]; then in the ditch turn right; jog to the logs and so on." I had about twenty riders in the class, and as each came to the gate he or she pushed or pulled, went through forward or backward (all had trouble) and on through the course. The obstacles were quite difficult and no one had a good trip.

The last rider approached the gate and, to my amazement, simply dismounted, opened the gate, led his horse through, closed it, mounted, and, much to my chagrin, completed the course in excellent fashion. My light-colored jacket darkened around the arms as I asked my ringmaster, "What instructions did I give for the gate?" He reminded me that I had said they could go through the gate any way they wanted but not to lose control. "I meant stay on the horse," I interjected, trying not to lose my cool. I could hear the buzzing of the "backgate lawyers" about the hole I'd dug for myself. I stood for a moment and sorted out what I had said—or rather what I hadn't said—marked my card, and handed it to my ringmaster. Oh, yes, I tied the last rider on top. He had interpreted my instructions differently from how I or anyone else had, but his interpretation was as valid as mine at the time.

Another dilemma, with a good track record, has become quite persistent. What do you do with a rider who doesn't quite conform to the rules governing appointments? Some are obviously not properly attired or lack the correct appointments as spelled out in the rules. These are easy to discard. But what about those who bend the rules or come close? What of those who sport some insignia or piece of equipment designed to catch the judge's eye? They attempt to project individuality but only succeed in vexing the judge who must sort out legal/illegal, proper/improper, penalty/disqualification—all of which takes time away from finding the best horse or rider.

Hunter under Saddle rules state traditional appointments. A horse comes into the arena, a good horse, with a Navajo saddle blanket cut down to a near English saddle size, not rounded or shaped, but a small Western-type pad, instead of the classic hunter-type pad. If the horse wins, a fad is launched allowing the trendy marketers to surface and create an abundance of Navajo pads in hunter classes. Not quite what was intended by the rule writers.

"Conservative colors" is another challenging area. To a color-blind person, anything goes; to the person whose closet holds monocolor, all else should be frowned on; to the one whose wardrobe rivals a Christmas tree, gaudy is best. What about more than the rules allow? Is a sweater over required attire okay in winter? What about insignias, chaps, saddles, pads, sweaters, all emblazoned with legal forms of advertising? What if a rider, on the best horse in the class, slips a forbidden finger between the reins as he or she is asked to back? Pretend not to see it, or throw the perpetrator out? A judge's dilemma once more.

In my opinion, individuality always has merit but should be within the realm of taste. (Good and bad also reflects a matter of opinion, of course.) Exhibitors who don't want to conform should think through their plan, as the judge must also. What will this do to the direction of the industry if this degree of unorthodoxy prevails? If this rider is placed on top with unconventional attire or appointments (even though technically legal), will it create a monster we'll have to live with until those who placed second and further down get the rules rewritten?

Exhibitors and judges have obligations to the horse show world to create and direct its future. Change, just for the sake of change, often can be detrimental to the overall good. Creativity, on the other hand, is always welcome as long as it doesn't interfere with tradition. That is the key word. Tradition is something tested by the annals of time. Gimmicks or novelty have always been short-lived.

Probably no other sport has as much tradition or history behind it as equestrian competition, and simple elegance has invariably been the norm. Whether English or Western, history gives us the right examples to follow. Understanding each piece of equipment and attire, why it was created and how it works, should have a bearing on change.

Judges are more impressed by proper, traditional appointments. Most appreciate well-tailored attire, well-groomed horses and riders, tack that fits the horse and is well cared for, hats that are shaped, chaps the proper length, hair neat and contained, tasteful earrings (if worn), and boots polished and fitted. The "hey-look-at-me" type of exhibitor, bending tradition and borderline legal, is generally frowned upon by the judiciary. Of course, in a class where only the horse is being judged, the best horse should win. But it's still hard to give the blue to a rider whose hat looks like someone sat on it, or whose spurs are upside down, whose crop is stuck in the boot tops, or who is chomping on gum. The wise exhibitor won't ever put the judge in the position of having to make that call.

Yet with show biz on the rise and tradition on the wane, I might just patent a few gadgets of my own. One is a case for small batteries so Western shirts and jackets can glow in the dark. Next, I've devised a color code for the service ribbons and medals worn on those majorette-type clothes (the ones with epaulets) so all judges will know where they've shown and won before.

And what's a poor judge to do when an exhibitor shows up in white tie and tails at 8:00 A.M.? Even Emily Post couldn't find a niche for that—unless some gent was just gettin' in from a night on the town.

EVALUATING JUDGES

I have often said, "The judge judges the horses and the people judge the judge." Their praise and/or criticism, well founded or not, travels rapidly in horse show circles. How often I've heard "He or she did a poor job"; or "So-and-so could have led in a donkey and he still would've won"; or "Finally someone judged horses instead of handlers." Whatever the case, word travels fast, loose, and is taken as gospel. Luckily, most exhibitors realize that there must be winners and losers in every event and sort facts from idle gossip for themselves. Keeping perspective is the important thing.

Because judging is only opinion (not right or wrong), we could do great harm to our industry if creativity or individual thinking were stifled; or if we refused to listen to new ideas or ways of looking at horses or classes. However, there should be some procedure or method for analyzing a judge's effectiveness.

There is no possible way for anyone to legislate innate ability; or to guarantee another's integrity; or to make all conditions of evaluation the same for every person at every show. How can anyone rate a judge who faces an average of three horses in a class as opposed to one who has an average of thirty at a given show? The straight relationship of numerical decisions is out of balance. Any attempted comparison has built-in distortions. Is there only one judge at the show, or more? Is there a backlash because one judge is so poor it makes the other look like a hero? Is there bad morale at the show because of conditions beyond the judge's control? What about the judge who is fantastic in one geographic area or type of class and poor in another? He may be a hero to the winners and something else to the losers.

I recently read an 1891 article published in a Chicago newspaper concerning an international horse show. The writer had praised the facilities and the horses, and then went on and on about how bad the judging was. The curious part was in the last sentence, where he stated that it was the first horse show he had ever attended. He had evaluated the show and the judges by becoming an expert in a total of three hours. I thought, How true, and it's an art that is still practiced today!

FIRST IMPRESSIONS

Everybody is a judge of something, and we're judging all the time. From morning to night we make judgments and decisions about all sorts of things, from the clothes we wear to the people we see.

Horse show judges are also judging all the time they're at a show, if only subconsciously. For instance, if they are walking from the parking lot to the show secretary's office and see an exhibitor acting unsportsmanlike or unruly or a horse causing trouble, they can't help registering the bad impression in their mind. The exhibitors are also judging judges as they preside over their classes, not only on their decisions but also on their appearance and manners, their authority and professionalism.

Although a judge's official work begins when all of the entries are gathered in the ring, the way they look on entering the arena has already provided an idea of their merits. Some horses are obviously too fat, too skinny, unfit or nervous. Some are obviously good movers, others bad. It's much easier to pick a winner from a good class than from a bad one. Selecting the best of a good class is also more satisfying than picking the least bad in a poor bunch.

In rail classes, the first clue comes when the horse enters the arena. Does it respond readily to the leg and go right into the gait called for? Or does it back off, resist changes, throw its head up in the air, or prance around? An experienced judge can usually tell how the "go" will turn out from the way the horse enters the ring and performs the first way around. This judge knows it's almost impossible for a bad mover with a sour attitude to have a go as good as that of a good mover with a cheerful air. The first impression is very important, and it starts the moment the horse passes through the ingate.

The rider herself makes an impression even *before* she comes through the gate, and sometimes it's one that can handicap her horse. I'm thinking of those riders who wait and pose at the gate, holding up the class; this is the last thing a judge wants. Judges have got a tough schedule that can keep them on their feet for eight or ten hours already, and they're trying to stick to the timetable. They can't do it if the class is delayed by exhibitors holding up at the gate.

Another tactic that usually backfires is making a show of letting the judge know which horse is whose, as when a trainer or owner ostentatiously accompanies a horse to the gate on the pretext of giving last-minute instructions. Don't think this influences judges. They take it for what it is: an effort to attract attention.

I've found that my first impressions are more often right than wrong. Of course, when a horse is shown in several different classes, it starts each class with a clean slate. The horse is up against a new set of rivals in a new performance, and the judge has to forget any earlier opinion. This is easy to do with a good horse and rider who may have previously committed some minor error. It's harder with a bad horse and rider who have already shown some glaring defect.

A simple way to improve your chances is to make it easy for the judge to pick you out for a ribbon. Wear your number so it's clear and visible and so the judge doesn't have to chase you halfway around the ring to find out what it is. The fad for numbers so small or fancy that they're practically unreadable only makes the judge's job harder.

Another false idea is thinking that you have to be first or last in the ring in order to attract the judge's attention. Naturally, you should plan your entrance and make the most of it, as actors and actresses do. But the main thing is to enter on cue, as they do. Promptness is just as important in the show arena as on the stage, and judges appreciate it.

POSITION

The importance of position begins when a horse is first conceived. The position of the embryo during pregnancy, the foaling position at birth, the nursing position, and the position the mare takes to protect her offspring will all affect an animal's future. The importance of position continues with the relation of the handler to the colt at first touch. The nose and mouth of the future begin with the position of the hackamore, snaffle, or both; their correct position is the essential base for all subsequent training.

The position of the horse's head to its body makes it easier for it to be in balance. From simple maneuvers, such as walk, trot, and canter, to more complicated movements, such as spin, stop, back, or sidepass—all must start with position as the foundation. Likewise, the total communication between rider and horse is achieved much more easily through proper position.

Position not only relates to the horse and training, but also to the location the judge takes when he or she walks into the arena. Some judges actually handicap themselves by choosing a poor position, and how they view a particular horse in a class will definitely influence their opinion.

Judges have historically viewed halter horses coming toward them one at a time. If they only observe the horse trotting directly away, they cannot judge the way a horse moves or any subtle unsoundnesses. Sometimes, from this position, even dead lameness can slip by. Nowadays judges are encouraged to watch a horse move on the profile; a side view can uncover many defects.

I've tried out every possible judging position before I found the one I think is best.

Experiments showed me that a performance viewed from outside the arena looks entirely different from what judges inside the arena are seeing. They also get an entirely different perspective if they are standing at ground level or slightly higher. The worst p lace to judge a pleasure or rail class is by standing and looking into the corner by the ingate or outgate, because that is where most problems for rail horses occur. If all judges see is just a few strides of a couple of horses at a time, they don't get a fair sample of each horse's performance. Another case of tunnel vision occurs when judges watch all the horses in profile along a certain spot on the rail. Again, by positioning themselves there, the judges see only a fraction of the round that the spectators are seeing.

The ideal position is to stand in a corner, just off the rail, and face the major portion of the ring. In this position, judges can view horses coming toward them, going away, and in profile. Judges who stand here get a much better view of the class—a full 350 degrees, losing a horse only for 10 degrees.

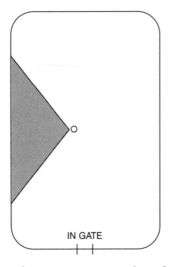

Judging position facing the rail on the long side of arena.

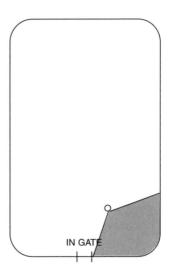

Judging position standing in corner facing the rail. This position is the least desirable—the epitome of tunnel vision.

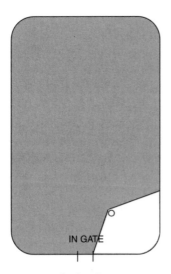

Ideal judging position—standing in corner looking into arena.

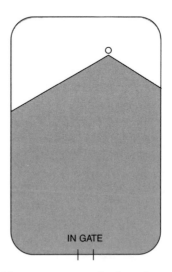

This position affords the judge an opportunity to see two or three riders coming into the arena at one time and about three-quarters of the ring.

JUDGING POSITIONS

Now I'll toss out another idea regarding the pinnacle of judging positions. I think the best way to view rail classes is from outside the ring, almost to a corner, and elevated to the height of the normal horse's eye. The advantage of this position is that the judge doesn't need to wander around to see the whole ring. No 10-degree segment is out of sight. From this vantage point, judges can look at all horses in the same way. (Of course, judges still can focus on just one as it goes around.) As judges have an obligation to see as much as possible of the entire class, I believe this out-of-the-ring, elevated position offers the best vantage point.

Hunter classes are normally judged from outside the arena, elevated in the middle of one side. This allows a broadside, or profile, view of the horse going over the fences. Coupled with being positioned on the opposite side of the arena from the in-and-out or combination, this allows the best possible judging position.

Reining and roping classes, judged from much the same position as the hunter, may provide a better view of how a horse uses the arena. From this location, it is easier for judges to assess the size and symmetry of the circles, the smoothness and length of the run-down, the turn-around, and to count the number of spins. Also, the judges' view is exactly the same as that of most spectators'.

Besides these aspects of position, the horse's position in the work order or lineup—in which some try to be first or last, or simply want to line up next to one that's uglier—greatly affects outcome. Competitors also haggle over position in the jumping order or the order of go for reining horses; naturally, the cutters all want to go last.

Those who believe there is a "pecking order" of who should win fight hard for their position or perceived position in the professional ranks. In every community there are so-called top trainers, those who have for one reason or another earned or promoted themselves into that position.

Position is a constant factor for those who compete. It seems no wonder, then, that winning in the horse show game depends so significantly on your awareness not only of your own position but of the position of the judge as well.

BALANCE

Let's do away with the bad-going, cheating, mechanical horses that have been dominating some areas because of the rider who shows them, and replace them with natural, good-moving horses.

Sounds easy, doesn't it? But the hard part is defining a good mover. While it's not difficult to see most of the time, it's tough to describe. Natural, yes; balanced, yes; free moving, yes; all of these are ingredients, but they must be put together in the right combination. To be a good mover, the horse must be allowed to go naturally, which means without restriction. Don't confuse this with head-set or speed.

All show horses must be balanced in order to perform. Balance is the ingredient that gives a horse that capable, ready look. What makes up balance? Simply a combination of impulsion and collection. Impulsion is the driving force; all movements are done with forward motion. A horse cannot perform if it's all strung out. Many horses, to escape pressure, raise the poll, lock the jaw, and invert the back, leaving their hocks trailing behind. A horse must be driven forward to have impulsion and gathered together to have collection. I liken it to squeezing an accordion. Balance has to come from both ends. The hands control the front end and the legs control the rear. When all of the ingredients are combined in the right amounts—the correct degree of collection and rate of impulsion—the top line becomes level and the horse is balanced.

Therefore, in most cases, moving the center of gravity back to where the horse can achieve this balanced position will enable it to move gracefully. If it's off balance, it will be either too much on the forehand and travel downhill, or too much the other way, climbing in front and hitching behind. All horses do not have the same balance point. You have to take the time to experiment by moving the saddle back and forth to find where the balance point is best and the easiest for each horse to carry the load. Some horses will never be good movers because of conformation defects; but all horses should be allowed to do their best. Breeders should emphasize good movement as well as other factors when making breeding selections.

Impulsion is directly related to the hindquarters, but it starts with the back, which must be strong and straight. Don't fall into the trap of thinking the shorter the back, the better for a Quarter Horse. A too short back can be as much of a fault as a long back. A back that is too short can hinder extension and flexion of the legs. If a short back is coupled with long legs, the horse usually ends up forging. The loin—the part of the horse that extends from the last rib to the hip—should have short, heavy muscles because it furnishes the support needed for the transmission of power from the hind legs.

Many people overlook the hind leg. It is what makes the horse go, and how it's used is related to balance. There is a definite correlation between hind leg and front leg. The thigh of the hind leg corresponds to the arm of the front leg. The stifle, gaskin, and hock of the hind leg are counterparts of the elbow, forearm, and knee of the front leg. Because the hind legs are like propellers, there must be good muscling through the thigh, stifle, and gaskin for the horse to move correctly. For a horse to have proper balance, the length of the gaskin and the forearm should be equal.

Most people fail to realize that the hock joint is the pivot of action. It plays an important role in propulsion. As the feet carrying the body strike the ground, the pressure is centered at the hock joint. When a horse achieves

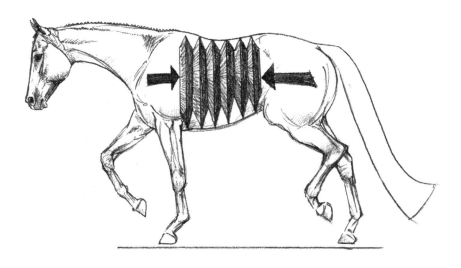

From both ends—collection with impulsion.

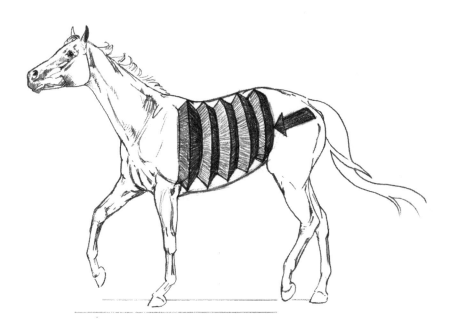

Disengaged—hollow-backed, poll raised, horse strung out.

COLLECTION IS ACCORDIONLIKE

the proper impulsion from behind and the proper collection by controlling the rate of motion, then it has freedom of movement, thus allowing the muscles to flex unrestricted.

The shoulder is an excellent place to observe good movement. If we restrict the horse too much, the shoulder cannot function at its best and the movements become choppy and hard. If the shoulder has the freedom to work, the legs move more easily and the concussion lessens, which results in a smooth, level top line of the back. If you notice the top line on all good movers, whether jumping, pleasure, cutting, or even racehorses, you will see the horse move with balance and grace, maintaining a flat, smooth top line regardless of gait.

I will not dwell on head position here because it is a subject of its own. But head carriage is directly related to collection. If the horse is to be collected or balanced, the head can neither be up, looking you in the eye, nor dragging on the ground, trying to plow a furrow with its nose.

Collection is not just related to the front end or limited to the head and neck; it is the gathering together of all parts of the horse. It is a subtle coordination of movement, not a jerk and spur. You actually *draw* the horse into a balanced position. Any restriction, either from overdoing or not doing enough, hinders the horse's ability to move properly.

Once the horse's balance point has been established, another essential factor to complete the picture is rider cooperation. How the rider distributes his or her weight will help or hinder the horse in maintaining its balance. If the rider is constantly shifting weight from in front of the motion to behind it, leaning from side to side, taking back on the reins, spurring up and taking back, or looking down at every change of gait, the horse must make adjustments to stay in balance. As a result, the horse's top line will soften, and the horse will show duress and resentment. All horses have a point at which they look and move the best. The main job of the rider is knowing what that point is, how and when to reach it, and how long the horse can maintain it.

For a horse to perform at its best, its body must be in a straight line. If a horse is going to cheat or break, it usually will lock its jaw on one side or the other. If it locks it on the left side, its right hip is escaping—a warning sign of breaking. The rider should feel this and move the shoulder and hip back into a straight line, by pulling on the right rein while engaging the right leg to move the body back into alignment.

Many people tend to try to make all horses look alike, and they happily jump on the bandwagon when each new fad appears. A trend is set with a particular horse that, when shown, demonstrates all the good qualities it possesses. The copiers take a horse of like substance but usually with fewer good attributes, and attempt to make it perform as successfully. It may work some of the time, but usually only until the horse figures out a way to cheat, at which point new problems arise.

Each horse has its own good qualities that must be accentuated and weak

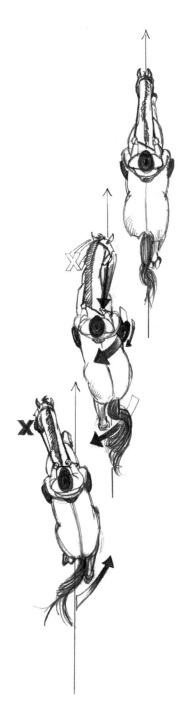

TO UNLOCK JAW ON LEFT SIDE
Simply move the right shoulder and hip back into line.

qualities that must be dealt with. Both showman and judge must recognize good and bad points. The new direction in showing and judging is to emphasize and reward the natural, good mover. But keep in mind that producing a horse that is a good mover doesn't mean reducing it to a mechanical, over-ridden piece of machinery totally created by humans. Such a horse will move in unnatural ways, and in the long run you'll have neither a happy, well-balanced animal nor one that impresses the judges.

TWO LITTLE WORDS

Two words not commonly related to winning or losing in the horse show ring correlate to the color of the ribbons received. The two words are "act" and "react." Winners act. Nonwinners react.

Those who consistently take home the blue always appear to be at the right place at the right time, are always visible to the judge, and never have trouble in the line. Their horses stand up for them at halter without a lot of placement, while others are always covered up, hollering "rail," lined up at the wrong end, or letting their horses wander around and gawk. The difference is that one exhibitor acts and the other reacts.

The rider or handler who acts is always on top of a situation before it happens, whereas the reactor adjusts after the error has been committed.

A good example is something as basic as showing at halter. I've seen people who allow their horses to "let down" all the time outside the ring or at home and do not demand their horses' full attention at all times. They let them wander, look around, and goof off at home or in the warm-up area. Then they wonder why a horse doesn't set itself up on the first command when it counts. I'm sure the horses have no idea when their owners want them to be serious and when they don't care if it takes two or three times to stand up properly.

The person who acts, though, has a different approach. Everytime this actor handles the show horse, the animal knows it must give its undivided attention, at home, in the barn, outside an arena, or in the arena. The horse of the handler who is in complete control knows that it must listen at all times. There is no question of whether it will stand up properly when asked.

Some exhibitors allow a horse to move a couple of steps when mounting at home and then get mad at the horse when it does so in a class. And some who allow their horse to cross-canter on the longe line wonder why they cross-cantered in the arena. Those who allow their horse to nuzzle and nibble, root in the bridle, turn its head, and do all kinds of annoying things when they are away from the show arena should not be surprised when the horse does the same thing when it enters the ring.

This situation is like children who have never been taught manners at home but are expected to behave in front of company. The children—or the horses—will do what they have been allowed to do no matter what.

This brings to mind an old fish tale of my first venture out to sea. I was with a real fisherman, the best. We got our tackle out and started to bait our hooks. I painstakingly put the bait on the hook so not a trace of metal could be seen. My compadre, in the meantime, had his line in the water a full ten minutes before I was ready. After I finished baiting the hook to my satisfaction and as I held it up admiring my handiwork, he said, "You sure give those fish a lot of credit for intelligence." And who do you suppose caught the first fish? There is a parallel for those who think the horse knows when it is supposed to be serious just by reading the handler's mind. The key to showing horses successfully is getting them to listen to you at all times under all conditions, whether at home or in the arena. To have top show horses, you must have discipline yourself. To be the kind of person who acts, you must know your horse and its idiosyncrasies and be able to head off any situation that could give you trouble in the ring.

If you're showing at halter, take the time to observe the other classes, or at least look at the arena for any points of distraction or problem areas, such as holes or uneven ground that might not do justice to your horse if you stand there. Don't wait to get into difficulty and then have to find a way out. If you want to win, don't leave anything to chance.

In performance classes, the same holds true. Check out the arena ahead of time. Ride in it, if you can, and read your horse's reactions to potential distractions such as speakers, banners, and shadows, and relate them to how your horse shows best. Observe the other horses in your class while you're warming up so you'll be aware of trouble ahead of time and can avoid that horse or person.

Prepare yourself and your horse by allowing enough time to get the basics, and tune your horse to listen to your every command. Learn to read your horse's personality. Pay attention if it backs off or becomes too aggressive, if it's spooky or tired. Take into consideration how your horse's personality traits relate to the surroundings. Learn to act ahead of time if your horse starts to cheat on the rail, fidget in the lineup, or drift while backing up. Correct the problem before it starts, not after it has begun.

Horses are not robots always reacting the same way every day, at every show. You can't afford to become a robot either. Be like the smart jumping horse rider who knows that if the horse is thinking about ducking out to the left, it will put its left ear back about three or four strides from the fence. If this happens, the rider has time to drop his or her left leg in and drive the horse more to the right, over the jump in the middle, saving what could have been a disaster.

There are instances like that at every show, no matter what division you're in. You must learn to pay attention to little details.

Everyone who is successful in the horse show business has one quality in common: the ability to know in advance how to show a particular horse in a particular class at a particular show in front of a particular judge. To sum it up, the blues belong to the ones who act; the reactors divide what's left over.

CHAPTER II

Conformation/Halter Classes

HOW THE JUDGE EVALUATES CONFORMATION

THE general purpose behind conformation classes is to call upon learned people to choose the horse that best exemplifies the breed. Those horses designated by the judge as the best conformed then become the horses most called upon to propagate the breed. Once you understand this simple, basic concept, you can better appreciate the tremendous impact that people who officially evaluate a horse's conformation will have on the future of a breed. Since the future of a breed rests in the hands of relatively few judges today, within a few generations erroneous or faulty concepts on the part of the judges can result in the loss of qualities that years of diligent selection have produced. Obviously, then, those people who evaluate a horse's conformation have a tremendous responsibility, and their decisions must be founded on deep knowledge of breed conformation.

It is the judge's responsibility to place the horses in the order of their excellence. To expedite this objective, the judge must decide when the good qualities exceed the bad or vice versa. Only by having a thorough understanding of the fundamentals of conformation can a judge form an opinion during the brief examination allowed during a horse show.

Judges are not the only group responsible for the conformation and type of a breed. They are only the agents or mechanisms by which a breed puts into practice its concepts of conformation. The associations must establish goals and inform the people who desire to judge the horses.

Many horse breeds have specific functions. By regularly selecting the best performers of a function or functions, a type develops. Type will be demonstrated by anatomical characteristics that establish a difference between breeds of horses. Conformation, therefore, is a broad term for anatomical structure. It has been defined as the form or outline of an animal, or the symmetrical arrangements of its parts. In my opinion, it is best described as the relationship of form to function.

Conformation of the modern horse has evolved to fulfill human needs. The horse has evolved as it has because human survival, as well as its own, depended on it. The roads of history are strewn with the bones of the horse. The modern horse has evolved by surviving nature's proving ground. Its conformation is a product of survival of the fittest. This gives us a basis upon which to evaluate the details of good or bad conformation (anatomy) that make the horse such a fascinating biological machine.

Three general areas must be considered when judging a horse's conformation:

1. Standard of excellence—established by the breed association—its concept of an ideal horse
2. Dynamics of equine locomotion—those anatomical structures that enhance the horse's athletic ability
3. Ability to perform and remain sound

Judges also must be very much aware of those anatomical structures that predispose to unsoundness. With these three factors in mind, the definition of relationship of form to function becomes very meaningful.

The dynamics of locomotion is the synchronization of the functions of the various biological systems that allows the horse to perform amazing tasks. The musculoskeletal system, of course, has the most effect on the horse's overall performance, a relationship that is best described by the statement that conformation (anatomy) is the key to the horse's method of progression. Besides conformation, a horse's dynamics can be affected by training, nutrition, development, physical fitness, health, shoeing, and temperament (to mention only some of the many factors). All of these factors can be altered, except for conformation, which a horse is born with and can be modified only slightly, if at all. Good and bad conformation is inheritable. This fact reinforces the importance of evaluating breeding horses for conformation.

The third factor upon which the evaluation of conformation is based is unsoundness. Those anatomical characteristics that predispose the musculo-skeletal system to injury when subjected to stress, strain, and concussion are of the utmost importance to consider. Conformation factors that distract from the efficiency of other biological systems are also considered under this general category—such as anything that interferes with the respiratory system, such as small nostrils or a thick throatlatch. The horse's conformation affects its dynamics of locomotion. It follows that its dynamics dictate its exposure to stress, strain, and concussion on the musculoskeletal system. Unsoundness often determines a horse's useful lifetime. Conformation then becomes the common measure of the horse's ability to perform and stay sound. This is a very significant correlation of conformation and the use of the horse, and it makes the following statement significant: Much of a horse's success or failure has been attributed to its conformation.

The three factors—standard of excellence; dynamics of locomotion; and lameness from stress, strain, and concussion—can be brought together to make the evaluation of a horse's conformation more meaningful. The standard of excellence implies beauty, symmetry, and balance. Balance is related to the center of gravity, which in the horse is located such that 60 to 65 percent of the total body weight is borne by the front legs. Therefore, any conformation defects that increase the stress, strain, and concussion on the front limbs should be carefully evaluated. By using this concept, a judge can attribute different degrees of importance to various defects. The result is a logical system by which a judge can decide when the good qualities exceed the bad or vice versa.

The evaluation of a horse requires systematic analysis of the sites and clinical symptoms of unsoundness. Very few unsoundnesses are actually inherited. However, the conformation defects that predispose a structure to stress, strain, and concussion are inheritable. It is therefore the judge's responsibility to evaluate the conformation defects that predispose the system to break down.

Soundness of the horse might be defined as that state in which there are no deviations from the normal that have resulted in or that will predispose the animal to pathological changes which interfere with intended use. Common unsoundnesses are side bones, ring bones, contracted feet, navicular disease, cocked ankle, laminitis, splints, carpitis, wind puffs, bog spavin, curb, thorough-pin, stringhalt, and bowed tendon. (These will be explained in the following pages.) A judge must exercise good judgment (based on knowledge) to determine the significance of these liabilities and must understand the difference between unsoundnesses and blemishes. For example, a splint or bog spavin is a minor condition when not accompanied by poor conformation or lameness. If a blemish is caused by some foreign agent (wire cut, etc.), it is of minor importance; however, if it is due to faulty conformation, such as inside splints or wounds over the inside sesamoids caused by the horse winging in enough to hit the side with the opposite foot, it is quite significant. These wounds are common to horses that are in at the knees, base wide, and toe out—and should be considered a major conformation defect.

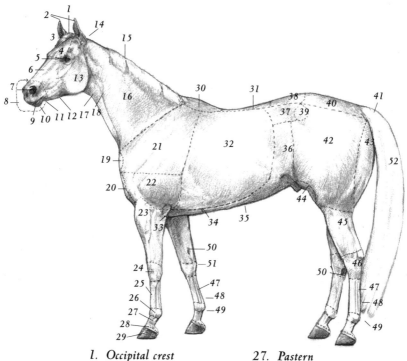

1. Occipital crest	27. Pastern
2. Ear	28. Coronet
3. Forelock	29. Hoof
4. Forehead	30. Withers
5. Eye	31. Back
6. Nose	32. Ribs
7. Nostril	33. Elbow
8. Muzzle	34. Brisket
9. Lower lip	35. Belly
10. Chin	36. Flank
11. Chin groove	37. Coupling
12. Branches of jaw	38. Loin
13. Jowl or cheek	39. Point of hip
14. Poll	40. Croup
15. Crest	41. Dock
16. Neck	42. Thigh
17. Throatlatch	43. Point of buttock
18. Jugular groove	44. Stifle
19. Point of shoulder	45. Gaskin
20. Chest	46. Hock
21. Shoulder	47. Suspensory ligament
22. Upper arm	48. Flexor tendon
23. Forearm	49. Fetlock
24. Knee	50. Chestnut, or callosity
25. Cannon	51. Trapezium
26. Fetlock joint	52. Tail

PARTS OF THE HORSE

EVALUATION

While there has never been a "perfect" horse, each breed association offers an ideal, which forms a starting point in your evaluation process. The judge's— and yours—quest is to find a horse that most closely resembles the breed ideal.

The breed ideal contains elements of four factors: balance, structural correctness, degree of muscling, and breed and sex characteristics. A thorough evaluation of conformation relies on defining these four areas as they relate to breed ideal and comparing elements of these traits of an individual horse to the breed ideal.

Of the four factors, balance is the single most important characteristic in equine selection. While research has demonstrated that all horses are proportional—meaning that the length of the head, for example, is directly proportional to the length of cannon bone—not all horses are balanced. Balance refers to the aesthetic blending of body parts and depends almost entirely on skeletal structure.

To gain a better understanding of ideal balance in an American Quarter Horse, there are several ratios that may be drawn in your mind's eye. View a horse from its profile, and imagine a straight line determining length of back (the distance from point of withers to croup) and one along the length of underline (point of elbow to stifle). In theory, the length of the back should be one-half that of the underline. Next, determine the top- to bottom-line ratio of the horse's neck. Draw an imaginary line down the top line of the neck (the distance from poll to withers) and the bottom line (the distance from throatlatch to neck/shoulder junction). Ideally, the top- to bottom-line ratio of neck should be two to one. Horses that deviate greatly from these two important ratios, becoming one to one, are often unbalanced.

What causes the deviations? Nothing is more critical to balance than slope of shoulder. As the shoulder becomes more vertically sloping, it shortens the top- to bottom-line ratio of neck. Not only does the top- to bottom-line ratio of the neck change, but the ratio of the length of back to the length of underline also changes. As the shoulder becomes straighter, the withers move forward, resulting in a longer back. But the length of the underline is not affected by the change in the shoulder angle. Thus, the straight-shouldered horse has a sort of tubular appearance.

Some say the ideal horse is a "square" horse, one that is roughly the same height at the withers as the distance from the point of the shoulder to the point of the buttocks. The length of its body is thus the same as the height from the ground to the withers. Others envision a well-balanced horse to be about the same distance from the fetlock joint to the underline as from the

In theory, the length of the back should be one-half that of the underline.

Ideally, the top- to bottom-line ratio of the neck should be two to one.

Some say the ideal horse is a "square horse," roughly the same height
at the withers as in the distance from the point of the shoulder to the point
of the buttocks. Points 1 to 2 should equal 3 to 4.

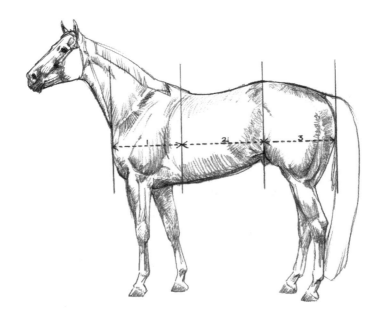

Dividing body into thirds.

underline to the top of the withers. This ratio perceives the depth of the body as having the same proportion as the length of the legs down to the fetlock joint.

My favorite ratio to determine ideal balance is the trapezoid. When judging a horse for conformation, the first step is to look at the body only from a side view. Divide it into thirds. The first third is from the point of the shoulder to the girth line, which is the line drawn between the back of the withers down under the chest behind foreleg. The middle third is from the girth line to a line drawn from the top of the croup down the flank. The rear third is from the last line described to the point of the buttocks. The horse should divide equally.

While observing the body, imagine a straight line being drawn from the point of the shoulder to the point of the buttocks. From there draw a line to the top of the croup. Then from there draw another line to the withers, and the last line connects back to the point of the shoulder. This figure is a trapezoid.

The sloping line from the withers to the point of the shoulders is an indication of the horse's speed and endurance. The other sloping line, from the point of the buttocks to the croup, is an indication of its power. The line from the top of the croup to the withers is the top of the bridge and indicative of top-line strength. It should be slightly longer than the saddle to be placed on the horse's back.

GOOD ANGLES
Trapezoid.

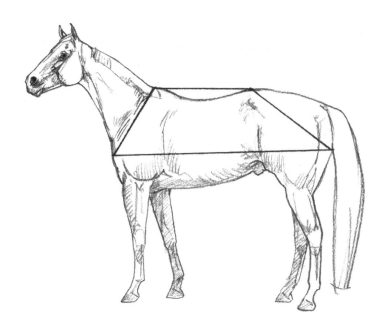

MISMATCHED ANGLES
Straight shoulder/sloping hind end.

MISMATCHED ANGLES
Too-sloping shoulder/steep hind end.

The key to this trapezoid and the usefulness of the horse is the bottom line, the longer the better. A horse that is divided evenly into thirds will have a short top line and a long bottom line. The two sloping angles are all important for balance. If the angles are equal or match each other in slope, the better the balance will be. Most horses are unbalanced; their angles are mismatched. Angles are the key to balance, whether the horse is being shown at halter or in a performance class.

Since a short top line and long underline are desirable, it is incorrect to compare shorter horses to taller horses, because horses of different sizes should not have the same length of body or underlines. The ratios themselves are important in determining balance, however, and these are affected directly by the slope of the shoulder. Moreover, when the shoulder is straight, other structural angles in a horse's body become straight, resulting in a horse with a short, steep croup, straight stifle, and straight pasterns. These latter traits are undesirable and contribute to a horse's lack of balance.

As balance is related directly to structure, the poorly balanced horse often lacks structural correctness and fundamental soundness. In general, the angle of the pasterns corresponds almost identically to the angle of shoulder, so that a horse with too much slope to its shoulder also will have weak, sloping pasterns. This condition, called coon-footed, may be so severe as to allow the horse's fetlocks to hit the ground as it moves. The ideal slope of shoulder is approximately 45 to 50 degrees; however, the angle may vary from ideal. You should not be overly influenced in demanding exact degree of slope of shoulder. Instead, concentrate on balance and blending of structure.

Once you have evaluated a horse's overall balance, its structure, muscling, and breed and sex characteristics can be judged more definitively by examining individual body components, starting with the horse's head.

HEAD

A horse's head can provide insight into its total conformation as well as its behavior. In general, there is no physiological benefit in having a "pretty head." However, most people don't like an ugly-headed horse, so selection is based on beauty. What makes an attractive head? The set of ears, shape of eye, size of nostril, depth of mouth, and overall proportions are important considerations. The ears should be proportional to the horse's head and sit squarely on top of it, pointing forward with an alert appearance. Any deviation in placement or carriage of the horse's ears detracts from the beauty of the head and thus from the horse's overall beauty.

Another useful tip in evaluating a horse's head is to measure visually the distance from the horse's poll to an imaginary horizontal line between the eyes. Ideally, this distance is approximately one-half the distance from the horizontal

Good Quarter Horse head.

Poor head: coarse muzzle,
Roman nose, pig-eye,
pendulous underlip.

line to the midpoint of the nostril. Thus, the eyes will be positioned one-third the distance from the horse's poll to muzzle. The width across the orbit of the horse's skull should be almost identical to the distance from the poll to the line between the eyes. Since horses are proportional, length of head is the same percentage of height for both tall and short horses. Therefore, the term "long headed" is somewhat a misnomer, as long heads are simply indicative of tall horses.

The head provides important clues in evaluating other factors, including behavior. Most notably, the eye often lends insight into a horse's disposition. Large, quiet, soft eyes—preferred and dominant among American Quarter Horses—normally indicate a docile disposition, while small, "pig" eyes are associated with horses that are sullen and difficult to train. Look for a bright, tranquil eye with a soft, kindly expression.

For American Quarter Horses, bulging, well-defined jaws are preferred, particularly in stallions, which are naturally deeper and bolder-jawed than mares. Pretty-headed horses always will have a well-defined muzzle, flaring into a refined chin and prominent jaw. For beauty's sake, look for large, flaring nostrils. Regarding depth of mouth, many horsemen and women claim that the shallower the mouth, the softer and more reactive the horse. Guard against horses that are thick-lipped and heavy across the bridge of the nose, for often these are less responsive to the bridle. Finally, make sure the horse is not parrot-mouthed (over on top) or monkey-mouthed (over on the bottom).

NECK

After evaluating the horse's head, move on to the neck. The throatlatch should be trim and refined, with the depth being equal to one-half the length of the head. If the horse is thick in the throatlatch, flexion at the poll is restricted, and the horse may not be able to carry its head correctly during competition because of an inability to breathe correctly.

Some horsemen talk about "long, thin necks" when, in reality, priority should be given to horses with an appropriate top-line to bottom-line neck ratio. Again, the top line of the neck to the bottom line should be two to one on a balanced horse. Invariably, horses with shorter necks are shorter-bodied, and since the horse is connected from its poll to tailset, a horse with a shorter neck may lack the flexion and suppleness desired for more advanced training, such as reining.

SHOULDERS

In addition to overall balance, the slope of the shoulder influences the length of stride. Thus, the straighter the shoulder, the shorter the stride. The angle of shoulder and pastern also serves to absorb shock when the horse moves. And the straight-shouldered horse will be shallow-hearted, as measured from top of withers to chest floor. Unlike the balanced horse, with legs that will measure approximately the same length as depth of heart, the straight-shouldered horse's legs will be longer than depth of heart. A straight-shouldered horse always will feel rough-riding compared to a horse with a desirably sloping shoulder.

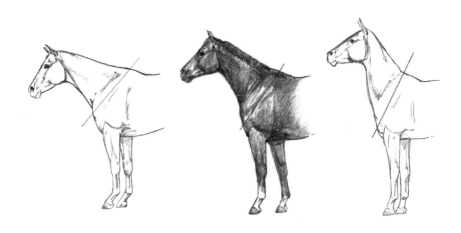

Neck set on low. *Average.* *Set on high.*

HEAD, NECK, AND SHOULDER RELATIONSHIP

WITHERS

The ideal withers are sharp, prominent, and slightly higher than the horse's hindquarters or croup. A balanced horse will appear to be sloping downhill from front to back. When the withers are higher than the croup, the hindquarters are properly positioned under the body and contribute to athletic ability. Strength of top line, over the back, loin, and croup, also is important in athletic ability and overall balance and soundness of the horse.

BARREL

Always evaluate spring of rib and depth of heart, as they indicate athletic capacity. Rule out horses that have a "pinched," flat-ribbed appearance and whose rib cages do not look rounded or convex.

HINDQUARTERS

When viewed from the side, the hindquarters should appear square. How the corners of the square are filled in will depend on the breed. American Quarter Horses are more desirably muscled, resulting in the hindquarters filling the square. The croup should not be too flat (which results in too much vertical action movement) or too steep (associated with a collected, but very short, choppy stride). The ideal American Quarter Horse has a quarter that is as full and as long from across the horizontal plane of the stifle as it is from point of hip to point of buttocks.

When viewed from the side, the hindquarters should appear square.

Muscling is one of the most important criteria in judging conformation in American Quarter Horses. It is important to realize that muscling is proportional (that is, as one muscle in the body increases, total muscle mass increases). Horses visually appraised as heavily muscled generally have greater circumference of forearm, gaskin, and width of quarter than lightly muscled horses. The horse is a balanced athlete that is muscled uniformly throughout.

FEET AND LEGS

Structure of feet and legs are major areas of consideration when evaluating a horse's conformation. When standing beside the horse, drop an imaginary line from the point of the buttocks to the ground. Ideally, that line should touch the hocks, run parallel to the cannon bone, and be slightly behind the heel. The horse with too much angle to its hocks is sickle-hocked, and the horse that is straight in its hocks is post-legged. Ideally, when viewed from the rear, any horse should be widest from stifle to stifle. Another imaginary line from the point of the buttocks to the ground should bisect the gaskin, hock, and hoof. It is not critical that a horse be perfectly straight from the ankles down as viewed from the rear. In fact, most horses naturally stand with the cannons parallel and toe out slightly from the ankles down. This allows the horse's stifle to clear its rib cage in flight, resulting in a longer-striding, freer-moving horse. However, when a horse is bowed in at the hocks and the cannon bones are not parallel, it is cow-hocked. Such horses have a tendency to be weak in the major movements that require work off the haunches, such as stopping, turning, and sliding. Occasionally you'll see horses that actually toe-in behind and are bow-legged. Most of them are very poor athletes.

The horse should stand on a straight column of bone with no deviation when viewed from the front. A horse that is "over at the knees" is buck-kneed, and the horse that is "back at the knees" is calf-kneed. Obviously, calf-kneed is the more serious condition since the knee will have a tendency to hyperextend backward. When the horse is viewed from the front, an imaginary line from the point of the shoulder to the toe should bisect the knee, cannon bone, and hoof, with the hoof pointing straight ahead. When a horse toes out, it is splay-footed, and the horse will always wing in when traveling. A horse that toes in is pigeon-toed and will always paddle out. The most serious of these cases is the horse that wings in. If the cannon bone is off-center to the outside, the horse is bench-kneed.

SOUNDNESS AND STRUCTURE

All horses should be serviceably sound. Young animals should have no indication of defects in conformation that may lead to unsoundness. (An unsoundness is defined as any deviation in structure that interferes with the usefulness of an individual.) Many horses will have blemishes—abnormalities that may detract from their appearance—but are sound. You should become familiar with all of the common unsoundnesses and learn to recognize them.

SKELETON OF THE HORSE

Many people are horse lovers, but only a few truly understand how this complex mechanism functions. Understanding the structure and functions of the skeletal system will result in more intelligent care and training of the animal. Studying the anatomy and physiology of this unique creature will enhance your expertise in the horse world. Keep in mind that anatomy and physiology are closely related to structure and function.

The skeleton of the horse is made up of 205 bones: The skull consists of 34 bones; the spinal column has 54 bones; there are 36 ribs, 1 sternum or breastbone, 40 bones of the thoracic limbs, and 40 bones of the pelvic limbs. The skeletal system gives the body form, protects many vital organs, and supports soft parts of the body.

Bones are divided into four categories: short, long, irregular, and flat. Short bones are found in the knee, hock, and fetlock; their purpose is to absorb concussion. The long bones are necessary for movement and supporting weight. Bones of the spinal column, the irregular bones, protect the central nervous system. Flat bones enclose and protect vital organs such as the brain, heart, and lungs.

Bones are covered by a membrane known as the periosteum. The periosteum serves as a protector for bones and, should a fracture occur, is the major site of healing. At times, injury to the periosteum will cause bony growths called spavins, splints, and ringbone. Keep in mind the following facts: Bones are attached to each other by ligaments; muscles are attached to bones by tendons; and joints are lubricated by synovial fluids. We will refer to various ligaments, tendons, and joints throughout.

SKULL

The horse's head seems considerably bulkier than is really necessary. Much of this bulk and weight is, however, associated with the teeth and jaws. The large size of the horse's head is related to its feeding habits. The skull consists of 34 irregularly shaped, flat bones that are united in early life by cartilage, which is later replaced by bone. As a foal ages, the union of the bones of the skull gradually becomes solid, and by the horse's eighth year, it is unyielding. The two halves of the lower jaw become united between the two central incisors when the foal is only two months old; until that time, the lower jaw has two separate halves. The hinged lower jaw is called the mandible, and the bones of the upper jaw that carry the upper cheek teeth are known as the maxillae.

The cranial cavity protects the brain and also supports and protects the

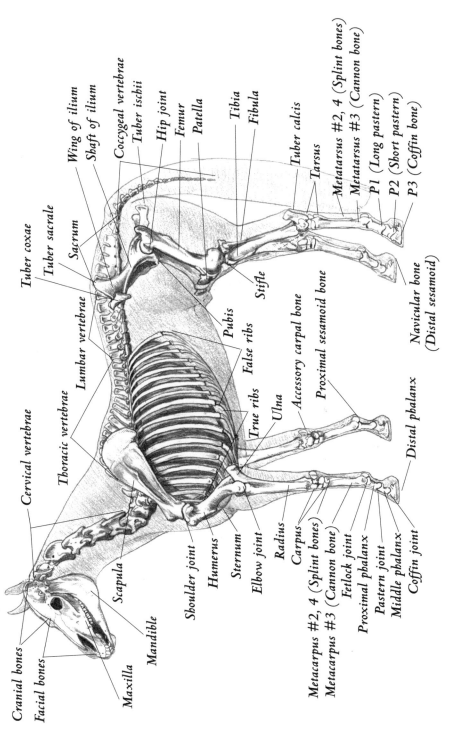

SKELETAL PARTS OF THE HORSE

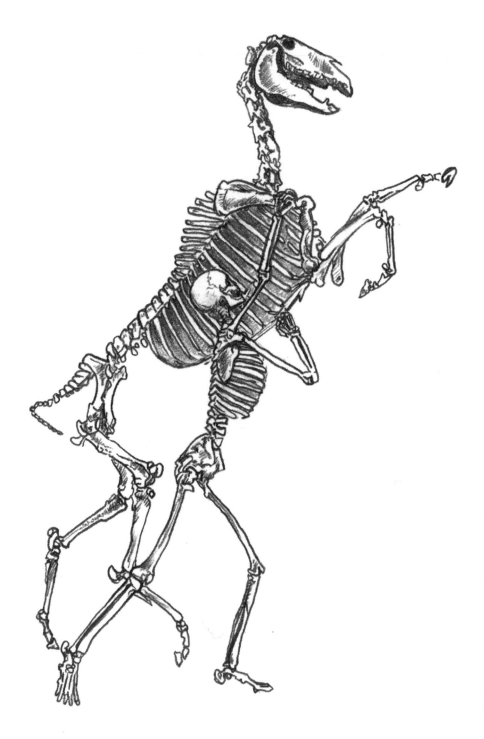

Skeletal relationship of horse to human.

eye in the orbital cavity. This bony enclosure also protects the nasal and oral passages. The relatively large size of the horse's head is due to the importance of mastication (chewing) for survival. The horse has strong, continuously growing teeth and large, strong jaws, which the upper part of the skull must be large enough to accommodate.

CERVICAL VERTEBRAE (NECK)

The horse's neck is made up of seven cervical vertebrae. The neck serves many purposes, including lowering the head to graze and to reach water in streams and lakes. The head is used as a pendulum to help maintain balance, and the neck's conformation and ability to move affects this process.

The cervical region is the most flexible part of the spinal column. The first vertebra, which is attached to the skull, is called the atlas vertebra, and permits extension and flexion of the neck and head. The second vertebra, the axis, allows side-to-side movement. This atlas-axis joint is sometimes referred to as the yes-no joint because it enables the animal to nod or shake its head. More important, these vertebrae enable the horse to shift its balance and assist in its ability to travel. Its sight will be restricted if the vertebrae do not allow adequate head movement. A short-necked horse has less use of its head than the horse with a properly conformed neck. An extremely long-necked

The position of neck bones regulates how a horse will carry its head and neck and influences the whole body carriage and gait.

horse is also at a disadvantage and lacks coordination and balance. Few people consider how important the neck is to the horse's ability to move properly. Avoid horses with extremely thick, beefy necks as well as those with especially thin, long necks. Also avoid ewe-necked horses, which carry their heads excessively high, cannot maintain proper balance, and may have restricted vision due to improper head carriage.

THORACIC VERTEBRAE

There are eighteen thoracic vertebrae. The first five constitute the withers, and the remaining thirteen make up the rest of the length of the back. The thoracic vertebrae serve as attachment for eighteen pairs of ribs. The first eight ribs are true ribs and are attached at the bottom of the breast bone. The last ten pairs of ribs are called false ribs. Together the ribs form a protective cover for the vital organs of the digestive, circulatory, and respiratory systems.

LUMBAR VERTEBRAE

There usually are six lumbar vertebrae; however, five are not uncommon, particularly in Arabian horses.

SACRAL VERTEBRAE

The sacral vertebrae contain five vertebrae that are fused together and are secured to the hip bones. These vertebrae underlie the croup of the horse.

COCCYGEAL VERTEBRAE

The coccygeal vertebrae (tail) vary in number, but usually fifteen to eighteen are present. These vertebrae become smaller as they proceed to the end of the tail. The last and smallest coccygeal vertebra is somewhat pointed.

FRONT LIMBS

The horse's front limbs are not directly attached to the vertebral column. The shoulder blade (scapula) is attached by muscles, not a bony structure. The radius and ulna form the upper part of the forearm. The knee (carpus) is made up of eight bones, and three metacarpal bones extend from the knee to the fetlock joint. The middle metacarpal is called the cannon bone, and the two smaller bones located on each side of the cannon are called splint bones.

HIND LIMBS

The hind limbs are firmly attached to the vertebral column by the pelvis bones. The femur is referred to as the thigh bone; the patella is a small bone of the stifle joint; the tibia is the main gaskin bone; and the fibula is a small bone fused to the gaskin bone. The hock (tarsus) contains seven bones and somewhat resembles the ankle and heel of humans. Like the front limbs, the hind limbs also have three cannon bones. They are called metatarsals.

PHALANGES

The first phalanx, or long pastern, is located just below the fetlock joint. The second phalanx is referred to as the short pastern, and the third phalanx, called the coffin or pedal bone, is surrounded by the hoof wall. The navicular bone is located just behind the coffin bone.

SUMMARY

Horses have varying degrees of arch to the spinal column. An extreme arch is referred to as roach back or hog back. If the backbone sags excessively, the horse is said to be "swaybacked." Either of these extremes represents undesirable conformation and is objectionable.

There is a close relationship between length of the vertebrae and the length of other parts of the animal. A horse with especially long vertebrae will have a longer tail, croup, loin, back, and neck. However, excessively long backs and loins are objectionable, since they will not be as strong as shorter backs. Be especially observant as you examine a horse's neck: extremely long or short necks will affect a horse's ability to move properly.

The skeletal system is amazing in its construction and equally amazing is its ability to function so efficiently. When assessing a horse's potential in performing maneuvers, consider first its skeletal system.

BODY SYSTEMS OF THE HORSE

The horse's bodily functions may seem quite complex, and to some, this topic may further seem unrelated to showing. Quite the contrary is true; in fact, all of the body systems are important when considering a horse's health, conformation, and ability to perform. Consider the following points:

1. Once feed or water has entered the pharynx, it cannot return to the mouth.
2. Horses cannot breathe through the mouth.
3. Wavelike contractions (peristalsis) move food down the esophagus; this is a one-way action from the pharynx to the stomach, making it nearly impossible for a horse to vomit.
4. Horses can choke especially when dry feed becomes lodged in the esophagus.
5. Parasites damage the delicate, sensitive systems of the horse. An immunization and parasite control program is vital to avoid harming a horse through neglect.

MUSCULAR SYSTEM

Muscles make up the largest tissue mass of the horse's body. There are three types of muscle: skeletal, cardiac, and smooth. The smooth and cardiac muscles are involuntary (automatic). Smooth muscle is located in the respiratory and digestive tracts as well as other areas. The skeletal muscles function as the horse moves; both long and short tendons attach these muscles to the bones. The flexor muscles cause flexion of a joint while the extensor muscles extend or straighten the joint.

The contractive process is a chemical reaction that produces heat within the muscle. This heat is very important in maintaining body temperature. Shivering is a muscle contraction that helps maintain heat in the body during cold weather. In hot weather the heat of exertion is released by sweating.

New horse owners seldom consider the importance of muscle conditioning. When muscles are overexerted without proper conditioning, muscle fatigue may develop. The importance of regular and consistent exercise cannot be overemphasized, since a careful conditioning program is necessary to help prevent muscle disorders.

RESPIRATORY SYSTEM

Oxygen is the most vital element to life, and a horse will die within minutes without sufficient oxygen. The respiratory system consists of air passages and the following organs: nasal cavity, pharynx, larynx, trachea, bronchi, and lungs. The main purpose of the respiratory system is to supply oxygen to the body and to remove carbon dioxide.

Movement of air in and out of the lungs is controlled by the contraction and relaxation of the diaphragm. The average rate of respiration is eight to sixteen times each minute. This rate increases greatly during strenuous activity.

Remember the following points:

1. As air enters the nasal cavity, it is warmed by a membrane lining the cavity.
2. The pharynx is an opening between the nasal passage and the mouth.
3. The larynx contains the vocal cords and prevents objects from being drawn into the trachea.
4. The epiglottis closes the air passage when food is being swallowed.
5. The trachea connects the throat to the lungs, and the lungs contain air sacs where the gaseous exchange takes place.

This very delicate system must be protected. Bacterial infection can cause pneumonia, and dusty, moldy feed can cause breathing difficulties. See that your horse is kept in sanitary surroundings and is not expected to consume forage that may cause digestive upsets or respiratory disturbances.

CIRCULATORY SYSTEM

Blood is necessary for the support of life. Blood removes waste products, carries nutrients, carries oxygen to the tissues, and provides immunity to disease.

The circulatory system consists of the heart, arteries, and veins. Arteries are thick-walled vessels that transport blood away from the heart. The capillary bed is the site of nutrient exchange, and the capillaries form small veins that unite with larger veins to return blood to the heart.

In general, the heart of a mature, resting horse will beat thirty-six to forty times a minute. (This rate is slower in draft horses and faster in Thoroughbreds.) Excitement, muscular exercise, and digestion are among the conditions that alter the heart rate, as does age. The heart of a ten-week-old foal will beat sixty to seventy-nine times per minute, while that of a five-year-old horse will beat thirty-six to fifty-seven times per minute.

URINARY SYSTEM

The urinary system is made up of the urethra, bladder, ureters, and a pair of kidneys. The kidneys, located in the loin area, clean the body of many waste products and control water balance.

Two muscular tubes (ureters) carry urine from the kidneys to the bladder. During urination, the muscular walls of the bladder contract and the urethra carries the waste products out of the body. The external organ of the urinary system in mares is the vulva; in geldings and stallions, it is the penis.

NERVOUS SYSTEM

The nervous system of the horse is highly sophisticated. It is a control mechanism that reacts to external and internal environment and stores memory for future use. The horse's sensitivity to touch, superb athletic ability, desire and willingness to please, as well as its low tolerance to pain, are all evidences of its uniqueness.

The nervous system is divided into the central nervous system, the peripheral nervous system, and the specialized sensory organs. The central nervous system is made up of the brain, brain stem, and spinal cord. This system regulates activities of the peripheral nervous system, which controls communication between the environment and the central nervous system. The peripheral nervous system is made up of the spinal and cranial nerves and is quite complex.

The specialized sensory organs are the eyes, ears, and nose. Horses have a highly developed sense of hearing and can hear sounds that humans cannot detect. However, some breeds differ in their ability to hear; lighter breeds tend to be more sensitive than heavier breeds.

ENDOCRINE SYSTEM

The endocrine system has long-range control over growth, digestion, and reproduction. This system is made up of ductless glands that produce hormones that influence many bodily functions. An improper environment can be detrimental to the workings of this delicate system.

REPRODUCTIVE SYSTEM

The reproductive system is also very complex. The female reproductive system is made up of the vulva, vagina, uterus, oviducts, and ovaries. The male reproductive system is made up of the penis, testicles, accessory glands, and ducts.

A successful horse breeder needs an in-depth knowledge of the anatomy of the male and female reproductive tract and an in-depth understanding of the estrous cycle, gestation period, hormonal changes, foal heat, infertility, castration, and sexual behavior.

I have introduced the systems of the horse briefly to establish in your mind the perfection and magnificence of this animal. These systems are delicate and must be considered as you ride and care for your horse. Horses must receive adequate feed, water, exercise to develop muscle and maintain these highly sophisticated bodily functions.

LIMBS OF THE HORSE

Many problems affect the horse's legs. Serious defects of the legs and feet are often overlooked, and the adage "no foot, no horse" may sometimes be a very apt observation.

SHOULDERS

The shoulder of the horse is attached to the thorax by cartilage, ligaments, and muscle. Although there is no body attachment that holds the shoulder to the thorax, the shoulder blade (scapula) serves as the main point of attachment to the body.

Most horse authorities agree that the shoulder should be "laid back" or sloped, ideally at a 45-degree angle. The shoulder also should be long and muscular. An especially long, sloping shoulder minimizes strain by distributing stress over a larger area. This type of shoulder is less prone to becoming stiff with overdeveloped muscles that are acquired in an attempt to withstand continual jar and strain. Shoulder damage can occur during racing, jumping, and the many other strenuous activities to which horses are subjected. Since

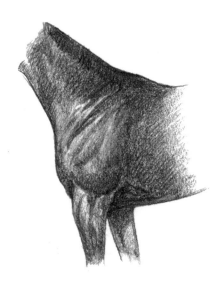
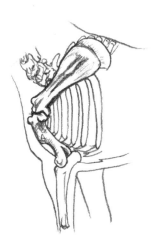

A desirable slope of shoulder. The shoulder blade (scapula) should slope back to such an extent that the leg can swing forward easily and freely, like a pendulum from the shoulder joint.

GOOD SHOULDER AND WITHERS

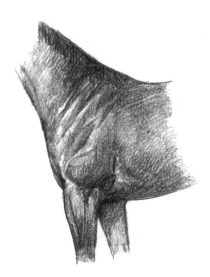

Straight or perpendicular shoulder.

POOR SHOULDER AND WITHERS

this desired slope decreases the angle between the humerus and scapula, concussion will be reduced. A long, sloping shoulder allows free forward motion while short, straight shoulders cause a shorter stride and increase impact as the foot strikes the ground. This short stride will not only cause more damage to the horse; it also will produce a less than comfortable experience for the rider.

FORELEGS

Proper set of the forelegs is very important if the legs are to function normally. The legs should be squarely set, and when viewed from the front, they should be straight so an imaginary line will bisect the foot, pastern, cannon bone, knee, forearm, and point of the shoulder. When viewed from the side, the cannon, knee, and forearm also should be in a straight line with the shoulder.

The forearm consists of two bones, the radius and the ulna, which extend from the elbow to the knee. The length of the forearm also plays a part in determining the length of stride; a long, well-muscled forearm is desirable. The cannon bone should be short and flat when viewed from the side. When viewed from the front, it should be centered in a wide, clean knee.

When viewed from the side, the legs should be nearly perpendicular to the underline of the horse's body. A properly shaped foreleg will allow freedom of movement and will minimize damage to the bone structure of the leg.

Few people think of evaluating the knee as they weigh various aspects of a horse's conformation. Yet some racehorse trainers consider the knees to be among the most important candidates for careful examination. As you view from the front, the knees should be placed squarely on the leg; horses whose legs break inward are termed knock-kneed while those with legs that break outward are termed bow-legged. If the cannon bone is not centered in the knee, also as viewed from the front, the condition is called bench or offset knee. The "open-knee" fault occurs when the joint bones are not large enough and a depression about the size of a finger crosses the middle, front surface of the knee. This characteristic is not considered a problem until after the horse is at least three years of age and the bones have stopped growing.

Two other undesirable faults of the foreleg include being buck-kneed and calf-kneed. An extremely buck-kneed horse will be clumsy and have a tendency to stumble excessively, but a slight case is not considered serious and seldom causes problems. Horses with severe cases tend to have bowed tendons and sesamoiditis due to excess strain on the flexor tendons and the sesamoid bone. Other terms sometimes used to describe this condition are knee-sprung, goat-knees, and over at the knees.

The calf-kneed horse stands with knees too far back, a condition that is especially damaging to the forelimb. Excess strain on the knee may cause the bones to chip, and permanent damage is very likely to occur.

Correct conformation.
A perpendicular line
drawn from the point
of the shoulder
to the ground
divides the leg
and foot into
two equal halves.

Toes out (splay-foot, or
toe wide). Narrow chest.

Toes in (pigeon toe).

Knock-kneed
(knee narrow).

Bow legs
(bow-kneed).

Base narrow
(feet too close together).

Base wide
(feet too far apart).

Bench knees
(offset knees).
Cannon bone is not
directly under forearm.

FRONT LIMBS VIEWED FROM THE FRONT

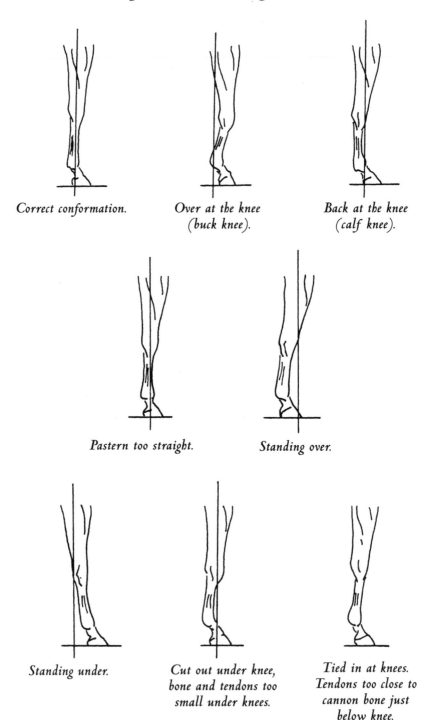

Correct conformation.

Over at the knee
(buck knee).

Back at the knee
(calf knee).

Pastern too straight.

Standing over.

Standing under.

Cut out under knee,
bone and tendons too
small under knees.

Tied in at knees.
Tendons too close to
cannon bone just
below knee.

FRONT LIMBS VIEWED FROM THE SIDE

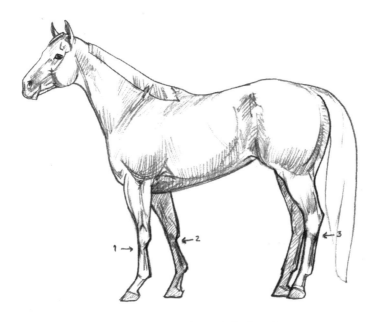

1. Back at the knee (calf knees).
2. Tied-in tendon.
3. Sickle hocks.

1. Over at the knee (buck knees).
2. Post-legged.

The fetlock joint, located between the pastern bones and the cannon bone, connects the leg to the foot. The fetlock should be examined for roughened hair and scars, which may be an indication that the leg in motion hits the opposite leg. Carefully examine this joint for stiffness and check for a strong, clean joint, free from bumps and injuries.

The pastern and fetlock joint will provide springiness to the horse's gaits. Pasterns should be moderately long and sloping to absorb concussion more effectively. Both slope and length of the pasterns will help determine smoothness and spring of stride. A pastern with excessive length and slope (coon-foot) will put strain on the sesamoid bones and tendons. Short, upright pasterns will not only cause a rough ride but may predispose the horse to ringbone, side bone, and navicular unsoundnesses.

Any serious examination of a horse—whether by a prospective purchaser or a judge—should include a visual check of the foot. First, the foot should be large enough to support the horse's weight. Second, the front

SIDE VIEW OF FOOT AND PASTERN AXIS

Normal front hoof and pastern axis, approximately 47 degrees (hind nearer 50 degrees).

Hoof and pastern axis less than normal (less than 45 degrees in front or less than 50 degrees behind).

Hoof and pastern axis greater than normal (greater than 50 degrees in front or greater than 55 degrees behind).

EXAMPLES OF BROKEN FOOT AND PASTERN AXIS

Broken hoof axis with toe too long and heel too low.

Broken hoof axis with toe too short and heel too high.

"Coon" foot. Weak pastern. The foot axis is steeper than the pastern axis.

EXAMINING THE FEET

feet should be more rounded than the back feet. Third, the heels should be wide and deep. Fourth, the hoof angle should be the same as the pastern. And finally, the hoof should be free from cracks and rings.

The foot is no less than amazing when we consider how it is constructed. The exterior of the hoof (hornywall) is the basic shell and wearing surface. This protective, horny wall is thickest at the toe and thinnest at the heel where it forms the bars under the foot to receive the frog. The center of the hoof is soft and sensitive and is called the frog; this V-shaped structure is located in the middle of the sole and acts as a shock absorber. The frog serves as a pump to the heart by increasing blood circulation from the lower limbs; it also assists the horse by providing traction as it travels.

The commissures are deep grooves located on each side of the frog, giving elasticity to the foot. The commissures should be kept clean to help prevent development of thrush, a disease that affects the cleft of the frog and is usually

Angles of pasterns and the arc a foot will follow as the horse moves.

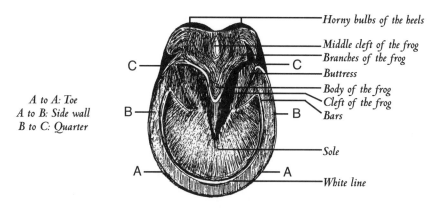

A to A: Toe
A to B: Side wall
B to C: Quarter

Horny bulbs of the heels
Middle cleft of the frog
Branches of the frog
Buttress
Body of the frog
Cleft of the frog
Bars
Sole
White line

STRUCTURE OF THE FOOT

caused by unsanitary conditions. The horny sole does not carry much weight, but it does protect soft areas of the foot from injury from rocks and other objects. Most of the horse's weight rests on the wall and frog area.

The perioplic ring, located where the hoof wall meets the hair of the leg, is an important part of the external portion of the hoof. It produces periople, which is a varnishlike substance that covers the outer surface of the hoof. Periople seals moisture in the hoof and prevents excessive drying. Moisture is extremely important in providing elasticity to the foot.

The hoof grows downward at a rate of about three-eighths of an inch per month. Horses in the wild wear their hooves off on rocky or sandy ground as they travel great distances in search of forage. Domesticated horses usually are confined to small areas, travel very little as they graze, and will therefore require hoof trimming every six to eight weeks.

HINDQUARTERS

The rear limbs of a horse are firmly attached to the spine by the pelvic bones. The hind limbs serve an entirely different purpose from the front limbs. The hindquarters provide force for moving the body forward, and since they do not receive a tremendous amount of concussion, this firm attachment does not damage delicate structures. Recall that the front limbs are attached to the spine and thorax by muscles that withstand concussion more efficiently than a bony attachment.

Breed types will vary somewhat in conformation, but certain points should be considered desirable and others undesirable. Extremes in length and slope of the croup should be avoided. Horses used as long-distance runners will have long, level croups, and short-distance runners will do well with slightly sloping croups. An exceptionally short, steep croup sometimes places excess strain on the hind legs. Excessive slope of the croup is termed goose-rumped. The croup angle dictates the way the horse moves best. A flat croup allows a long flowing stride, while a steep croup causes the hind leg to be more forcefully driven into the ground. The steep croup is favored by ropers who need horses that can start quickly, run at great speed for short distances, and stop quickly.

MUSCLING

The amount of muscling in the hindquarters can depend on the horse's bloodline and its purpose. Horses used for pulling heavy loads will naturally need more muscling than those used for speed.

The length and set of the cannon bones, the femur and tibia will affect the horse's gaits and potential speed. The femur should be inclined forward, downward and somewhat outward. The tibia should be long, increasing the area for muscle attachment, thus providing more driving power for the hindquarters and increasing potential speed. An especially short tibia will decrease the length of stride. The gaskin muscles are formed on the tibia. A gaskin that overlays good bone structure and is well muscled both inside and out will provide greater balance and reduce unsoundness.

The hock joint should be strong, wide, clean, and well defined, not rough or puffy. This joint is the hardest-working joint of the horse's body, and it should receive special consideration as you evaluate a horse's conformation. The angle of the hock, when viewed from the side, should not be too straight or especially acute. A line drawn from the point of the buttocks should touch the back of the hock and cannon bone and then continue to the ground, where it will strike three to four inches behind the hoof. A sickle-hocked horse has excessive angulation of the hock, the most common fault of the hind limbs. This fault places extensive strain on the plantar ligament

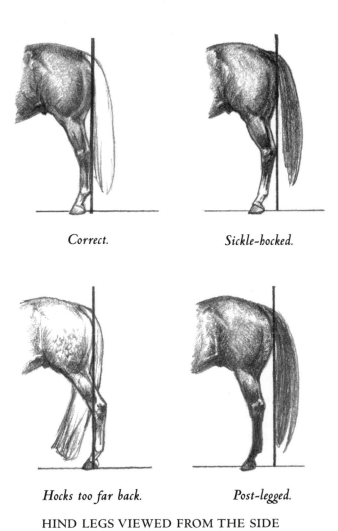

Correct.   *Sickle-hocked.*

Hocks too far back.   *Post-legged.*

HIND LEGS VIEWED FROM THE SIDE

and sometimes causes a curb to develop. Sickle hocks are sometimes referred to as curby conformation. Horses that are camped out have difficulty getting their legs under themselves in order to move properly. These horses have difficulty collecting themselves and tend to jab their legs into the ground.

When viewed from behind, lines dropped from the point of the buttocks should bisect the hocks, cannons, and heels, equally dividing the leg. This viewpoint also will reveal base-wide, base-narrow, cow-hock, and bowleg faults. Few horses have base-wide conformation of the rear quarters, but the base-narrow fault is quite common. Excess muscle on the outside of the leg will cause a horse to be base-narrow and place strain on the outside of the

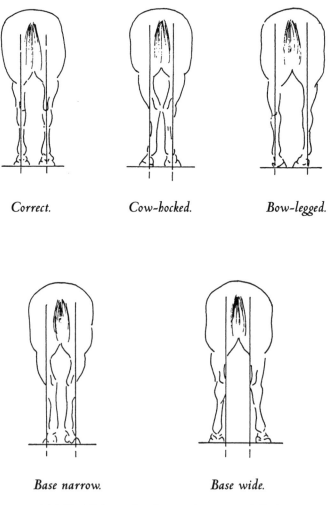

Correct.   *Cow-hocked.*   *Bow-legged.*

Base narrow.   *Base wide.*

HIND LEGS VIEWED FROM THE REAR

leg. The cow-hocked horse stands with the hocks inside the parallel line. This places excess strain on the inside of the horse's leg, which may, in turn, cause a bone spavin. The bowlegged horse will seem stiff in the hindquarters, and its straight-forward movement will be impaired.

Good legs and feet are essential if your horse is to be used in strenuous activities, but some serious leg faults may hamper its performance even though it is used only for light riding. Never purchase a horse if its conformation or disposition suggests that it will be unsafe. The legs and feet are of utmost importance, but also consider eyesight, coordination, inherited characteristics, vices, and possible nuisance habits acquired through an incompetent handler.

EQUINE BLEMISHES AND UNSOUNDNESSES

Regardless of breed or type, certain characteristics are desirable and others undesirable. Some breeds are better suited for speed and long-distance riding; others are conformed ideally for jumping; still others are more muscular and excel in activities that require great strength.

Let's take a closer look at the Quarter Horse's various parts individually and see how conformation may enhance or hinder its ability to perform well and remain sound. As you make a general assessment of equine conformation, keep in mind the following points.

The head should be attractive and well proportioned to the rest of the body. The shape of the head will have an effect on eyesight, balance, and the ability to breathe properly. The ears should be carried alertly and the eyes be prominent, clear, and large. A broad forehead indicates intelligence, while a long, narrow head indicates plainness and is less desirable. The head should be triangular when viewed from the side and front, the jaws large and powerful, and the head should taper down to a refined muzzle. There should be no unevenness or mismatch of upper and lower jaw. A horse with an overbite ("parrot mouth") or undershot jaw will have trouble eating and usually will be a poor keeper and thus it will be hard to keep fit. The nostrils should be large and capable of great dilation. (Remember, a horse cannot breathe through its mouth as a human does when out of breath, so it needs to be able to take great gulps of air through the nostrils when running hard.)

The neck should be in balance with the rest of the body, and the head should be attached properly to the neck to allow a clean throatlatch that is trim and capable of great flexion. The neck is important as a means of lowering the head for grazing, and its length will greatly determine the ability or inability of the horse to shift its center of gravity and maintain balance. A short, thick neck often results in an unyielding, stiff throatlatch that limits suppleness and balance. Ideally, the neck will be slender, clean in the throat, and capable of flexion, which will enhance balance and length of stride. The

Overbite (Parrot mouth).   *Undershot.*

HEAD AND JAW

"ewe-necked" horse has a concave top line accompanied by a depression in front of the withers and usually has a sagging bottom line. This type of horse will have difficulty when asked to flex at the poll and consequently will not be suitable for Western pleasure or any other performance class. It will have a tendency to throw its head upward rather than to accept the bit. The opposite extreme of the ewe neck is a "cresty neck," in which excess fatty deposits line the crest of the neck. This fault greatly restricts flexibility. In some instances this excess fat causes the crest to fall off to one side of the neck. Beauty and refinement of the head and neck are important not only for looks but will also affect movement and balance.

The horse's chest should not be too wide or too narrow. If the chest is too narrow, leg interference may occur because the horse will move with a crisscross motion. If the chest is too wide between the front legs, the horse may paddle and have a rolling type of gait.

The horse's height is measured from the highest point of the withers, the tallest fixed point of its body. The withers should be high enough to hold a saddle and prevent it from slipping from side to side. Prominent withers allow greater flexibility and coordination because ligaments and muscles that attach the neck to the thorax are freer to move. Higher withers are usually accompanied by long, sloping shoulders, and this extra length of muscle will result in lighter, freer movement. Be aware that excessively prominent, thin withers are a fault, and the saddle may cause soreness and injury if rubbing occurs on the withers. Horses with low, round withers often have a heavy front end and usually move poorly. Withers that are too low are termed mutton withers. This fault will restrict movement of the shoulder, usually shortening the length of stride. Flat withers cause difficulty in a riding horse because the saddle will not stay in place. The excessively tight cinch the rider uses in an attempt to stabilize the saddle may cause sores to develop.

The thorax of the horse is sometimes referred to as the trunk, middle, or barrel. The thorax is formed by the spine at the top, ribs on the side, and cartilage and breastbone at the bottom. The ideally shaped thorax will supply adequate space for the heart and lungs and will provide a large area for muscular attachment of the shoulders and legs. The "slab-sided" horse has less space for air intake, has less staying ability, and is limited in its ability to carry weight. The "round" barrel appears to have well-sprung ribs, but the ribs will not carry down a sufficient distance along the sides. Horses with this type of barrel may have difficulty maintaining balance due to legginess.

FORELIMB BLEMISHES AND UNSOUNDNESSES

A horse should be evaluated for soundness and serviceability. A good horseman or woman should be able to recognize blemishes and unsoundnesses, understand how they may affect the horse's usefulness, and know what causes these faults. A horse may be sound for one purpose but unsound for another. For example, crippled and lame horses sometimes are used for breeding but cannot be used for riding. Experience and study is necessary to determine how serious an unsoundness is. Unsoundnesses that are a result of faulty conformation usually are considered the most serious since they may be inherited. Unsoundness also includes other serious faults that interfere with the horse's usefulness. Blemishes, on the other hand, are abnormalities that do not normally affect the horse's usefulness. Rope burns, wire cuts, and shoe boils generally are considered blemishes.

Splints are bony growths on the cannon or splint bones. A splint can be considered either an unsoundness or a blemish, depending on the location and whether lameness is present. The most common causes of splints are overworking a young horse, hard stops, fast turns, galloping on hard surfaces, slipping, or getting kicked. "Bench-kneed" horses are especially prone to develop splints because extra strain is placed on the inner splint bone. Some splints are caused by interference from the opposite front foot. The use of splint boots or heavy bandages reduces splint formation in young horses. Usually a splint will "set" with rest, and the inflammation will become only a bony blemish.

Sidebones develop when lateral cartilages, immediately above and toward the rear quarter of the hoof, become ossified. This bony growth may be of genetic origin, may develop from injuries, or may be caused by concussion. The condition is seen more commonly in draft breeds and in horses that toe in or out. The calcification is considered an unsoundness in young horses

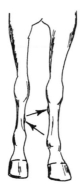 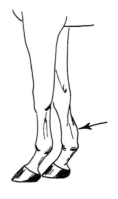

SPLINT

A bony enlargement in the groove formed by the splint and cannon bone. It may be high or low, forward or back (occasionally on the outside).

BOWED TENDON

An extension behind the flexor tendons, caused by tearing or stretching.

CANNONS—COMMON BLEMISHES
AND UNSOUNDNESSES

because it may result in contracted heels and abnormal foot growth, which causes permanent lameness.

Ringbone is a bony growth on the first, second, or third phalanges. While the forefeet are most commonly affected, this condition may occur on any foot. It is caused by strain on ligaments of the coffin and pastern joints, concussion from work on hard surfaces, straight pasterns, and the toe-out and toe-in conditions. The name ringbone was given to this particular condition because the bony enlargement can encircle the pastern bone.

Bucked shins, enlargements on the front of the cannon bone, are located between the fetlock joint and the knee. Bucked shins usually occur during the first few weeks of strenuous training and are especially prevalent in young racehorses. This enlargement usually occurs in the front legs and is due to injury of the periosteum (the membrane that covers all bones). New bone growth (exostosis) causes a "bucked" appearance to the leg.

A **bowed tendon** is an inflammation and enlargement of the tendon behind the cannon bone. This condition may be caused by long, weak pasterns, long toes, excessive strain, fatigue, or improper shoeing. Generally, however, it results from severe strain and may occur anywhere along the cannon bone. This condition is extremely serious since few bowed tendons heal totally.

A **shoe boil** (capped elbow) is a soft swelling at the point of the elbow and is usually caused when the elbow bursa is irritated by the hoof when the animal is lying down. Serious lameness rarely develops, and this condition is considered a blemish.

Wind-puffs (windgalls) are enlargements of the fluid sacs (bursa) and are the result of hard work, especially on hard surfaces. Wind-puffs are located around the pastern or fetlock joints and may appear on the front or the back feet. Many older horses have wind-puffs, which are an indication that they have been worked very hard. These enlargements are not usually serious.

Popped knees are the result of inflammatory conditions of the joint, bones, or ligaments. Popped knees are caused by concussion and trauma, and are most common in racehorses but will occur in other horses that are worked especially hard. Bad conformation, such as calf-knees, may predispose a horse to this problem. Horses with popped knees seldom regain soundness and will not withstand hard work.

Sand cracks or **cracked hooves** usually occur when the feet have been neglected. Dry, brittle hooves of unshod horses are most apt to develop cracks. These cracks, which may cause lameness, can be prevented by keeping the hooves flexible with moisture and by keeping the feet properly trimmed or shod.

TOE CRACK

A split in the front of the hoof wall. May be partial, complete, high, or low.

SIDEBONES

Ossification of the lateral cartilages resulting from injuries that cause calcium to accumulate and harden.

QUARTER CRACK

A split in the quarter area of the hoof wall that runs toward the heel.

SEEDY TOE

A separation of the wall of the hoof near the toe. Cracks starting on the bearing surface are usually due to improper care. Cracks originating at the coronary band are usually caused by an injury.

RINGBONE

A bony enlargement surrounding the bones of the pastern.

FEET AND PASTERN SOUNDNESS

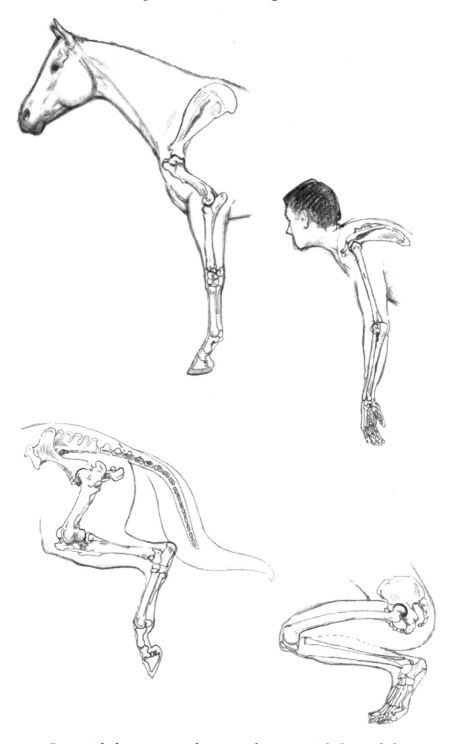

Parts of the horse corresponding to similar parts of the human body.

HIND LIMB BLEMISHES AND UNSOUNDNESSES

The hind limbs are the primary propulsive force; consequently, most blemishes and unsoundnesses of the hind limbs are the result of sprains and strains rather than damage from concussion. Front-leg unsoundnesses such as splints and ring bone can occur on the hind legs but are less frequent.

The horse's stifle corresponds to the knee in humans.* A horse is said to be **stifled** when the kneecap slips to a location above and to the inside of its proper location. The stifle and hock are then unable to flex. The patella (kneecap) can sometimes be returned to its normal position manually, but severe cases may require surgery.

A **curb** is a firm enlargement at the rear of the leg just below the point of the hock. It develops when stress causes the plantar ligament to thicken. This problem can be caused by sickle or cow hocks, kicking, or even a direct blow. A curb caused by faulty conformation is more serious and may result in chronic lameness.

A **capped hock** is an enlargement at the point of the hock that is caused by bruising when the horse kicks the walls of its stall, trailer gate, or any other solid object. This enlargement is unsightly but usually isn't considered serious unless it affects the horse's ability to work.

A **bone spavin** (jack spavin) is a bony enlargement located on the inside and front of the hock. Faulty conformation such as sickle hocks or cow hocks may predispose a horse to bone spavin due to excess stress on the inside of the hock joint. Horses with narrow, thin hocks are especially susceptible. Bruises and sprains also may cause this serious unsoundness to develop.

A **bog spavin** is a filling of the natural depression on the inside, front portion of the hock joint. This type of spavin may be caused by straight hocks, strain, and/or nutritional deficiency. A bog spavin caused by accidental trauma, such as a kick by another horse, is treated more easily and is less apt to affect serviceability.

A **thoroughpin** is an enlargement in the web of the hock and can be moved to the opposite side of the leg by palpation. This condition is caused by strain on the flexor tendon, which causes synovial fluid to enter the hollow of the hock. Thoroughpins are rarely serious and are usually considered a blemish.

This summary has not covered all equine blemishes and unsoundnesses but has introduced you to many potential problems. To develop a talent for identifying and evaluating all the conformation faults, blemishes, and unsoundnesses, you will need much practice and experience.

---

*It is interesting to note that almost every part of the horse (except the tail) corresponds to a similar part of the human body. The stifle is the same as the human knee and has the same kneecap (patella). The horse's "knee" on its foreleg is comparable to the human wrist and even has the same seven bones. The hock joint in the hind leg is similar to the human ankle. The cannon bone in a horse is like the human middle finger, and the fetlock joint compares with the middle knuckle on that middle finger.

CURB

An enlargement below the point of the hock. This fullness is due to an enlargement of the ligament, tendon sheath, or skin. Can be caused by structural defects such as cow-hocks or sickle-hocks.

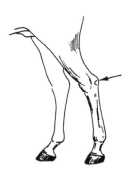

CAPPED HOCK

An enlargement on the point of the hock, usually caused by bruising.

BOG SPAVIN

Any inflammation or swelling of the soft tissues of the hock.

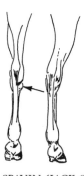

THOROUGHPIN

A puffy condition in the hollows of the hock. It can be identified by movement of the puff, when pressed, to the opposite side of the leg. Caused by strain on the flexor tendon.

BONE SPAVIN (JACK SPAVIN)

A bony enlargement that appears on the inside and front of the hock at the point where the base of the hock tapers into the cannon bone.

HOCKS—COMMON BLEMISHES
AND UNSOUNDNESSES

MOVEMENT OF THE HORSE

Most aspects involved when evaluating a horse have been discussed earlier. Regardless of how you will use a horse, certain points of conformation should be stressed. For example:

1. Is the head well proportioned to the rest of the body with adequate width between the eyes?
2. Is the chest deep and wide?
3. Are the front and rear legs straight and squarely set?
4. Is there adequate muscling over the croup and through the rear quarters?
5. Are the shoulders and pasterns sloping at a 45-degree angle?
6. Is the back short and strong?
7. Are the ribs well sprung?
8. Are any unsoundnesses evident?
9. What has caused noticeable blemishes?
10. Are the hooves large, dense, and wide at the heels?

As you evaluate a horse, you should consider these points plus its manner of moving, or gaits. Before domestication, the horse had four natural gaits: the walk, trot, canter, and gallop. These gaits have been modified and others have been added through training and selective breeding. "Gait" (walk, trot, and so on) refers to a specific movement, while "way of going" (rough, smooth) refers to the nature of the movement. "Action," on the other hand, is used to describe the amount of flexion in the knees and hocks.

As you observe the horse's movement, keep in mind that movement should be straight without wasted motion; it also should be brisk and not sluggish; it should be free and regular without lameness; and the stride should be long, not short and choppy.

NATURAL GAITS

The **walk** is a slow, flat-footed lateral gait. The sequence of hoofbeats is: left back, left front, right back, right front. When both feet on one side strike the ground before the feet on the opposite side strike the ground, the movement is called a lateral gait. The walk is a slow, four-beat gait that should be springy and regular.

The **trot** (jog) is a two-beat gait in which diagonal feet strike and leave the ground at the same time. When one forefoot strikes the ground simultaneously with the hind foot on the opposite side, the movement is called a diagonal gait.

The **canter** (lope) is a three-beat gait in which two diagonal legs strike the ground between beats of the unpaired legs. The legs that strike the ground separately are called lead limbs.

The run or **gallop** is a fast, four-beat gait. This natural gait is an extended canter in which one hind foot strikes the ground, followed by the other hind foot. The front foot on the same side as the first striding hind foot then strikes the ground and is followed by the last or leading front leg. With speed, the middle diagonal beat of the canter will become two beats rather than one, producing a four-beat gait.

ARTIFICIAL (ACQUIRED) GAITS

Training must accompany natural ability and conformation to bring a horse to its full potential. No horse, regardless of how it is used, will reach a high degree of proficiency without training. But do not make the mistake of trying to train a horse for something that does not suit its conformation and natural abilities.

Even though carefully trained, a horse will revert to untrained behavior if subjected to an inexperienced, careless rider. Less experienced riders should not purchase finely trained horses and expect them to continue performing at this highly trained level. Proper and frequent schooling is important to prevent the highly trained horse from reverting to an ordinary mount.

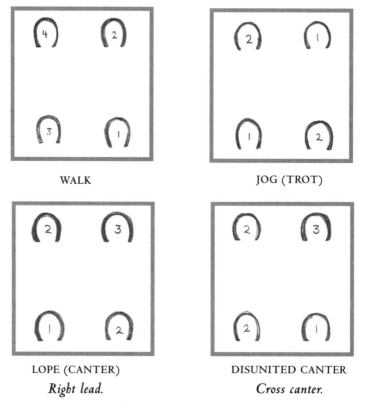

WALK

JOG (TROT)

LOPE (CANTER)
Right lead.

DISUNITED CANTER
Cross canter.

FOOTFALLS OF THE HORSE

DEFECTS IN MOVEMENT

The flight of the foot should be perfectly straight, since any deviation will cause stress to the legs and may lead to unsoundness. Watch for the following common faults when you observe a horse's movement:

- **Forging** occurs when the hind foot strikes the sole of the front foot on the same side, usually during the slow trot.
- Pigeon-toed horses have a tendency to throw the front feet outward as they move; this is known as **paddling.**
- Heavy movement rather than the desired light, springy movement is termed **pounding.**
- **Scalping** occurs when the hairline at the top of the hind foot hits the toe of the front foot as the horse strides forward.
- Short, straight pasterns and straight shoulders predispose horses to a short, choppy stride referred to as **trappy.**
- **Winging** is the inward deviation of the front feet and may result in interference.
- Excessively wide-fronted horses tend to **roll** from side to side as they move. This rolling motion is unpleasant and an undesirable type of action.
- **Lameness** can be detected by a characteristic bobbing of the head as the affected foot strikes the ground.

The horse's ability to move gracefully, as well as straight and true, will depend on its conformation. Any of the listed defects of movement may be present in varying degrees. Always consider implications of future unsoundness when a defect is present.

I've described only a few types of faults to stimulate your desire to look further and study for yourself. After noting the good qualities and the bad ones of whatever horse we're looking at, we always must take into consideration its "way of going," or what makes a "good mover"—terms often used but seldom understood. I'm going to be somewhat technical now and explain what "way of going" actually means.

The **pace** refers to the rate at which the horse moves, and the **action** implies flexion of the knees and hocks; the **stride,** then, means the distance from the point of breaking over to the point of contact of the same foot. The **direction,** or trueness, is the line in which the foot is carried forward during the stride; **rapidity** or promptness is the time consumed in taking a single stride, while **power** is the pulling force exerted at each stride. The **height** also must be noted; it is the degree to which the foot is elevated in the stride indicated by the arc. **Spring** is the manner in which the weight settles on the supporting parts of the body at the completion of the stride. **Regularity,** the rhythmical precision with which each stride is produced, is a must for soundness.

When judging a horse, you must consider the way of going and the gait; together they are the basis of every champion and can be summarized in a few words: the horse's ability to coordinate its action and move in good form. When you look at a horse's conformation, see it for what it is in relation to what it can do.

PROCEDURE FOR JUDGING A HALTER CLASS

Horses will walk to the judge one at a time. As the horse approaches, the judge will step to the right (left of the horse) to enable the horse to trot straight to a cone placed fifty feet away. At the cone, the horse will continue trotting, turn to the left, and trot toward the left wall or fence of the arena. After trotting, horses will be lined up head to tail for individual inspection by the judge. The judge shall inspect each horse from both sides, front and rear.

All stallions two-years-old and over shall have two visible testicles. All mares and stallions shall be examined for parrot mouth. The judge should excuse from the ring all lame horses, cryptorchids, and parrot-mouthed horses prior to final placing. The judge should line the horses to be placed in a head-to-tail order according to preference.

HALTER JUDGING EXAMPLE

As noted previously, judging is an effort to find the horse that most closely fits what could be considered the industry ideal. It is a positive process. When evaluating a class of halter horses, there are four major considerations:

- Balance and/or quality
- Muscling
- Structural correctness
- Breed and sex character

When evaluating a class only on these characteristics, you can use a chart to aid you in placing a class.

Rank the individuals in the class on balance, muscling, structure, and then on breed and sex character. Total the numbers for each horse, and place the horse with the smallest total first in the class. Suppose a class was evaluated as follows for the main criteria:

HORSE #	BALANCE	MUSCLING	STRUCTURE	B & S CHARACTER	TOTAL
1	1st	2nd	1st	1st	5 pts.
2	2nd	1st	2nd	2nd	7 pts.
3	3rd	4th	3rd	3rd	13 pts.
4	4th	3rd	4th	4th	15 pts.

You would place this class 1-2-3-4. This is a relatively easy way to begin placing halter classes and can be efficient in keeping placings objective and positive. However, a judge will use this method less frequently as he or she becomes more accustomed to formally evaluating horses.

LAMENESS

Bringing together the components of balance and structural correctness, the horse must be able to move as a durable, well-balanced athlete. One criterion of movement is the ability to be sound of limb (not showing lameness). The degree of lameness that allows a horse to perform is based on the American Association of Equine Practitioners' definition of what constitutes the various degrees of lameness.

AAEP GRADING SYSTEM

0 degree – Lameness not perceptible under any circumstances.

1 degree – Lameness is difficult to observe; not consistently apparent regardless of circumstances (such as weight-carrying, circling, inclines, hard surfaces, etc.).

2 degree – Lameness is difficult to observe at a walk or trotting a straight line; consistently apparent under certain circumstances (such as weight-carrying, circling, inclines, hard surfaces, etc.).

3 degree – Lameness is consistently observable at a trot under all circumstances.

4 degree – Obvious lameness: marked nodding, hitching, or shortened stride.

5 degree – Minimal weight-bearing in motion and/or at rest; inability to move.

SIGNS OF LAMENESS

A. Head goes up when lame forelimb strikes the ground with exception of shoulder lameness, which is very rare.

B. Bilaterally symmetrical forelimb lamenesses are characterized by shortened, stilted gait rather than head nod.

C. Hip is hiked up when lame rear limb strikes the ground, and head tends to drop when lame rear limb strikes the ground.

D. Attitude, willingness to go forward, and expression can be important indicators of lameness.

MECHANICAL VS. PAINFUL LAMENESS

A. Mechanical lameness is more common in the rear limb and is due to a mechanical problem, such as shortened muscle or tendon. Intermittent upward fixation of patella in the slow-jogging pleasure horse is mechanical, as is fibrotic myopathy.

B.   Post-legged horses have a difficult time doing the slow jog as their stifles tend to lock or catch when the limb is extended behind them.

C.   Subtle mechanical lameness often is not a detriment to the horse's performance but may be unattractive.

LAMENESS VS. WAY OF GOING

A.   Winging, paddling, forging, climbing, and so on are not lameness problems but are cosmetically undesirable in some events. Horses with these problems usually do not have an increased incidence of lameness problems but are considered "bad movers."

B.   Bad movers are defined by style and tradition rather than by medical factors.

C.   Bad movers may or may not be penalized for their way of going. This is a judge's prerogative and not a medical consideration.

ACCEPTABLE VS. UNACCEPTABLE LAMENESS

A.   Protection of the horse, prevention of abuse, and public relations must be considered at all times.

B.   A horse showing lameness greater than or equal to three degree should not be allowed to compete in any event.

C.   One degree lameness is subtle, inconsistent, and not a serious threat to the horse at this time.

D.   The two degree lame horse is the problem. If it is a two– degree with a willing, go-forward attitude, it should be allowed to compete. If the horse is a two+ degree lame, appears unable to perform, it should be excused from showing.

E.   If you are in doubt about a horse, watch it go both directions in the corners at a trot, establishing a rhythm in cadence with its footfalls by tapping your foot or nodding your head.

F.   Remember that lameness must be consistent to be considered a problem: Is a horse consistently lame in the left front every stride at a trot to the left? Or did it take four lame steps and then recover completely?

G.   What to do with the horse who becomes lame during performance: If it is becoming more lame as it goes, it should be stopped and excused from the ring. If a horse completes its work and is noticed to be obviously lame when leaving the ring, this becomes a judgment call and may or may not be penalized.

H.   When in doubt, remember that your obligation to the horse should come before your obligation to the exhibitor. If your decision was honestly in the best interest of the horse, you should not be criticized.

CHAPTER III

Western Performance Classes

WESTERN PLEASURE HORSE

THE most discussed class at Quarter Horse shows is probably the Western pleasure class. Don't let that word "pleasure" mislead you into thinking this division is a piece of cake. It's one of the most competitive of all and one of the most difficult to judge. The performance requirements may sound simple: the walk, jog, lope, extended gaits, with halts and backups thrown in from time to time. But it's not so simple to produce a winning performance.

No division has undergone so great an evolution as the Western pleasure classes. Many years ago, the horse that could stay on the proper lead the longest could eventually win a pleasure class. In the intervening years, just about every head position one could dream up has gone in and out of fashion, and we have, for the most part, survived the epidemic of the four-beat lope.

The horses we use for Western pleasure also have changed in the conformation department. Today we have more athletic horses. To win now, a horse must be attractive to the eye, especially when in motion, and it must be a good mover, fluid and balanced. Regardless of breed, the horse must have good angulation: a long sloping shoulder to allow freedom, a long forearm to allow fluid movement, a short cannon bone, and a pastern that correlates with the angle of the shoulder to provide a cushioning effect to concussion.

The back must be level and strong with a good hip angle for driving power. The horse must travel square and true, be in rhythm, and give the appearance of being soft—"kissing the ground," as they say. No longer can a horse hit the ground hard at every gait, be sullen and resentful, and win the pleasure classes. Not the major ones anyway.

The head and eye must be appealing with a look of intelligence.

Today, though, more than these points must be considered when judging the class. As we become more sophisticated in selecting and showing, we must upgrade the evaluation system, or criteria, by which we pick a winner. Even though the horses are shown in a group, each individual must be judged and compared to all the other individuals in any given class.

All horses are not built alike, and all horses do not go alike. So, the individual, how it travels, how it looks, and what it does, is of primary importance. An individual that travels in balance, soft and fluid, will beat one that is heavy and uneven. Some horses, because of their conformation, have a longer stride or longer reach. Horses of different sizes go in a way that is different from that of their shorter or larger counterparts. Each should be given credit for how it performs the required gaits, even though the horses are shown in a group.

Sometimes riders allow the first horse into the ring to set the pace, and everyone follows in lock-step, making it look like an elephant train, with each animal's head hooked to the tail in front. The first horse in the class should not dictate the speed or length of stride of any other horse being shown. A rider shouldn't hesitate to pass another if that's the way his or her horse shows best.

You've all heard the cliché "Show your horse to its best advantage." Nowhere is that more true than in the Western pleasure class. If, in a class, one rider must pass another, his or her horse should be able to move out with a minimum of urging. Conversely, if the rider has to slow down to get a better advantage or get out of a crowd, his or her horse should come back willingly without resentment or duress.

Every horse will tell you where it needs to carry its head for maximum balance, but you must pay attention. Watch your horse move naturally in a field or corral. See where it puts its head when it's moving around. Try different head positions, and when the horse's top line (from withers to croup) becomes level, you'll see where the head should be carried. This should be done at the trot to get the horse accustomed to a change in head position, or set, and at the lope to determine the exact position of the head as it relates to the neck and how it comes out of the body.

The throatlatch also plays a major role in head position, as does the length of the neck. A thick throatlatch, in any breed, will not allow for flexion. Head set then, by its very nature, should be related to what each horse actually needs in order to go in form and be balanced.

In judging, of course, we need to place the best horse on top. In the pleasure classes it should be the one that is balanced, is a good mover, and that most assuredly gives the appearance of being a pleasure to ride.

From the judges' standpoint, and most definitely depending on where they stand in the arena, the view they get or the angle they focus on plays a major role in the overall outcome of the class. Regardless of the type of horse, the animal must be seen to be judged. If judges stand in the corner and look at three-quarters of the ring, they see quite a bit more than judges who look at one spot on the wall and see a horse only for a split second as it passes by.

The first gait requested is usually the **walk**, which is the horse's basic natural gait. You might expect all horses to walk in more or less the same way, but there's probably more variety in performing this gait than any other, between the two extremes of the horse that plods listlessly along and the hot horse that needs continual checking to keep it from breaking into a faster gait. Some horses walk in a perfectly straight line, and others wobble left and right or bob up and down.

The pleasure walk is a four-beat, flat-footed gait that should be free and easy, willing rather than forced, forward-moving in a straight line and in balance.

When evaluating the walk, judges should begin by observing the whole horse, seeing if it's walking with straight, firm movements and no shuffling or stumbling. They are looking for a free and easy gait, not the fastest in the ring but one the rider can slow down or speed up on command. Judges also should notice the horse's behavior toward others. Is it aggressive, pushy, nervous? Or is the horse paying attention only to the rider, as it should?

The exact distance for showing the walk is up to the judges. It shouldn't be a marathon, but it should be long enough for them to form an opinion not only of the walk but of the horse as a whole. Too often, however, the walk is used merely as a transition from one gait to another.

Some judges proceed quite rapidly into the **jog**, a diagonal two-beat gait that gives a clearer picture of the horse's mechanical movement. It's a gait that shows up faults such as forging, winging, crossing over, interfering, and lameness. You'll also see some horses that sway from side to side or bobble up and down, and some that simply trudge along with bended knees. With any luck, there will be others performing a true diagonal two-beat gait.

The principal indication of a good jog is the top line, which should remain level. A level back is, after all, what makes a horse pleasant and comfortable to ride, and a good pleasure horse should maintain a level top line no matter what it's doing with its legs. Next, judges should notice if the horse is moving in cadence, a regular rhythm like a military parade. It should move straight, with a smooth, elastic step that doesn't jolt the rider out of the saddle. Every part of its body, from head to croup, should work together to produce a smooth, coordinated movement. As at the walk, the horse should be able and willing to jog faster or slower on command, and rapidly make transitions to other gaits if asked to do so. These transitions are of critical importance to judges.

It is very difficult for judges to view all of the gait transitions of all of the horses in a Western pleasure class at one time. However, when judges are looking for differences between two horses that perform equally well, they can focus on the transitions. The change from one gait to another should occur smoothly without resistance in the bridle. The transition should be clean with no delays, extra steps, half steps, or stumbling.

The third gait required of a Western pleasure horse is the **lope**. Here again, you see a lot of variations. The most important point in the lope is for the horse always to be on the correct lead and to maintain it as long as necessary.

The best spot for judges to evaluate the lope is from a corner, where they can observe the horses not only from the side but also coming straight toward them and going straight away. When a horse is heading toward you, you can spot at once if it's holding its head straight or to one side, if it shoulders in or out or puts a hip to the inside. You'll also see how it reacts to passing another horse or being passed. And when you get the profile view, you can see whether the horse's top line is level. This is just as important at the lope as it is at the other gaits, because the horses that win ribbons in this class should be comfortable, smooth and easy, a real pleasure to ride.

Although all of the gaits are important when judging the pleasure horse, a key indicator of a horse's movement potential is its ability to lope well. A lot of horses can walk and trot well, but few are superior lopers. This is probably because the trot has a two-beat rhythm, which is a naturally balanced, cadenced gait, and the stable, four-beat walk is often relaxing for the horse. Thus it would be a little more difficult to ruin a horse's trot or walk than it would be to ruin its lope.

If you'll think about it, this explains why, in most performance classes, the lope (or canter) is the essential gait. The only classes that are won at the walk and trot are Walk-Trot, Pleasure Driving, and perhaps Trail. All the others depend on the horse's ability to lope. The horse lopes through the reining and Western riding pattern, after a steer or calf, through the games classes, and canters over fences.

It's no wonder the lope is emphasized. There have been many good trotters, but the percentage of really fine lopers has been slim. If a horse is a good loper, it will most likely change its leads correctly. The lope is the gait that will really show whether a horse has natural balance and can use its hindquarters like an athlete.

The lope (canter) is an asymmetrical gait in which the legs on each side of the body perform entirely different movements. There are no mirror-image motion patterns, as at the walk and jog. It is a three-beat gait. There is, however, a brief period during which the horse is momentarily airborne, when all four legs are off the ground.

Loping is a forward and slightly upward motion. The horse should drive from its hocks, sending the energy forward and slightly up in order for it to use the rest of its body correctly. When we ask or allow a horse to travel downhill, the energy progression is forward and down. This restricts the front legs, causing the knees to jerk up, which, in turn, interrupts the natural rhythm and balance and breaks up the fluid motion.

After observing the lope, judges go into their own "druthers": head position, speed, purity of gait, manners, attitude—whatever their own preferences may be along these lines. All people do not like the same things in a horse. Perhaps a better way to say it is that all people emphasize different qualities that they consider important.

The next step in the procedure is to line up all the horses in the ring. The judges generally look at their conformation and appointments, as they are asked to back up individually. Sometimes the backup can become the deciding factor between contestants. Let's say that two or more first-class Quarter Horses have performed faultlessly from the moment they passed through the gate and even proved to be equally good examples of the breed. Then they are asked to back up. If one of them does it well enough, but at the same time opens its mouth and throws its head in the air, and if the other steps backward just as readily, at the same time giving to the bridle and flexing at the poll, responding willingly to the rider's demand, the judge's decision is clear and irrefutable. He's found his winner.

Head set, or head position, is a much overrated evaluation. Some people, even judges, place their total emphasis in a Western pleasure class on the horse's head position when, in fact, it should be one of the least-counted evaluation points. In every division and with every horse, the head set is, and should be, different, depending on the job and the horse's conformation.

Some people try to impose a supposedly "correct" head set on a horse. But if it isn't suited to the horse's conformation and activity, it can be not only incorrect but also dangerous.

There are three different kinds of head set: the right one for a given horse, insufficiently flexed, and overflexed.

"Insufficiently flexed" and "overflexed" cover a wide range of degrees, and judges score them accordingly.

The most common fault nowadays is overflexing, when the trainer imposes a head carriage at the jog or lope with the horse's poll held lower than the withers. If a horse is overflexed, behind the bit with the poll held low, it can't see where it's going. All it can see is the ground. It's obviously too much flexion. On the other hand, you don't want it to be a star-gazer either. Ideally, its nose should be carried slightly below the vertical so it can see where it's going and not be gripped in a vice. The position of the poll is the key point. Held too high, it hollows the back and hinders free movement; held too low (lower than the withers), it results in a sort of plodding downhill action.

In the Western pleasure division you see a wide variety of head sets—or lack of same. The horse's action depends on its individual conformation. Its head and neck act as a counterbalance to help it produce effective mechanical movements. It cannot perform effectively if it is overflexed (a horse with its chin on its chest is also in the best position to resist or run away), underflexed (with the poll lower than the withers), or stargazing. All of these exaggerations make it difficult for the horse to function in the way it was built to do.

Frankly, I can't see the point of imposing artificial restrictions and unnatural gaits on our horses, when they are among the greatest natural athletes in the world, with the most beautiful natural movement. The original idea of a head set was to help the horse move in balance at all gaits. But when it's carried to extremes, it can be more of a hindrance than a help. We judges shouldn't reward excesses but rather choose the winners on the basis of the smoothness and efficiency of their movements, their willingness in responding to the rider's commands, and above all their balance.

Every horse requires a little different ingredient to aid balance. Balance traces back to the symmetrical arrangement of the horse's parts. Different gaits require different degrees of collection and impulsion, but balance should be one of the main areas of evaluation. Balance is a direct result of collection and impulsion. The head set is directly related to the particular horse and its balance-position requirements.

A horse whose neck seems to grow straight up out of the withers, or one whose neck is naturally arched, should be trained to carry the head in a near-vertical position, depending on how long the neck is and how clean the throatlatch. A horse whose neck is attached lower should carry a lower poll, again depending on the length of neck and throatlatch. There's not much you can do about a ewe-necked horse, aside from giving it a head set with which it's comfortable. Head set is important because it can either help or hinder the horse's movement, and therefore its performance. The best policy is to find out what head position permits each individual horse to function at its best and then develop it until it has become natural to it.

When more than one judge officiates in a class, there are bound to be some differences of opinion due to individual preferences for style of movement. Also, due to the different vantage points of the judges, one may have seen something that greatly alters his or her placings, while the other judge(s) may not have seen the problem.

When there are several go-rounds before the finals, it is important for both judges and exhibitors to clearly understand what method of placing is being used in the finals—a composite or clean slate.

Using the composite system, the final placing of each horse is determined by the total of its scores in the finals plus the go-rounds. The clean slate system uses the go-rounds to determine which horses will show in the finals. Each horse entering the finals has an equal chance to win because the previous scores are erased.

The pleasure horse division often has more entries than any other. It also often poses more problems for the judge than any other. We try to pick the horses that look and act as if they'd really be a pleasure to ride and own, not simply the ones that make the fewest errors.

What exactly is it that makes a horse a pleasure to ride? It's not extraordinary athletic ability, as in a jumper. Some famous jumpers have been hell to ride. The closest I can come to defining the essential quality is "a good attitude." The horse's attitude, good or bad, is apparent to the judge whether the horse is simply walking along in a well-placed position or doing something more demanding, such as making a transition.

The ideal pleasure horse has to be a good mover at all three gaits, make smooth transitions, and carry its head in a natural position according to its conformation. The horse should maintain a level top line, be relaxed but alert to the rider's cues, show expression, and act as if it would be a pleasure to ride.

As judges, we need to look at the overall picture of the movement of the Western pleasure horses and reward those with exceptional balance and attitude. While doing this, it would be judicious to break up the performance into segments, as they do in Olympic figure-skating competition. The judges score the competitor's performance in many categories and the award is given for how well the components of the performance fit together. We judges need to look at our job in much the same manner.

FAD FORMATION

Judges see many fads come and go. Some are beneficial and some are not. Judges can perpetuate these fads or kill them off, depending on their preferences.

In the Western pleasure division, many things depend on the judge's opinion: Head set, for example, lends itself to fad at every turn. One year everyone turned their horse loose, to plow a furrow with the nose and cover it with the tail, nose out and strung out behind. After that came the year of the overflex, with the chin almost buried in the chest.

Then came the near ruination of the Western pleasure horse with the four-beat lope. It started out simple enough, as most fads do, with a particular horse winning everything (sound familiar?); it was a brilliant show horse and probably the best-balanced horse ever to come down the pike. Well, this horse could lope slowly in balance and cadence, with a natural head set (for his body and pretty neck) held nearly to the vertical. This horse practically floated when he moved and hence was champion at nearly every show.

Well, those who continually got second and third or on down the line decided it was fashionable to go slow at the lope with the head set copied from the winning horse. Now, unfortunately, all horses are not as well balanced or carry themselves as well as the champion did, so the trainers started riding them more and snatching them back more and more.

If you remember the chapter on conformation relating primarily to form to function, you know that the first place a horse gets tired is in its back. So, when we ride the daylights out of a horse, its back tires and soon softens (especially if it's out of natural balance). When the back softens, the head comes up, and when that happens—what do most trainers do?—hit the horse on the head, of course, to make the head go down.

Now we have a horse that has a tired back and can't put its head up for fear it'll get clobbered. The next defensive thing the horse does is put its hip to the inside for relief. This, coupled with a continual breaking of gait, naturally makes the trainer spur it up. The tired back can't seek relief by putting the head up nor by changing its body angle or breaking gait—so the poor horse, to escape all of this, fakes it. It lopes in front and trots or shuffles behind, which creates the relief the horse is seeking and feels smooth and slow to the trainer. The trainer has just taught the horse an unnatural four-beat lope.

Judges who were afraid to go against the trend of slow and overflexed kept placing these horses, and soon all the horses in the class were going that way, until one or two judges had the courage to defy the fad and place good-moving horses at the top. Only then was the fad broken. If judges had not been lax at the start, however, this fad never would have caught on or reached the magnitude it did.

In the pleasure division, one fad after another holds sway, even concerning color. People copy the winner. The judges responsibility is to make the best horse win, not the one that goes along with the fad that's current at the time. Judges must set the trend, not follow someone else's lead. Silver, types of bits, lengths of reins, manes, and tails, speeds of gaits—are all subject to fashion and change.

Change is necessary, of course, but only for the good of the horse, not just for its own sake. In the Western pleasure division, the pendulum keeps swinging back and forth, so watch for it to come your way. Every horse goes just a little different—and rightly so. The balance points are not the same on all horses. The horse should go as it is designed to go, and the one that is the best mover overall (assuming that all perform correctly in the mechanical sense), natural, light, free and giving the apparent ability to be a pleasure to ride, should emerge the winner, regardless of who or what is considered "in" at the time.

GUIDELINES

With all the extremes that have penetrated the Western pleasure class over the years, the presentation of slow, lethargic, droopy-headed horses has drawn the most complaints from the public. The appearance, training techniques, and exhibiting of some pleasure horses drew widespread criticism among spectators and members of the American Quarter Horse Association. They complained that the horses were going so slowly that you couldn't tell the difference between the gaits. It wasn't a true jog; the horses were walking in front and jogging behind, or vice versa.

In an effort to improve the image of the Western pleasure horse and the breed, the AQHA adopted judging guidelines as to what is acceptable and unacceptable, and they are outlined as follows:

- Horses that carry their heads so that the point of the ear is lower than the withers.
- Horses that are flexed behind the vertical.

(These two rules are the extremes. Ideally, a horse should carry its head no lower than level, and its nose should be in front of the vertical.)

- Horses that are excessively slow (at any gait).
- If light contact with reasonably loose rein is not maintained.
- Horses that appear sullen, dull, lethargic, emaciated, drawn, or overtired.

Horses that commit one of these faults, regardless of how they move, are not to be placed any higher than a horse on the incorrect lead or one that is bolting or bucking.

These rulings came about because judges weren't judging as the rules were written. The guidelines simply provided more clarity and reiterated the rules already in existence. Judges should look for horses that move well and carry their heads in the proper position. I've never yet seen a horse that moved well when carrying its head too low or overflexed. The only time I've ever seen a horse willingly put its head that far down is when it's going to graze, roll, or buck you off.

However, head carriage alone is not the only criterion by which to judge the pleasure horse. There are more factors to consider than the levelness of the head. Judges should look for good horses: horses that are balanced, have good forward motion, a willing attitude, and good conformation.

BACKING INTO THE BLUE

Maybe people don't realize just how important the backup is. Put yourself in the judge's shoes. You've got the pleasure class just where you want it on the rail, a good winner, a close second and third, and on down the list. You call for the lineup and disaster strikes. Your top horse throws its head up and refuses to back, your second-place horse backs sideways all the way around its neighbor, and the horse you thought would be third drops its nose, flexes, and marches backward like a slot machine hitting the jackpot. Naturally it's going to move up on your list to become the winner.

Don't get me wrong; the whole class is not decided on the backup alone. Nevertheless, you shouldn't overlook its importance and how it looks to the audience. Most specifications say "Stand quietly and back readily," and the judges can all read. I know some judges who cop out and back the line only a couple steps, but that is not what it's all about. The backup demonstrates

UNACCEPTABLE

*Reins too long; head so low it is
cutting off air by breast collar.*

ACCEPTABLE

*Reins and head good; ears should be up but
horse might be listening to rider.*

ACCEPTABLE

Reins and head carriage good; ears up.

WESTERN PLEASURE GUIDELINES

ACCEPTABLE

Head set good; slightly in front of the vertical. The horse at the jog looks bright and pleasing to the eye.

UNACCEPTABLE

Horse is way overflexed; nose behind the vertical; reins too tight; horse is not happy.

UNACCEPTABLE

Head too low and reins are way too long and loose.

UNACCEPTABLE

Head too low and slightly overflexed; looks artificial (manmade).

WESTERN PLEASURE GUIDELINES

many things, not least of which is attitude. If a horse pins its ears and wrings its tail even though it backs, it is showing duress and resistance and should be penalized. If it throws its head up and looks the rider in the eye with a wide-open mouth, it is also demonstrating resistance and should be marked down. Backing crookedly, sideways, or turning is a major fault. So why do so many exhibitors and judges overlook the obvious? The horse should back smoothly and straight and give to the bridle regardless of the class.

I think everyone practices backing at home and I'm sure all goes well. Why, then, is there such a problem in the arena? Most of the time it's pilot error. Riders—even professionals—get nervous, causing anxiety and a tendency to hurry up and get it over with. When the judge approaches, all signs of calm, cool, and collection fade, leaving a case of the jitters. A little patience is all it takes. *Ask* the horse to back, don't tell it.

Where a rider lines up will have a bearing on how the horse backs. If the horse is somewhat lazy and the rider lines up at the opposite end from where the judge starts, waking up the horse might take slightly more pressure because of the length of time it has had to unwind. By the same token, if the horse is nervous and anxious, with time it may become more so and might not pay attention to the rider when the judge gets there. If the horse stands next to a horse that kicks or bites, it might try to get away by moving sideways. Being prepared to back willingly is as essential as taking the proper lead.

I for one want to see a horse back more than a step or two. If the horse has been schooled properly and the rider is giving the correct signals, the horse should back as far as the rider wants. The mouth is a telegraph station or a tattle-tale on all other working parts of the horse's body. It will tell you which parts are working properly and which ones aren't, if you pay attention. The mouth ties in the drive line from the poll through the neck, shoulders, and rib cage (or body) directly to the hindquarters, which is the horse's driving force. The backup then becomes a series of communication aids, using a combination of hands, seat, and legs, not just a pull and jerk on the reins.

I received the following letter, which I'd like to share with you. It deals with whether a rider should look backward before or during the backup.

Dear Mr. Burt,

I had a situation arise the other day that I need your opinion on. When I have given advice to our students regarding position while backing their animal in line for a pleasure or horsemanship class, I have told them to keep their head raised, eyes ahead, and back the requested distance.

While lecturing the other evening, one of the audience commented that, at several shows, different judges have placed riders down for not looking back to see where they are going. There are certainly two different sides to this: (1) While in line, you should know where the riders are on each side, and know what was behind you when you came in line.

Assuming that there would be no wanderers in the arena, nothing should have moved into the line of travel...hence, no need to look back. (2) Going on the theory that one would not back a car up without looking back, one should not do any backing on horseback without a backward glance.

There has been nothing written about this particular phase of horse-manship that I have come across, and I would appreciate your comments....

In answer to the letter, I find the backup occurring in two different ways, so I have a position on both. First, if most of the riders are in a straight line, with a basic view of what's taking place around them, and if all of the other horses are standing still (having used logic and left plenty of room on either side when lining up), and if the judge wants them to back right from where they are, then the action is all in front and that's where head and eyes should remain. That is, of course, if they back in a straight line. If the horse drifts, the rider should naturally look back to see where they are going or if they are causing someone else a problem. This again depends on whether the lineup is in the center of the ring, as they most generally are, and the judge is in front of them and the next class has not lined up behind them.

On the other hand, if the judge happens to walk down the rear of the line and not in front, or if the next class has come in behind, I think it advisable to take a quick look at where the judge and other horses are standing so as to not back over the judge or into the horses.

Sometimes a judge will call the riders forward from the line one by one and ask them to do some sort of a maneuver and then to back into the lineup again. This situation is tricky. The rider should look back and get oriented before barging backward into the line. Looking back at this time seems obvious because all of the action is behind the rider and he or she could easily end up in the wrong slot, especially if his or her place in line has been narrowed by someone having difficulty maintaining position.

Generally speaking, then, look where the action is, whatever the direction. A most important rule of thumb in any class is: When in doubt, try using plain old common (horse) sense.

REINING

Unlike cutting or working the cow, reining is an event in which the rider dictates a horse's every move. It is classical horsemanship fine-tuned into an art form that is entertaining and exciting to watch. As it is a highly competitive sport, reining horses today are some of the most sophisticated types of show horses. They have to possess certain qualities. My friend and fellow horseman Bob Loomis says it so well: "The true mixture of a great reining horse is one with a golden mind, athletic ability, a huge heart, and lots of guts. The horse has to be extremely well broke; one that allows a rider to handle it, moving all of its working parts effortlessly. Just as significantly, however, it must have a good mind and display a good attitude."

The numerous patterns in the rule book insure that the participants have a diversified test of difficulty to assess the agility of the reining horse. The basics, however, remain the same, no matter what part of the routine comes first or how many turn-arounds are requested.

Circles and figure-eights, for instance, are used to show balance and control. It's the quality of the circles (size and shape) that becomes important. If they are executed correctly, the horse should be in the proper body arc (head to tail) with the hindquarters going in the same direction as the nose. A horse that has its head looking in one direction and its tail going in the other is not in a proper body arc. The horse needs to demonstrate flexibility in the rib cage to perform proper circles and direction changes.

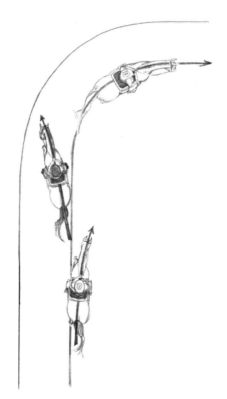

The horse at the top has the proper body arc.
The two following are incorrect with the head looking one way
and the tail going the other.

HORSE SHOULD BE IN PROPER BODY ARC (HEAD TO TAIL)

Lead changes should be executed in the same place each time, and the horse must change both in front and behind or it will be greatly penalized. The horse's body arc also must change as it changes leads. Often this change is very slight to the untrained eye, but the arc should change nevertheless. While changing leads, the horse should not show duress or resentment, such as excessive tail switching, jumping through the change, tossing the head, or gaping the mouth. It should be fluid and demonstrate control and position.

Two of the most common problems when changing leads, as Bob Loomis attests to, is anticipating the change and crossfiring (when the horse is on one lead with the front leg and on the other with the hind leg). Anticipation is caused by practicing too many lead changes without correctly positioning the body. Crossfiring is the result of a horse changing leads with its shoulders first and being stiff in the hip. A horse should change leads with its hind legs first. When a horse is allowed to drop its shoulder into the circle, it puts its hip out of position, and eventually it will start dragging a hind lead. In other words, the horse will change in front and not behind.

Another common fault that should not be overlooked is a horse that "shoots through" or stampedes at the change point, which breaks up the form and continuity of the figure-eight.

Circles and figure-eights (which seem like rather simple tests) can demonstrate many things to judges. They must then place a value on each element. For example, is it worse to drift around or miss a lead change for a couple of strides? Is an open mouth worse than backing sideways? Is head-throwing a greater evil than bouncing off the wall? Judges must rely on their own knowledge and experience in assigning penalties to each of these faults.

Many people think the run-down is only a means of getting to the place to slide or turn around. Not true. The run-down, an extremely important factor in the overall picture, shows the horse's willingness to do what is asked.

Some also interpret the run-down to mean "how fast?" Speed may work for some exhibitors, but only if the horse can handle it in form or if it's requested. Horses should perform at their own level and never sacrifice form for speed.

The run should be smooth and even. The horse should be penalized heavily if it starts slow and continues slow three-quarters of the way down, but then stampedes the last two or three strides and is pulled to a stop. The horse must run all the way into the stop and not shut off partway down or back off at the end. It should run steadily and straight all the way to where it is asked to halt.

The point in the testing that gets the "oohs" and "aahs" from the crowd is the sliding stop. Many times reining classes become sliding contests even though that's not the way they were designed. In assessing the stop, judges have to consider more than just how long the slide is.

Position, attitude, and execution are the most important factors in judging this phase. Position must come first, for if the horse is not in position, the rest will not follow. In short, the horse just can't stop. Position is the horse's

Position, attitude, and execution become most important factors
in judging the sliding stop.

overall picture, from the way it holds its head when pulled, to how the body arc remains and the legs stay together well under it. Position also includes how the horse handles the ground: If it pops out of the stop, walks out, stops crooked, throws its head, gapes its mouth, stops on its front end, or elevates too high in front, the judges will know that the horse is off balance.

Proper balance, which is the result of proper position, becomes evident, as does how hard the horse must be pulled when asked to stop. Position of the rider has a great deal to do with the overall picture. Riders can pile up minus points if they simply lean way back, pull, and holler "Whoa." If they bounce out of the saddle or fall on the neck, the picture becomes distorted, giving the impression that the horse is not really able to perform.

Whatever spins or turning maneuvers are called for, position remains the key. It may be a simple quarter turn, half turn, rollback, or spins from one to four turns in different directions. If a horse "kicks out of gear" on the turn, lunges forward, hangs up, arcs one way and turns the other, wanders, jumps around or swaps ends, it would be heavily penalized for being out of position.

The severity of the penalty is at the discretion of the judges, as is the interpretation of the speed at the turn. Flexibility and handiness are what are wanted. The horse should use its pivot foot properly and drive off its hocks with impulsion while turning around. This also must be done without any signs of duress or resentment.

The backup should be straight and well cadenced to illustrate a willingness to respond.

Judges must then relate all these items to the overall routine of each horse in the class, consider their own preferences when it comes to speed and handiness (depending on the type of class or what a particular horse can handle and still maintain position), compare one performance to the other, and pick a winner.

The reining horse should be willfully guided or controlled with little or no apparent resistance and dictated to completely. Any movement by the horse on its own must be considered a lack of or a temporary loss of control and, therefore, a fault that must be marked down according to severity of deviation. After deducting all faults against execution of the pattern and the horse's overall performance, credit should be given for smoothness, finesse, attitude, quickness, and authority of performing various maneuvers.

The basis of scoring is from 0 to infinity, with 70 denoting an average performance. After each horse works, the score is announced. According to the rule book, any type of bit that is free from mechanical devices may be used. Curb chains are permissible provided they are at least one-half inch in width; free of barbs, wire and/or twists; and lay flat against the horse's jaw. A complete set of scoring rules can be found in the current AQHA rule book.

There are some basic ideas as to how the class is judged.

Run-downs are made from one end of the arena to the other, from one side to the other, or to the center. They can be executed in the middle or along the side of the arena, depending on the pattern. They are the lead-in to a stop and turning maneuver or rollback, a stop and back, or a stop. The horse should demonstrate a relaxed, fluid attitude when starting a run-down and,

The horse should use its pivot foot properly and drive off its hocks with impulsion during turning maneuvers or spins.

throughout the maneuver, a controlled speed consistent with the size of the arena and ground conditions. All runs should be executed in a straight line.

Credits always should be given when deserved, such as for running in a straight line; guiding with a minimum of rider commands; using controlled speed; and maintaining an even, natural stride throughout the maneuver. Faults also are considered, such as: resisting rider commands in any way; indication of a reluctant attitude (gaping mouth, pinning ears); jumping into a maneuver; failure to maintain a distance of twenty feet from the walls, run in the center of the arena, or run in a straight line; anticipation of the rider's commands.

Circles are a controlled maneuver at the lope in a designated area of the arena. They must be made in the appropriate geographic area of the arena, and right and left circles must have a common center line in the middle of the arena. The horse must begin on the correct lead from a walk and show a clearly defined difference in the speed and size of each small (slow) and large (fast) circle. Also, the slow right circles must match the slow left circles and the fast right and left should be identical. The horse must lope in an even, fluid manner with a minimum of rider contact and/or commands. The transition of size and speed from large to small, or the reverse, must be accomplished in an even fashion with a minimum amount of contact from the rider and no visible resistance from the horse.

Again, credits are:
- Speed and size of circles must be executed with the same precision, going to the right as to the left
- Controlled, fluid motion by the horse
- Clear definition of speed and size between large and small circles
- Transitions made in the center of the arena
- Minimum of contact between the horse and rider

The faults are:
- Any resistance to rider's aids on the part of the horse
- Excessive or prolonged contact between the rider and horse
- Resistance to commands from rider by the horse as indicated by gaping mouth, overflexing, or a change in size or speed of a circle that indicates rider is not in control
- Any indication that the horse is reluctant to complete the maneuver (during transitions, head out of position, gaping mouth, ears pinned, etc.)
- Uneven strides or overflexing that detract from the fluid nature of the lope
- Unclear definitions of speed and size

- Speed and size of circles inconsistent, not the same to the left as to the right
- Failure to have a common line between right and left circle in the center of the arena
- Jogging into the lope

Lead changes are the act of changing the propelling side of the horse's body when changing the direction traveled at a lope. The lead change must be executed at a lope, with no change of gait or speed and at the exact location dictated in the pattern description, and in one stride. A horse should be considered out of lead if both front and rear leads are not changed within one stride. It is desirable that, when running around the ends of the arena, the horse is on the correct lead when starting to turn the corner.

Credits are:
- Maintaining a fluid motion and constant speed through the lead change
- Minimal contact between horse and rider
- Executing the change in the exact position in the arena dictated by the pattern
- Demonstrating a willingness by the horse to be guided through the lead change and into the correct position for the next maneuver

Faults are:
- Any indication of resistance to the rider's commands
- Excessive contact or application of commands by the rider
- Any change in speed or temporary loss of the rider's ability to control speed and direction
- Anticipation of lead change by the horse

Spins are one or more 360-degree turns executed with the inside hindquarter (pivot) remaining stationary. When spinning, the horse's propulsion is from the front legs, and continuous contact should be made with the ground and one front leg. The location of the hindquarters should be fixed at the start of the spin and maintained throughout the spins. The spins should be executed at the exact position in the arena indicated in the pattern description.

Credits are:
- The use of controlled speed while maintaining correct positioning
- Starting and stopping the spins without excessively altering the position of the hindquarters
- Fluid, consistent motion
- Light contact and commands by the rider
- Consistency in positioning, speed, and rider commands in left and right spins

Faults are:

- Failure to maintain the position of the hindquarters
- Any resistance to rider's commands or the necessity of the rider to use excessive commands or contact
- Both front legs leaving the ground (hopping)
- Overextension causing the horse to move ahead and alter hindquarter position

Rollbacks are maneuvers that combine a stop, a turn over the hindquarters, and an exit in one fluid motion. They must be executed with no more than a slight hesitation after the stop, and the horse should not step ahead or back up prior to the turn. The horse should be in a position to lope off in a straight line when exiting a rollback.

Credits are:

- Fluid motion with fixed hindquarters
- Light contact and commands from rider
- Exiting turn in the correct position for the next maneuver

Faults are:

- Resistance to the rider's commands
- Excessive contact or commands by the rider
- Failure to maintain position of hindquarter
- Stepping out of stop or backing up prior to rollback
- Exiting turn other than in a position to begin the next maneuver (over or under turning)

Stops are the act of slowing the horse from a lope to a stop position by bringing the hind feet and hocks under the horse in a locked position and sliding on the rear shoes. The horse should enter the stop position by bending the back, bringing the rear legs and hocks farther under the body while maintaining forward motion and ground contact with the front legs. Throughout the stop the horse should continue in a straight line, and the position of the hocks and rear feet should not vary relative to each other. The rear feet should remain in a constant position once entering into the stop, and the horse should not pick up one or both hind feet nor should the back position be altered, causing the horse to stand up. The head and neck should be in a slightly flexed position consistent with the arch of the back.

The credits are:

- Distance traveled in a smooth fashion
- Entering into the stop on command of the rider, but without excessive contact or commands by the rider
- Stopping in a straight line

- Maintaining an even rhythm through loose and fluid contact with the ground and the front legs
- Use of light contact only by the rider

The faults are:

- Picking up either and/or both hind feet
- Leaving the stop position (standing up) at any time throughout the stop
- Failure to enter into the stop as soon as dictated by the rider
- Sliding in a crooked fashion
- Resisting the commands of the rider or excessive contact by the rider (head up, gaping)
- Walking ahead and out of the stop
- Backing up at the end of the stop, except as dictated in the pattern description or as necessary to maintain balance
- Excessive lifting of front legs from ground

The **backup** is the horse moving in a reverse motion in a straight line a required distance. The horse should begin the backup in a controlled manner, without hesitation, until directed to stop by the rider.

Credits are:

- Use of speed while retaining a relaxed attitude
- Lightness of contact and commands from rider

Faults are:

- Hesitation in starting or during the course of the backup
- Failure to back up the distance required in the pattern
- Resistance to the rider's commands or the use of excessive contact or commands by the rider (ears pinned, mouth open)
- Failure to back up in a straight line

Each horse begins with a score of 70 and, as each maneuver is completed, the judge adds or subtracts from the composite score depending on the level of performance. Each maneuver is scored as follows: minus 1 = very poor; minus ½ = poor; 0 = average; plus ½ = good; plus 1 = very good. At his or her discretion, a judge may add or subtract an additional ½ point as warranted, for good and poor performances. At the conclusion of the pattern, the judge may add to the composite score a mark between minus 1 and plus 1 as an assessment of the overall pattern (definition of the pattern, smoothness, way-of-going, general appearance).

When a penalty is applied under this system, the maneuver is graded independently. For example: If a horse has a good right spin but incurs an over spin, the spin will be credited (plus ½) and the overspin will be deducted (minus 1) from the composite score. It's a good idea for judges to keep a running composite score and alter this score as each maneuver is completed.

A SCORING EXAMPLE

PATTERN		70
1st maneuver	Spins right—good	$+ \frac{1}{2} = 70\frac{1}{2}$
2nd maneuver	Spins left—average	$0 = 70\frac{1}{2}$
3rd maneuver	Circles right/lead change—average	$0 = 70\frac{1}{2}$
4th maneuver	Circles left/lead change—average	$0 = 70\frac{1}{2}$
5th maneuver	Run around end of arena, rundown, stop and rollback—good	$+ \frac{1}{2} = 71\frac{1}{2}$
6th maneuver	Run around end of arena, rundown, stop and rollback—good	$+ \frac{1}{2} = 71\frac{1}{2}$
7th maneuver	Rundown, stop and back—average	$0 = 71\frac{1}{2}$
	Backed crooked and jerky	$-1 = 70\frac{1}{2}$
Overall		$0 = 70\frac{1}{2}$
Composite of run		$0 = 70\frac{1}{2}$

SHOW PREPARATION

It's one thing to show a good horse that doesn't have any bad habits and bring it all the way through to become a finished performer. It's quite another thing to show a problem horse or change bad habits. The latter requires a different way of approaching a horse's mind. For years I took horses that had a bad start and tried to make them into something that you could show. It'll teach you a lot about judging and showing horses, but it's a tough way to learn. It takes a lot of concentration. I know many trainers who, if they could show horses as well as they prepared them, would be awfully tough to beat. There's a lot of pressure in the show ring, and you have to learn how to handle the pressure and utilize what you've accomplished beforehand.

A large part of judging or showing a reining horse is learning how to execute the reining patterns. You can have a horse trained to do everything, but if you have a tendency to rush yourself in a pattern, you won't execute each maneuver to its fullest extent. You have to complete it and then release your horse's mouth before asking it to go to the next maneuver. That takes a lot of discipline on your part. If you haven't gone over the pattern in your mind and know how you're going to execute each part, you'll wind up shortchanging yourself somewhere, and it won't be the horse's fault. On the other hand, when preparing at home, you should execute all the individual parts, but you should never run a whole reining pattern or else your horse will learn to anticipate the maneuver and become stale.

You also have to know your horse's weaknesses. If it needs a little help getting started into a spin or more preparation for a lead change, you must program that into your execution of a pattern ahead of time. If a horse that doesn't change leads naturally isn't prepared two or three strides before it changes, it is liable to drag the hind lead. Or if a horse has a sticky side on a spin, you need to give it more time, ask it a little more slowly, or maybe tip its nose in just slightly. If you're riding a horse that is lazy, you will have to build more fire under it prior to showing it. A real hyper, nervous kind of horse will need more time to become relaxed and quiet before the show. It's better to take that extra time to do it right than to rush it and blow it completely.

The important thing to remember, however, is that doing it right does not necessarily mean doing it exactly the same way for each horse or exactly imitating a more accomplished competitor. Showing takes a lot of thought precisely because you have to tailor your goals to the particular situation you face. For example, some people lean forward to speed a horse up and run fast circles, then lean back and relax to bring him down slower. Other people do just the opposite, lean back a little bit and drive with their thighs and hips to get a horse to speed up and make faster circles, and then raise up and relax to bring a horse down slower. You also can teach a horse to increase speed by taking hold of its mouth a little bit, letting it take the bridle and run with a slight pressure on the reins, which is basically the same thing a racehorse does. Judges know that there are different, perfectly legitimate ways to accomplish the same goal, so it is the outcome that you should focus on. The main things are to develop consistency and to control a horse's body position so that you both stay in balance.

You have to develop a system of communication signals that your horse understands. To develop that, you have to know how a horse moves and functions, how it uses its legs, and how its head moves in relation to its body when it's running, stopping, changing leads, or turning around. Particularly at a gallop, the horse's head is not stationary. As a horse's head moves, it uses it as a balance tool. So, as you ride, your hands need to move in rhythm with the horse's head. I see many riders who are bumping their horses' mouths on every stride, because their hands are coming back as the horse's head is going out. The constant bumping makes a mouth lose its lightness. It's like wearing a watch on your wrist; the pressure is always there, so you become unconscious of the watch being on your wrist. If you're always putting pressure on the horse's mouth, when you really ask it to do something, it's been preconditioned to ignore you. If you ride in rhythm, staying out of the horse's mouth except when you're asking it to do something, you'll receive a lot more response.

To win, you know you must instill both confidence and discipline. The secret is knowing when to peak the horse at the right time not only to condition the body but the mind as well.

THE PATTERN

Judges focus on the pattern very precisely, and the secret to performing an accurate pattern is knowing where you are in relation to the center of the arena at all times, without turning to look at the markers. Even a small movement of your head shifts your weight in the saddle enough to miscue your horse and trigger an early change. You must get into the habit of "feeling" for the marker out of the corner of your eye without actually looking for it by moving your head. Practice a few times with a helper on the ground who can tell you when you "cheat" (turn your head) and can alert you if and when your pattern begins to lose its shape.

To the judge, the shape of the pattern is an important element of your run. If your pattern is sloppy, your run will seem sloppy even when your horse is responding accurately to your cues. And if your horse's performance has some rough edges, an accurately ridden pattern will help smooth them over. Circles should end where they began and be round, not oval or irregular. All large circles should be the same size, and distinctly larger than the small circles, but they shouldn't come closer to the fence than eight feet or you may be marked down for using a barrier to turn your horse. Small circles should be of matching size, as small as possible without provoking resistance from your horse.

When the instructions specify that a maneuver be performed at the center of the arena, it should be at the center—or no more than a stride or two from dead center. The judges, positioned at the center of the long side, will be particularly aware of any deviations on the long way of the arena because it's easier for judges to see a horse in profile. Conversely, they won't be quite so attuned to minor deviations from a three-quarter angle when the horse performs maneuvers on either end.

There's more to a winning run than just doing the maneuvers well. Many little strategic considerations combine to produce the polished, neatly laid-out pattern that judges want to see. Most have more to do with thought and planning than with your horse's ability or your innate talent as a rider.

Concentrate on a smooth and accurate pattern. Start slowly. If your horse performs the early maneuvers well, you can ask for a little more brilliance as the pattern progresses, but hold your top speed to somewhere between medium and a fast lope. Judges would rather see a slow run performed fluidly and accurately than a fast one that is full of faults.

Every part of your run, from the entrance through to the exit, should be second nature by the time you reach the competition, not because you've overpracticed the pattern but because you've mentally gone through it many times.

Judges and riders should carefully study the arena. If it's a different size from the one you've practiced in, plan how to alter the pattern to fit it. Check the ground. Dry ground with two or three inches of soft topping over a firm base is ideal and allows the horse to slide and turn around freely. But if the ground is wet with deep, heavy footing that could bog a horse down and bounce it up out of its slides, plan to keep your speed conservative. Your horse may not slide very far, but at least it'll stay in the ground. Before warming up, watch two or three runs. They'll tell you things about the state of the arena that you may have missed. If the riders seem to have trouble turning on their circles, the arena may be narrower than it looks. If they seem to be running out of room as they lope toward their slides and rollbacks, it may be shorter than it seems.

If possible, time your warm-up so that you finish with just one or two horses to go before your turn. That way your horse won't lose its readiness. Use the warm-up to supple and settle it. This is not the time for training. If it's fresh in the warm-up, plan to keep the pattern slow, at least in the opening circles.

Mistakes are bound to happen. Expect them and don't let them rattle you. If you forget the pattern, keep going; you may be able to ride through your momentary blank spot. If you do go "off pattern," you'll be disqualified, but you may—and should—complete your ride anyway and as best you can. If your horse misses a lead or crossfires, keep loping and cue again immediately and more forcefully. It'll probably correct its error, but if it doesn't, just continue on the wrong lead. You'll lose some marks, but if you stay cool and don't upset your horse, your mistake won't necessarily affect your next maneuver.

Judges today are giving horses credit for what they do and not just scoring faults. If you maintain a mental image throughout the pattern of how you're going to show your horse and stick to it, your plus points could outnumber the faults and your efforts may be rewarded.

TRAIL HORSE

The trail horse class is not only for professionals but for amateur Quarter Horse owners of backyard horses as well, often one they've raised and trained themselves. The horse may not be halter-horse pretty or talented enough to make a reining horse, but if it's been well trained and had experience handling the different obstacles you're apt to come across on a trail, it's got a chance of winning or placing in a trail horse event. Its chances increase as it adds age and experience.

Judges begin with certain criteria: A trail horse should be careful and willing; it should have personality instead of behaving like an obedience machine; and it should deal with the obstacles on the course with promptness and confidence. The rider also plays a role, and his or her job of keeping basic control over the horse is more important as the courses get more challenging and intricate. Another factor is the speed with which the horse negotiates the course. It shouldn't be a headlong rush, but it shouldn't be slow-motion either. The performance should attract and hold the attention of the judge, spectators, and other exhibitors.

A trail horse is asked to cope with different obstacles, guided by the rider. It should deal with them confidently, but always under the rider's control. These obstacles include such challenges as opening a gate, passing through, and closing it; riding over at least four logs or poles; and backing through a prescribed obstacle course.

Additional optional tests may include:

- Carrying objects from one part of the arena to another
- Wading through water
- Riding over a bridge
- Side-pass
- Serpentine obstacles
- Standing steady while the rider puts on a slicker
- Taking letters out of a mail box
- Coping with any other obstacles apt to be found on a natural trail (subject to the judge's approval in view of the likelihood of running into them during a normal trail ride)

Trail courses have changed a lot. They used to be hair-raising survival contests that seemed to have been concocted by sadistic course designers who had never ridden on a trail themselves or even in an arena—or so it seemed to the judges and contestants. Now they're more realistic. It takes a lot of thought to draw up a good trail course. Designers also have to consider the material available for building it. But what they should keep most in mind is that the class should be a true test of the horse's ability to handle simulated trail obstacles, not a series of traps to see how many riders and horses can get hurt.

Among the most familiar obstacles on the course is the gate, which may be opened and closed in various ways, such as push-away, pull-toward, back-through, and so on. Logs, which are strewn about to demonstrate the horse's ability to step through an obstructed course without reluctance or panic, give the judge a good idea of the horse's handiness and eye-foot coordination. Course designers can set the logs in various ways: in a straight, curved, or zigzag line, or one that requires the horse to back up at the end, which demonstrates its flexibility.

In trail classes, judges are interested in the horse's attitude just as much as where it is putting its feet. Even when a horse gets through and over the obstacles, if it does so in a sulky way and seems to be stressed by the ordeal, or if it simply charges madly through them, judges take this into account.

Aside from the usual obstacles, there are optional ones. Their usefulness and fairness depends on where they're placed on the course. Part of the judges' job is to check and make sure that no unreasonable demands are made.

*Walking over logs shows a horse's willingness and ability
to pick its way through a maze.*

Because it's practically impossible to reproduce at home all of the different obstacles you may find in the arena, trail horses should be trained not so much to handle particular obstacles but to obey the rider's commands, whatever they may be.

The three essential qualities of a trail horse are calmness, agility, and control. Some horses are born with a calm disposition and even temperament, and these are the ones you should look for if you want to show a trail horse. You won't get anywhere in this division with a nervous horse. Some trail obstacles are even called "calmness obstacles," because calm horses take them in their stride, while high-strung horses balk or shy away from things such as bridges, water, ditches, holes, and tarpaulin and plastic sheets, and look scared about carrying a sack filled with cans or a shovel, or when the rider puts on a slicker. All horses are naturally wary of water if they can't see the bottom. They'll willingly ford a clear stream, but they balk in front of a shallow mud hole. There's the same problem with bridges. With patience and practice, you can get some nervous horses to conquer their fearfulness. But it's easier to start off with a horse that's got a calm disposition.

Some horses are born with natural agility, but this too can be developed through patient training and experience. Some horses seem clumsy only because they don't know how to deal with an obstacle they've never seen before.

Arena obstacles to test agility consist mostly of walk-, trot-, and lope-overs of various shapes and dimensions. Naturally agile horses aren't fazed by them, but others can get into a lot of trouble, perhaps because they lack depth perception or because they're simply not very smart. Some of these cases are hopeless.

When watching a horse perform over a trail course, judges look at the whole horse, not just its feet. For example, a horse that gazes around the grandstand while negotiating the obstacles faultlessly would still be marked down for lack of style. It should have dropped its head slightly—not down to the ground (although this seems to be the current fashion), but low enough to look where it's going and where it has to put its feet to get there. At the other extreme, a rider who hoists her horse's head up on a tight rein usually will end up with faults for rubs or knock-downs.

This is not to say that the rider shouldn't always be in charge. Otherwise, few horses would be able to negotiate the obstacles that absolutely require rider guidance. Gates, side passes, back-throughs, corners, and turns on the forehand and hindquarters all require not only rider control but also good training and good riding. It's easy to steer a horse that's moving forward to the right or left with the reins. But if you want it to move diagonally, sideways, or backward, you have to give it leg signals too.

In theory, the rider controls directional movement ahead of the cinch (the shoulders) with the hands (reins) and directional movements behind the cinch (hindquarters) with the legs. For example, a simple push-away gate requires a combination of hand and leg signals: side-pass to put the rider in position to open the latch; backup so the horse's head won't hit the gatepost; pushing the gate open; riding through. As soon as the rider's knee has cleared the gate, it moves the horse's hindquarters out of the way to make room for closing the gate; the opposite leg then moves the horse back to the gate's "closed" position. This principle applies to all kinds of gates. It's a lot simpler than it sounds!

The side-pass is a maneuver made by pushing the horse's shoulder in the direction of movement. Most mistakes are due to the rider having the horse's front end on the pole because he doesn't remember that the center of the horse is actually *behind* his leg, generally about where the flank cinch is attached.

Other frequent requirements are turns on the forehand and hindquarters in a square or circle, during which the horse has to place all four feet inside the prescribed area and make a full 360-degree turn to the right or left.

I also give bonus points—for example, if the horse looks carefully at strange obstacles but takes the familiar ordinary ones in stride, or if it responds spontaneously to the rider's aids instead of giving a robotic response. I like a trail horse to seem eager but not rushed, alert and energetic but not nervous or worried. The overall impression should be gentle and light. The horse and rider should form a harmonious partnership, and I can spot this right away. I'll give bonus points to the horse that handles the obstacles in a relaxed, alert, and responsive manner. In a winning partnership, the rider should be the guide and the horse should respond willingly and cheerfully to the commands.

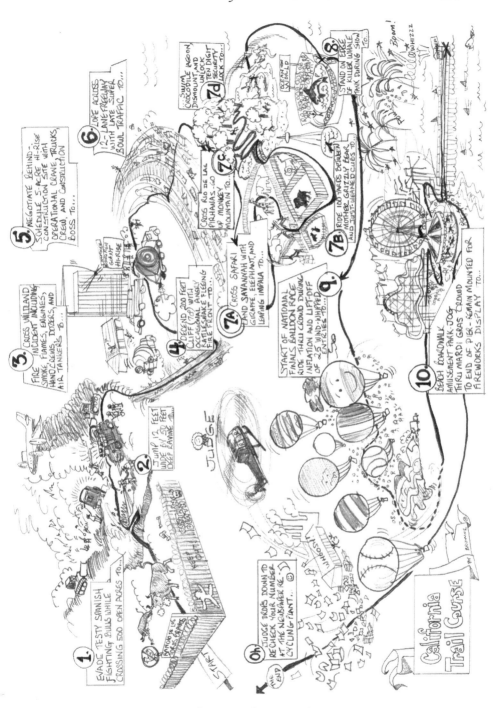

Trail course à la naturale.
The Medal of Honor is awarded if you survive this course!

A good trail horse course can be covered easily in 120 seconds or less and includes at least fifty feet of jogging and loping. This gives judges a good idea of what kind of a mover the horse is.

Riders must understand exactly what they're asked to do on the course. Judges always should try to give clear instructions, such as: "The gate is a push-away to the right, so take it in your right hand. You can slide your hand along the top as long as you keep it under control. Push the gate away from you and step through. Then close it." Judges always should allow time for questions. Although a diagram of the course is posted so the riders can see what to expect in the arena, most exhibitors need verbal instructions too.

Over the years, most judges have devised their own scoring systems to keep a running count of each obstacle. I have always preferred the positive method, giving points from 1 to 5 for a few entries and 1 to 10 for larger classes. This system lets me give points not only for the way a horse handles each obstacle but also for its attitude, the way it approaches and moves on. I consider attitude extremely important.

Now that the class has grown in popularity, the AQHA has standardized the system for judging trail to help make scores more uniform. Judges are encouraged to use scribes to record the numbers. This not only facilitates tallying the scores but also allows judges to stay focused on each entrant.

The scorecard makes it easy for judges to record a horse's performance on each obstacle as soon as it is completed. Each obstacle has a column and is given a value of 0 to 10 points, with 0 being perfect. The fewer the faults, the fewer numbers have to be added up after each contestant. Columns also are provided for scoring the gaits (between obstacles) and a horse's manners, attitude, and style.

When a horse does not execute an obstacle according to the pattern, does not attempt, or refuses, it is given a "no score" for that obstacle. Using 0 to 10, it would receive a 10 for the obstacle in question. Putting a circle around the 10 reminds the judges to place this contestant after the other entries that have completed all the obstacles on the course.

If, for example, a tie exists after tallying the obstacle scores of all contestants, judges can use the special column (last) for a tie-breaker. The score in this column is a number between 1 and 100, with 70 being average. Even though attitude, manners, and style are taken into account at every obstacle in the individual scores, this overall grade can be used to separate two horses with equal performances. The gait score column is depicted by a number between 0 and 10 and assesses the ability to demonstrate the required walk, jog, and lope on the course. This score is added to the obstacle work and will be reflected in the total obstacles column.

A hypothetical course along with a scorecard depicting four contestants' performances is on pages 104–105.

WORKING COW HORSE

DRY WORK

Old-time vaqueros worked cattle with horses that they trained with infinite patience and care. No steps were eliminated in their training processes, and the result was a light-mouthed horse capable of spinning and stopping on the proverbial dime. Many of the vaquero methods are still used in preparing horses for today's show ring.

The working cow horse event is broken down into two segments. The first is a dry work or reined pattern, similar to the reining horses; the second is a prescribed cow work. Both phases must be completed to qualify for an award. Each portion is scored on the basis of 0 to 100, with 70 denoting an average score. In the event of a tie, the entry with the highest cow work will be declared the winner.

In the reining or dry work, the horse should make a smooth run. There should be enough speed to allow judges to determine whether the horse can move out and still handle itself in the arena. It shouldn't be fighting the bridle. In changing leads, there should be a fluid and distinct change with no dragging. When it's time for the horse to stop, it should go to the ground and come to a halt and pause until the next signal is given. Its hind legs should be up under it, with its rear end almost literally sitting in the arena dirt. The front feet and legs should be flexible, gently paddling as the horse comes to the stop.

A horse and rider must complete a number of required maneuvers in a pattern.

When the arena gate opens and the horse enters, it should immediately give an impression of being willing and responsive. The animal's facial expression—ears, mouth, and eyes—will relay this message. Are the ears working, or are they pinned back in resentment? Are the eyes popped open from fear, or are they relaxed in appearance, looking for something to do? Is the horse chewing or gaping at the bit because of fear or frustration?

A good horseman or judge will notice these things and even more. Remember, how the rider prepares the horse to begin the pattern is important. First impressions count.

The next step is usually the figure-eight executed at a lope, showing flying changes of leads. The horse should lope in a fluid forward motion. The change of leads should be a natural maneuver for the athletic horse. If the horse is late with its change, doesn't change behind or even change at all, it will be penalized according to the severity of the offense.

Next, judges look closely at the circles. Both circles, right and left, should be the same. The consistency, size, speed, flow, and placement are all considered.

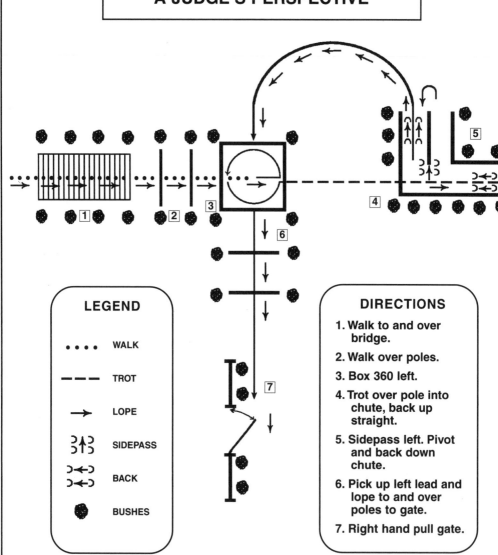

A JUDGE'S PERSPECTIVE

LEGEND

•••• WALK

--- TROT

→ LOPE

ᣮᡧᣮ SIDEPASS

ᗡ←ᗡ
ᗡ←ᗡ BACK

● BUSHES

DIRECTIONS

1. Walk to and over bridge.
2. Walk over poles.
3. Box 360 left.
4. Trot over pole into chute, back up straight.
5. Sidepass left. Pivot and back down chute.
6. Pick up left lead and lope to and over poles to gate.
7. Right hand pull gate.

SCORED GAITS

1. HORSE HAS SMOOTH, EVEN GAITS THROUGHOUT.	0
2. HORSE NEVER TRULY LOPES CORRECTLY; NOT A GOOD MOVER, BUT MANAGES TO PERFORM DUTIES.	3
3. HORSE IS ANXIOUS AND HIGH, RIDER HAS TO KEEP A TIGHT HOLD TO STAY IN CONTROL.	5
4. HORSE VERY RELAXED BUT IS INTERESTED IN OBSTACLES; LOPES AND TROTS CLEANLY.	0

ATTITUDE, MANNERS, STYLE
1. 82   2. 68   3. 60   4. 90

OBSTACLE 1 BRIDGE

1. Touches horse on the neck. — 10
2. Steps off side of bridge. — 7
3. Hesitates to go on bridge; rider must use leg. — 3
4. Horse walks over bridge smoothly, with head down, looking where it is going, with ears up and alert. — 0

OBSTACLE 2 LOGS

1. Horse nicks log one time. — 1
2. Horse knocks over a log with no other faults. — 4
3. Horse skips a space between logs and has one nick. — 5
4. Horse nicks two logs but very lightly. — 1

OBSTACLE 3 BOX

1. Horse steps out of box. — 5
2. Horse ticks front of box walking in and walking out. — 2
3. Rider turns horse the wrong way in the box but is totally clean. — 10
4. Horse steps into box cleanly, negotiates turn, and steps out smoothly with no touches. — 0

OBSTACLE 4 BACKUP

1. Horse misses trot over pole going into backup, but backs without incident. — 5
2. Horse scrapes along backup pole inside, touches three times. — 3
3. Horse hits trot over pole going into backup, then touches poles two times backing up. — 4
4. Horse hits trot over pole, trotting into backup, then has one light rub backing up. — 1.5

OBSTACLE 5 SIDEPASS

1. Horse hits poles two times during sidepass, then drags pole with its front foot when pivoting. — 4
2. Horse sidepasses unevenly, seesawing front to back, but does not hit poles. — 3
3. Horse sidepasses evenly but is chomping the bit and wringing tail throughout. — 3
4. Horse sidepasses evenly and smoothly, but rider takes way too much time looking back and forth, detracting from the overall picture. — 1

OBSTACLE 6 LOPE OVER

1. Horse picks up the wrong lead for two strides, then rider switches to correct lead, continues correctly over the poles. — 3
2. Horse picks up correct lead but breaks to a trot while approaching poles and changes to right lead over poles. — 7
3. Horse hits last lope over pole while building up speed over the series. — 2.5
4. Horse lopes smoothly with cadence and rhythm over poles. — 0

OBSTACLE 7 GATE

1. Horse goes through the gate forward when course calls for a back through. — 10
2. Rider drops gate, lets go, but regains control and completes obstacle. — 7
3. Horse bumps into sides of the gate and is nervous and fidgety. — 4
4. Horse negotiates gate smoothly, but grabs at a plant near the gate with its mouth. — 1.5

AQHA TRAIL SCORECARD ORDER OF AWARDS

Entry Number	Total Obstacles	1 BRIDGE	2 LOGS	3 BOX	4 BACK	5 SIDE	6 LOPE	7 GATE	8	9	10	Scored Gaits	Attitude Manners Style
1	-38	(10)	1	5	5	4	3	(10)				0	82
2	-36	7	4	2	3	3	7	7				3	68
3	-36½	3	5	(10)	4	3	2½	4				5	60
4	-5	0	1	0	1½	1	0	1½				0	90
5													
6													

ORDER OF AWARDS: 1. Fourth   2. Second   3. Third   4. First

The horse's head and neck should be either straight or curved slightly toward the center, never toward the outside of the circle. The horse should be moving away from rein pressure without resistance, giving the appearance of power steering. There should be no increase or decrease in speed unless asked for by the rider. The horse also should remain and appear to be relaxed during the execution of the circles.

After the completion of the circles, the horse should prepare for the run-down to the other end of the arena. The run-down can be made just off the rail or in the middle, depending on the pattern. The run should be straight and true, maintaining speed up to the stop.

Does the horse wait for the rider to send it running to the other end of the arena, or does it look like a runaway? Also, did the rider have to spur the animal to reach a high speed or have to whip it with a romal to go forward? These are all questions the judges ask.

Now that the horse is running down the arena, is it anticipating the stop, trying to stop when not asked for? If the horse is guilty of any of these infractions, it will be penalized according to the severity.

The stop is the audience's favorite part of the pattern. Unfortunately, some judges seem to place the entire class by the stop.

At whatever speed the horse is traveling when asked to stop, it should do just that. Stop. The hindquarters should melt down into the ground, then slide forward while the front end continues to run or pedal. Thus, the forelegs stay out of the way of the hind legs. This will allow the horse to remain balanced during its sliding stop. When the horse stops, it should do so in one smooth motion—not a skating slide, then come up, then go down and slide some more.

While the horse is stopping, the judges will look at the entire picture of the horse and rider. Is the horse's mouth shut? How is the head position? Does it stay in the ground? Also, is the rider pulling the bit "through the horse's tail," forcing it to stop, or does the rider simply ask for and receive a pretty, balanced stop?

After the stop is complete, judges look for a rollback, a spin, or more. As in the reining class, a good horse, when asked to spin, will very fluidly and rapidly turn its front end around the hip and will continue to do so until told to stop. When the horse is spinning, the front legs should cross over one another while the hind end remains stationary.

Once again, judges consider the entire picture. Does the horse look fluid and snappy while remaining flat in the spin, or does it have to hop around to complete it? Also, does the horse look broke, or does the rider have to pull on the horse, maybe even prod it a little to complete the spin?

If the horse stops or freezes up in the spin, that's a major fault. After the completion of the spins, the horse should run to the other end of the arena, stop and repeat the spins (reversing the direction).

After this, the horse will run back to the center of the arena, stop, settle, and back up. The backup should be straight and quick with no hesitation, tossing of the head, or opening of the mouth.

The final piece of the pattern is the pivot (off set) or spin. No matter which, the spin or pivot should display control, snap, and correctness. After all of this, the horse also should be able to walk calmly and quietly from the arena.

To rein a horse is not only to guide it but also to control its every movement. The best-reined horse should be willfully guided and controlled while showing little or no apparent resistance. The horse should be dictated to completely, and any movement on its own must be considered a lack of control.

All deviations from the written pattern must be considered a lack of or temporary loss of control, and be scored as such.

Credit should be given for smoothness, finesse, attitude, quickness, and authority of performing various maneuvers, while using controlled speed. This raises the difficulty level and makes the performance more pleasing to watch and more exciting for the audience.

The methods used to teach a horse the various maneuvers required for the working cow horse class are identical to the methods described in schooling the reined horse and are basic to all performance horse training. However, their application varies according to the different patterns.

COW WORK

To the cowboy who earned his living working cattle on a ranch, a good finished cow horse was like his own right hand. A really good one could outthink and outmaneuver the most ornery cow, thanks to its speed, agility, flexibility, strength, and balance. This much sought after combination of qualities used to be called "cow savvy." A good cow horse could chase hard after a cow, head it, squat, turn, and come out of it at such lightning speed that the poor cow would think at least two horses had gotten the better of it.

It is safe to say that most working cow horse classes are won along the fence. A horse may gain or lose points in the reined work, but usually a cow horse class will separate itself in the cow work. Even within the cow work, a horse can be impressive in the boxing maneuvers and be pretty fancy circling a cow in the center, but the horse that takes a cow down the fence, turns it correctly, and stays with it is the one that usually ends up on top.

Cow work in the arena is designed to simulate actual ranch work. But it's almost impossible to give each contestant an equal chance when so many variables are involved: the size and quality of the cattle, the ring layout, and footing. Cows that have already been used in roping and cutting events may have been soured by their previous experiences and there's no telling how they'll behave. Not being able to provide enough cattle for a contestant to get another chance with a second cow if the first one turned out to be unworkable is a frequent problem for judges and show managers.

The following depicts a typical cow-working pattern: After your cow enters the arena, box it or hold it at the prescribed end of the arena for a sufficient time, then let it out down the fence, make a turn or two each way on the fence, then bring it to an open part of the arena and circle each way. When the judge has seen enough, he or she will announce or whistle for the contest to end.

Since this is a reined cow horse type of class, the rider is permitted to rein the horse during the entire procedure. When the cow is released into the arena, judges watch both the horse and the cow as they size each other up. The cow's first moves determine what the horse is going to have to do. A tired old cow that plods into the arena and then stands there in a daze needs a different kind of control from the one that charges in and tries to stampede into the grandstand. Judges give different values to all of the different tactics employed. A horse that can make a dull cow look like a clever one will get points for it. And a horse that can dominate a cow that's on the rampage and get it to settle down will score extra points too. It's only fair for judges to take into account what kind of cow each horse has been allotted.

A slow steer sometimes can really come apart when the rider lets it down the fence. However, good judges can see when the rider is letting the cow down the fence and hasn't lost it at the end by either overworking or undercontrolling. When the cow is let down the fence, the horse has to be fast enough to get to its head and make the turnback. Some horses like to run shoulder to shoulder with the cow until it's turned, or at least helped to turn, by the arena corner.

Riders who are always in control of their horse's speed, who send it to the cow's head for the turnback, impress the judges. The horse should drop in on the cow, follow it around, regain control when coming out of the turn, and then handle the cow along the fence for the turn in the opposite direction. But usually when the cow ducks back, the horse isn't fast enough in the turn to be in a position to head it again. Then the cow can hang up and run to the other side of the arena, and the rider has to chase it around instead of taking charge and forcing the cow to go where he or she wants it to.

There are lots of different theories about cow work. Some say that the horse should stay away from the cow and shut it off at a right angle. Others say that the horse ought to follow the cow and intimidate it into turning. What the judge is looking for in this phase of the work is a genuine cow horse who anticipates the cow's every move and is prepared for anything that can happen. All horses don't react the same, and neither do all cows. So the final judgment has to be a combination of how hard the cow is to handle and how cleverly the horse has handled the cow it had the good or bad luck to draw. Some cows act so tired they'd make the greatest cow horse in the world look bad. Others you could work on a pogo stick.

The event continues with holding at the end of the arena, then two or more turns on the fence (left and right), and finally it's time to "wrap him up," in other words, finish the cow off. The horse is asked to shoulder the cow or handle it in a close tight circle in both directions without using the fence to help. To do this

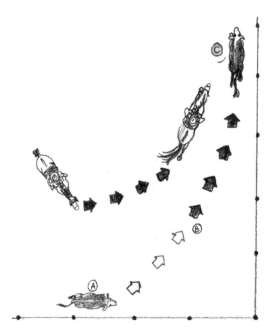

Here a rider holds his horse up in the center of the pen, allowing the cow to cut the corner (point A to point B). When the rider does allow his horse to move toward the cow (point B), the cow has a comfortable lead (a margin designated by the white arrows). Even if the horse moves stride for stride wtih the cow from here, it is still outrun by the time it gets to the fence (point C). From then on the run becomes a game of catch-up, with the horse having to run faster than the cow to overtake it, and the horse's momentum naturally carries it past the cow in a turn, allowing the cow to gain the advantage.

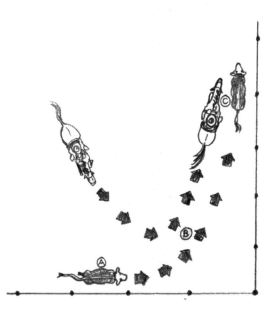

A remedy is shown. After boxing, the rider drives his horse toward the cow (point A), causing the cow to move toward the fence. As the cow cuts the corner (point B), the rider can position his horse on the cow's shoulder and let the horse rate with the cow as both proceed down the fence (point C). Here, the horse has maintained the working advantage.

A COMMON PROBLEM WHEN JUDGING A COW HORSE CLASS
Not shaping the cow up properly for the run down the fence.

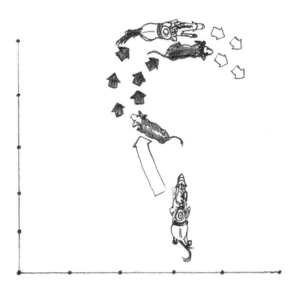

Losing the working advantage during circling begins when the rider reins the horse up as the cow naturally drifts away from the fence. When the rider releases, he picks up the same lead as the cow and tries to maneuver the horse to the outside shoulder. Because the horse is running a larger circle than the cow, it is difficult for it to get to the shoulder. Then circling becomes a game of catch-up.

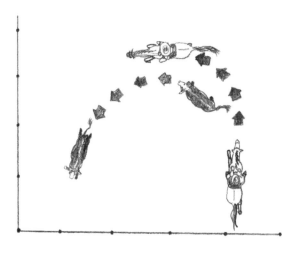

A remedy for this problem. As the cow drifts toward the left, the rider should take the horse off in the opposite lead as the cow and drive it toward the cow's inside shoulder. The cow, then, is forced to change leads, and the horse should be able to remain at the cow's shoulder throughout the circle.

A COMMON PROBLEM WHEN CIRCLING

well the cow has to have reached just the right spot, and the horse has to be fit enough to have the energy left for handling this part of the test with vigor, instead of huffing and puffing while chasing the cow around in a circle. This is where there's no substitute for experience, both the horse's and the rider's. You must be able to tell exactly when you should make your move—soon enough for the cow to be fresh enough to make the rider look good, but not too soon, when the cow is so fresh that you run the risk of losing it in the center. You have to make your timing decision and then carry it out.

Many times problems can be avoided by proper boxing and reading of the cow. If it's chargy, work it a bit harder before taking it down the fence and get in close. Don't make it a horse race. Instead, let the horse rate the cow. When going down the fence, watch the cow's actions, especially its head positioning. Cattle that enter the arena and run down the fence high-headed will usually drop their heads when they're thinking about turning. This should be a clue to turn it. If the cow starts lowering its head as it runs, it's probably running out of air, so it's time to get it circled.

The biggest problem I see when judging is that many riders never get the horse to the cow's shoulder, where the horse has the advantage. If the cow breaks right, the horse should leave on the left lead and get to the inside shoulder. If the cow breaks left, you should leave on the right lead. After the first circle, drive the cow toward the center of the arena before changing directions.

With good horses and fresh cattle, cow work can be a spectacular event, even a fine art. The show management should provide sufficient cattle so the same ones don't have to be worked over and over again, which gives the earliest competitors a distinct advantage. Also, there should be enough cows so that

Rider should get to the cow's shoulder where the horse has the advantage.

the rider who has drawn a bad one can, at the judge's request, be given another one to work.

In scoring each go, the judge gives penalty points for:
- Bad manners, such as biting, striking, or running over a cow: 3 points (simply nuzzling the cow with nose or lips when working or circling should incur no penalty)
- Running past the cow: 1 point for every (horse's) length past
- The horse failing to show control of the cow when circling: 2 points
- Hanging up on the fence, exhausting the cow before circling, failing to hold the cow at the end of the arena during boxing: 3 points
- Any deliberate spurring or use of the romal in front of the cinch: 5 points

The following are causes for a zero score:
- A horse that turns its tail to the cow
- Any unnecessary roughness to the cow
- Use of two hands on the reins during the cow work
- Running over the cow when circling it, causing the fall of horse and rider; being out of control, crossing the path of the cow and endangering the rider and horse

Other faults that judges take into consideration are:
- Exaggerated opening of mouth
- Hard or heavy mouth
- Nervously tossing the head and lugging on the bridle (signs of unwillingness)
- Halting or hesitating
- Anticipating the rider's commands (often due to overtraining)

Now for the positive. The qualities of a good working cow horse are:
- Good manners
- Willing response to the rider's commands
- Being agile, smooth, keeping the feet under the body at all times, displaying balance and control of movements
- Stopping with hind legs well under it
- A light mouth that responds to a light rein, especially when turning
- Maintaining a natural head position (according to the individual conformation)
- Being able to work at a reasonably fast speed while remaining under the rider's control
- Finally, the most important of all and the main ingredient of a winner in this class: taking total control of the cow and never losing it for a moment

WESTERN RIDING

The Western riding class often has been described as Western-style dressage, and there's some truth in the comparison. The main difference is in the kind of movements the horses have to perform. A dressage horse's movements are highly refined, even to the point of looking artificial, although many of them are fashioned after the battlefield maneuvers of mounted cavalry. In the Western riding event, the horse has to perform maneuvers that have been adapted from the pleasure, reining, and trail classes, so they too are mostly a competitive version of movements and maneuvers that can be of practical use in certain circumstances.

A good Western riding horse has to be alert and attuned to the rider, with no sign of resistance (especially not in the mouth or rib cage); it has to have a good mind so that it accepts the rider's commands willingly, without charging or anticipating. Another desired characteristic is a good attitude. Manners can be taught, but attitude, good or bad, is an inherent trait that is readily discernible by what the horse does with its head, eyes, ears, and tail. It is more noticeable during a transition period but can be seen throughout the entire performance. How the horse reacts to *any* situation will give the observer an indication of its disposition.

Its head carriage depends on its conformation. Never forget that a horse's natural head position and way of going are determined by such unchangeable things as length of neck and where the neck comes out of the shoulder. Judges shouldn't penalize a horse for being more high-headed throughout a pattern than they personally prefer. If the horse performs well, it should be rewarded for its good athletic ability and not penalized for the particular kind of conformation it was born with.

If a horse has its head and nose way up in the air, usually it is trying to counteract some form of duress. To get its head in this position, it must drop its back, which makes it become strung out and definitely not in the bridle. This can happen at the walk, trot, lope, or while backing up.

The other extreme is the horse that puts its head on its chest. This overflexed position allows more weight to be put on the front end, which in turn disengages the hindquarters. Again, the horse is resisting the rider's demands, which puts it out of balance and also affects its mental attitude.

Some horses, because of a more vertical head carriage, require a little more collection to be balanced. Those that naturally carry their heads lower, flexing more at the neck than at the poll, require less collection to travel in balance. Any overdone movement, such as take back, pick at, check, or bump, only causes a horse to become overflexed, sour-eared, and switchy-tailed because of constant duress. The loose-rein rider puts the horse off balance by having more weight on the forehand, causing it to wallow and roll its body.

Because most of the pattern is performed at the lope, a horse that is strung out behind will not be supple, balanced, or a smooth loper. When the hindquarters swing well under the horse, the underline of the horse should contract and the top line arch slightly at the loin. A horse that has a hollow back is not capable of reaching under with the hindquarters and having the back flex in a rounded manner.

To compensate for the propelling of the hocks under from behind, the front end (neck or poll) must raise slightly to counterbalance the thrust from the hindquarters. Such a frame allows a horse to lope slowly and with collection because its weight is settled on its haunches. This is the refined lope of a Western dressage horse and is attained through invisible aids given by the rider.

Precision is one of the qualities of an ideal Western riding performance, but it should never be achieved at the expense of smoothness and form. For example, a horse that performs lead changes at the exact prescribed spot but in a bunched-up, tense manner should not be placed above a smoother, more natural mover that has made the lead changes correctly but perhaps not exactly at the right spot every time. The horse also should maintain a consistent speed throughout the pattern and not increase it during lead changes or when loping down the center.

Good judges of this class should be horsemen and women themselves who watch each horse's performance with a horseman's eye, looking for the good points instead of trying to catch some slight mistake. They should base their final decision on the talent and cooperation of the horse and rider, instead of basing their score only on negative penalties.

Today judges have to have a scoring system that enables them to make a decision they can back up by their score sheet. The scoring system must allow judges to consistently produce a numerical tally based on how each element is performed throughout the pattern. To give this overall viewpoint, judges must be able to give credit for positive maneuvers during a performance, in addition to accurately recording mistakes that are made. Mistakes often stand out in judges' minds. If there isn't a system for recording the good maneuvers along with the mistakes, it's easy for judges to lose sight of the overall picture in a performance.

An equitable scoring system should allow good and bad maneuvers, along with transitional mistakes, to be recorded at the exact moment they occur. Judges should not have to rely on memory recall. Now that there are twenty-five or more contestants in a class, judges *have* to have a more sophisticated scoring system at their disposal. It's impossible to remember every maneuver that each horse made during the class.

The Western riding scoring system resembles the one used for reining. Judges, utilizing scribes to write down the maneuver and penalty points, call out the points so that they never have to look away from contestants. Judges routinely exert more energy and thought assigning maneuver points than they do penalty points. Penalty points are pretty concrete—judges and everyone else can see when the horse makes a mistake at a transition point, and these errors are recorded. However, the maneuver points involve more of a judge's opinion on the quality of lead changes and the horse's way of going. A contestant's final score is compiled from two series of numbers assigned throughout the pattern as either maneuver points or penalty points.

Printed score sheets are used. If the score cards are posted, exhibitors can see exactly what the judge liked about their horse and what the horse did wrong.

Of course, personal opinion always enters into it to a certain extent. Some judges like to see a really fresh horse and don't mind if it looks around a bit as long as it remains in proper form. Other judges are more fussy over the horse's businesslike attitude. Judges can use the just-described scoring system to reflect their personal opinions. It all boils down to a combination of judges' acuteness of observation and the occasional need to make a subjective call.

The Western riding pattern #1 begins at the walk. The contestant then picks up the jog and moves toward the log. The horse must jog over the log without hitting it or rushing.

After crossing the log, the horse should begin to lope. Failure to start loping within twenty feet of the log after crossing it at the jog is considered a fault and should be penalized. A rider should use the arena to his or her benefit, moving farther away from certain cones when necessary and riding deep into the corners to aid positioning. Riding deep into the corner for the turn helps to line the horse up so it approaches the line of five pylons with its body straight. A horse cannot change leads if its body is bent.

When a horse fails to make a lead change, it's usually because the horse is out of position when the change is called for. Timing is crucial when executing a flying change of leads. If the rider's timing is off, the horse often will change in front but fail to make the change behind until the next lope sequence. The rider should ask for the change just before the leading foreleg is grounded. This allows the horse to make the change behind first, then complete the lope sequence with a change of leads in front. If properly done, the change of leads should be performed in a single sequence of the three footfalls, changing both front and hind feet in the same sequence.

For some reason, riders often attempt to force or spur a horse through the change. Overriding almost always results in the horse expressing its resentment by anticipating the change, speeding up, wringing its tail, throwing its head up, or a combination of all these faults. The horse should move forward on a lead change, not up and down and then forward.

The rider who is late (beyond the designated change area) in making the first change will be pushing at the next cone, and by the time he or she has reached the fifth pylon, the initial error has compounded to the point where the last

Horse should jog over the log without hitting it or rushing.

change of the first line is way out of position. But if the rider had changed slightly early on the first cone, he or she would have insured the success of the rest of the pattern. Judges should take these things into consideration.

The horse's speed down the middle of the arena should be the same as throughout the pattern. Some riders think they can cover up lead changes that haven't gone so well by speeding up. They should remember that excess speed is not desirable in a Western riding horse and should be penalized. As riders prepare for a soft, quiet stop, they should time their commands so that the horse ends up ten feet beyond the center of the arena, where it's in position to finish the pattern correctly by backing to the center. Speed in the backup here doesn't gain points either. In fact, it may incur penalties if it results in loss of control and form.

The scoring system for this event is as follows: A contestant enters the arena with an average score of 70 and receives pluses or minuses, ranging from plus 1½ to minus 1½ as **maneuver** scores. Up to plus 1½ points can be given for each transitional maneuver for such things as exceptional lead changes, an even pace throughout the pattern, manners, and disposition. As many as minus 1½ maneuver points can be deducted for excessive mouth opening, anticipation of signals by the horse, or early lead changes.

A separate line on the scorecard keeps track of mistakes made throughout the pattern. These are **penalty** points, and they range from 1½ point to 5 points, depending on the severity of the disobedience. The entire maneuver's scores, penalty points, and disqualifications can be found in the AQHA rule book.

Judges have to remember that while Western riding is not a stunt or a race, it still should be performed with reasonable speed. They have to judge the horse on the quality of its gaits, changes of lead, responsiveness, manners, disposition, and intelligence. In these judgments, they should look for and give credit to smooth, even gaits with the horse starting and finishing the pattern in the same regular cadence. The horse's precise and easy changes of lead, with both front and hind legs at the exact center between the markers, are equally important. The horse's head carriage should be relaxed enough to respond to the rider's hands with a moderate flexion at the poll, and it should perform the pattern in a relaxed manner, without breaking gait or changing stride.

Now let's examine more closely the two Western riding patterns and their respective scorecard examples.

Horse should approach the line of five pylons with its body straight.

AQHA WESTERN RIDING PATTERN I –

Contestant 1

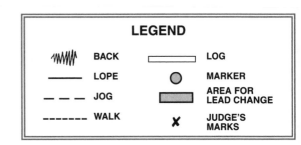

LEGEND

wwwww BACK   ▭ LOG

—— LOPE   ● MARKER

— — JOG   ▭ AREA FOR LEAD CHANGE

------- WALK   ✗ JUDGE'S MARKS

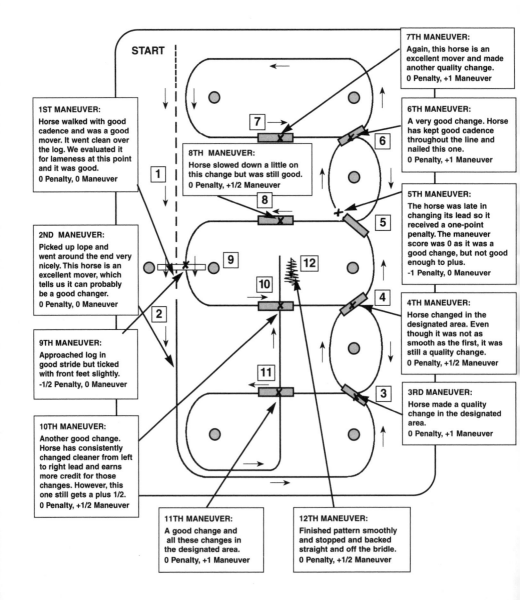

START

7TH MANEUVER:
Again, this horse is an excellent mover and made another quality change.
0 Penalty, +1 Maneuver

6TH MANEUVER:
A very good change. Horse has kept good cadence throughout the line and nailed this one.
0 Penalty, +1 Maneuver

1ST MANEUVER:
Horse walked with good cadence and was a good mover. It went clean over the log. We evaluated it for lameness at this point and it was good.
0 Penalty, 0 Maneuver

8TH MANEUVER:
Horse slowed down a little on this change but was still good.
0 Penalty, +1/2 Maneuver

5TH MANEUVER:
The horse was late in changing its lead so it received a one-point penalty. The maneuver score was 0 as it was a good change, but not good enough to plus.
-1 Penalty, 0 Maneuver

2ND MANEUVER:
Picked up lope and went around the end very nicely. This horse is an excellent mover, which tells us it can probably be a good changer.
0 Penalty, 0 Maneuver

4TH MANEUVER:
Horse changed in the designated area. Even though it was not as smooth as the first, it was still a quality change.
0 Penalty, +1/2 Maneuver

9TH MANEUVER:
Approached log in good stride but ticked with front feet slightly.
-1/2 Penalty, 0 Maneuver

3RD MANEUVER:
Horse made a quality change in the designated area.
0 Penalty, +1 Maneuver

10TH MANEUVER:
Another good change. Horse has consistently changed cleaner from left to right lead and earns more credit for those changes. However, this one still gets a plus 1/2.
0 Penalty, +1/2 Maneuver

11TH MANEUVER:
A good change and all these changes in the designated area.
0 Penalty, +1 Maneuver

12TH MANEUVER:
Finished pattern smoothly and stopped and backed straight and off the bridle.
0 Penalty, +1/2 Maneuver

AQHA WESTERN RIDING PATTERN I –

Contestant 2

		DRAW #	ENTRY #		1	2	3	4	5	6	7	8	9	10	11	12	TOTAL PENALTIES	TOTAL SCORE
AQHA JUDGE'S CARD WESTERN RIDING PATTERN I		1		PENALTY					-1				-½				-1½	74½
				MANEUVER	0	0	+1	+½	0	+1	+1	+½	0	+½	+1	+½		
				TOTAL	70	70	71	71½	70½	71½	72½	73	72½	73	74	74½		
				PENALTY														
				MANEUVER														
				TOTAL														
		2		PENALTY	-½		-½		-3-3								7	62
				MANEUVER	-½	0	-½	0	0	0	+½	+½	+½	0	0	-½		
				TOTAL	69	69	68	68	61	61	61½	62	62½	62½	62½	62		

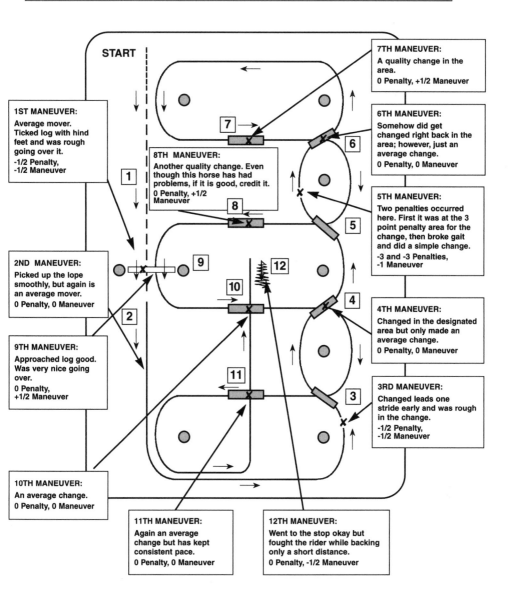

START

7TH MANEUVER:
A quality change in the area.
0 Penalty, +1/2 Maneuver

1ST MANEUVER:
Average mover. Ticked log with hind feet and was rough going over it.
-1/2 Penalty, -1/2 Maneuver

8TH MANEUVER:
Another quality change. Even though this horse has had problems, if it is good, credit it.
0 Penalty, +1/2 Maneuver

6TH MANEUVER:
Somehow did get changed right back in the area; however, just an average change.
0 Penalty, 0 Maneuver

5TH MANEUVER:
Two penalties occurred here. First it was at the 3 point penalty area for the change, then broke gait and did a simple change.
-3 and -3 Penalties, -1 Maneuver

2ND MANEUVER:
Picked up the lope smoothly, but again is an average mover.
0 Penalty, 0 Maneuver

9TH MANEUVER:
Approached log good. Was very nice going over.
0 Penalty, +1/2 Maneuver

4TH MANEUVER:
Changed in the designated area but only made an average change.
0 Penalty, 0 Maneuver

3RD MANEUVER:
Changed leads one stride early and was rough in the change.
-1/2 Penalty, -1/2 Maneuver

10TH MANEUVER:
An average change.
0 Penalty, 0 Maneuver

11TH MANEUVER:
Again an average change but has kept consistent pace.
0 Penalty, 0 Maneuver

12TH MANEUVER:
Went to the stop okay but fought the rider while backing only a short distance.
0 Penalty, -1/2 Maneuver

AQHA WESTERN RIDING PATTERN II –
Contestant 1

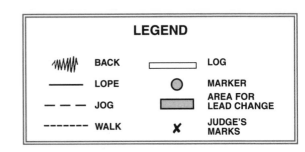

LEGEND

∿∿∿	BACK	▭	LOG
——	LOPE	●	MARKER
– – –	JOG	▬	AREA FOR LEAD CHANGE
- - - -	WALK	✗	JUDGE'S MARKS

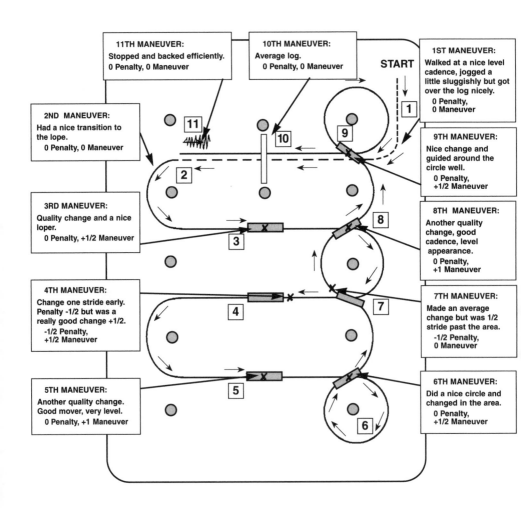

11TH MANEUVER:
Stopped and backed efficiently.
0 Penalty, 0 Maneuver

10TH MANEUVER:
Average log.
0 Penalty, 0 Maneuver

START

1ST MANEUVER:
Walked at a nice level cadence, jogged a little sluggishly but got over the log nicely.
0 Penalty,
0 Maneuver

2ND MANEUVER:
Had a nice transition to the lope.
0 Penalty, 0 Maneuver

9TH MANEUVER:
Nice change and guided around the circle well.
0 Penalty,
+1/2 Maneuver

3RD MANEUVER:
Quality change and a nice loper.
0 Penalty, +1/2 Maneuver

8TH MANEUVER:
Another quality change, good cadence, level appearance.
0 Penalty,
+1 Maneuver

4TH MANEUVER:
Change one stride early. Penalty -1/2 but was a really good change +1/2.
-1/2 Penalty,
+1/2 Maneuver

7TH MANEUVER:
Made an average change but was 1/2 stride past the area.
-1/2 Penalty,
0 Maneuver

5TH MANEUVER:
Another quality change. Good mover, very level.
0 Penalty, +1 Maneuver

6TH MANEUVER:
Did a nice circle and changed in the area.
0 Penalty,
+1/2 Maneuver

AQHA WESTERN RIDING PATTERN II –

Contestant 2

	DRAW #	ENTRY #		1	2	3	4	5	6	7	8	9	10	11	12	TOTAL PENALTIES	TOTAL SCORE
AQHA JUDGE'S CARD WESTERN RIDING PATTERN II	1		PENALTY				-½			-½						-1	73
			MANEUVER	0	0	+½	+½	+1	+½	0	+1	+½	0	0			
			TOTAL	70	70	70½	70½	71½	72	71½	72½	73	73	73			
			PENALTY														
			MANEUVER														
			TOTAL														
	2		PENALTY		-3		½		-5	-5						13½	53
			MANEUVER	0	-½	0	-½	0	-1	-1	0	-½	0	0			
			TOTAL	70	66½	66½	65½	65½	59½	53½	53½	53	53	53			

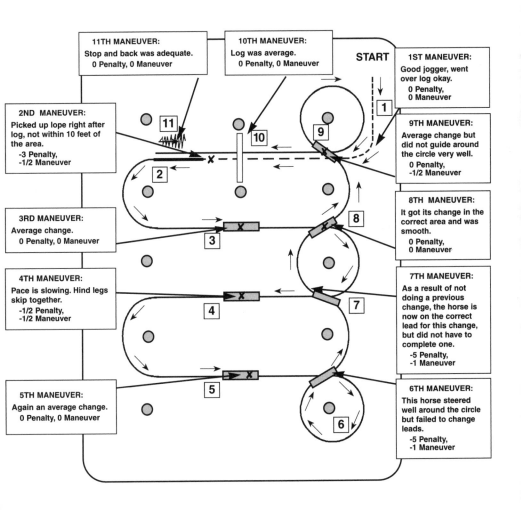

11TH MANEUVER:
Stop and back was adequate.
0 Penalty, 0 Maneuver

10TH MANEUVER:
Log was average.
0 Penalty, 0 Maneuver

START

1ST MANEUVER:
Good jogger, went over log okay.
0 Penalty, 0 Maneuver

2ND MANEUVER:
Picked up lope right after log, not within 10 feet of the area.
-3 Penalty, -1/2 Maneuver

9TH MANEUVER:
Average change but did not guide around the circle very well.
0 Penalty, -1/2 Maneuver

3RD MANEUVER:
Average change.
0 Penalty, 0 Maneuver

8TH MANEUVER:
It got its change in the correct area and was smooth.
0 Penalty, 0 Maneuver

4TH MANEUVER:
Pace is slowing. Hind legs skip together.
-1/2 Penalty, -1/2 Maneuver

7TH MANEUVER:
As a result of not doing a previous change, the horse is now on the correct lead for this change, but did not have to complete one.
-5 Penalty, -1 Maneuver

5TH MANEUVER:
Again an average change.
0 Penalty, 0 Maneuver

6TH MANEUVER:
This horse steered well around the circle but failed to change leads.
-5 Penalty, -1 Maneuver

ROPING EVENTS

All three judged roping events—calf roping, dally team roping (heading), and dally team roping (heeling)—are direct descendants from the daily work on cattle ranches of the West, where the Quarter Horse was used to rope and brand or doctor cattle.

While some of the smaller calves could be roped, tied, and worked on by one cowboy, team roping was used for larger cattle. One cowboy, known as the header, would rope the head or horns of the animal, while another, the heeler, would rope the hind legs. The heeler would then hold his end steady while the header continued to pull, taking the animal's hind legs out from under it and laying it on the ground. The animal was then rendered helpless, allowing a third cowboy to do whatever work was necessary.

Upon completion of his job, the cowboy doing the doctoring would release the header's rope and then, while the heeler continued to hold the hind legs tight, remount his horse. Then the heeler would ride his horse forward, loosening his loop, and allow the doctored animal to regain its feet and rejoin the herd.

Competition among the ranches was keen, and in the early 1900s, many of them began meeting on common ground where the cowboys could match their talents in the various jobs at which they were particularly adept. These included roping, and since almost none of the cowboys missed loops, speed became the winning factor.

Rodeos emerged from these ranch competitions, along with a new breed of cowboy, the rodeo cowboy. Some of them became roping specialists, whittling away at the elapsed time required to complete a run until it became shorter and shorter.

When the AQHA was established in 1940, roping was among the events contested in its first shows, because many association founders were ranchers who felt that roping was a true test of the Quarter Horse. Roping events continue to be featured in most Quarter Horse shows today, and in some areas, they attract more entries than any others.

In calf roping, the ideal run begins with the horse walking quietly into the roping box, turning around and standing, quietly but alert, and under control at all times. Then rider and horse leave the box at a cue from the roper, run to a spot directly behind the calf, break down to the same speed as the calf, and remain there until the roper has thrown his rope. At that time, and as the roper starts to the ground, the horse should stop on its rear end and begin backing up, keeping the rope tight as the roper throws the calf. The horse should continue to keep the rope tight as the roper ties the calf, walks back to the horse, and remounts. Only then can the horse, at a cue from the roper, walk forward and allow slack to come in the rope.

Team roping is broken down into two events, heading and heeling. The perfect heading run would be for the heading horse to assume the same position in the box as that of the calf-roping horse, quietly and under control. At a cue from the roper, it should run from the box to a spot just off the steer's left hip and remain there until the header throws his rope and "dallies" (wraps) it around the saddle horn. At that time, and at a cue from the roper, the horse should drop its left hind leg into the ground, "setting" the steer (slowing its rate of speed and turning its head to the left), and lead it off to the left. As the heeler ropes the hind legs and stops the steer, the heading horse then, at a cue from the roper, should "face," or wheel around to the right, and come to a stop when it is facing the steer.

The heeling horse should be mannerly in the box and then run to a spot off the steer's right hip as the animal runs down the arena. When the header has roped the steer and turned it off, the heeling horse should come to just off the steer's left hip and remain there until the heeler throws his rope. Then the heeling horse should stop on its rear end (much like a calf-roping horse) and absorb the jerk of the steer hitting the end of the rope. It should not move in any way until after the heading horse has faced and the run is completed.

These are the ideal runs in each of the events. But few horses or runs are perfect, and rules cannot be written to cover every situation. So judging in this case is really just a matter of judgment, which should be based on certain established criteria. If two calf ropers have similar runs, but one drew a harder-running calf, that horse should place higher because it had to work harder. If two headers had equal runs but one completed the run quicker, it should place higher. When in doubt, use logic.

CALF ROPING

There are four key elements to a calf-roping run: scoring in the box, running and rating, stopping, and working the rope. In each phase, not only should speed and correctness be demonstrated, but the horse should appear to enjoy its task. Also, the smoother and more fluid the run, the better the score. Even though the run should be done quickly, a fast run should not place higher than a slower one, if the slower run was more correct.

It is the judges' responsibility to check the Western type of equipment on all entries. Even though the type of bridle used is up to the contestant, judges may prohibit the use of bits or equipment they consider to be severe. Mechanical hackamores are commonly used in this event, and they are legal. However, any part of the hackamore that runs across the bridge of the nose must be covered.

In calf roping, a **neck rope** is required. This is a piece of rope tied around the horse's neck that is not secured to either the headstall or the saddle. The neck rope is a safety measure and prevents the horse from running off after the roper has roped the calf and left the horse. A contestant's rope must be run from the saddle horn through the neck rope and back to the roper's hands. **Tie-downs** and **keepers** are optional, but if a keeper is used, it may be fastened only to the noseband of the tie-down, never to the bridle or the bit. Neither **jerk lines** nor **tack collars** are allowed.

Judges should stand on the left side of the arena (roper's left), about halfway down, where they can see the horse in the box. They should not stand at the box, as they cannot adequately see the run from that position. The person running the roping chute informs the judges if a contestant breaks the barrier.

Calf roping is scored on the basis of 0 to 100 points, with 70 denoting an average performance. The roper is being judged from the time his number is called and he starts toward the roping box until he rides his horse forward to loosen the rope following the conclusion of the tie. During this time, a roper can either lose or gain points depending on a horse's performance.

The horse should be under the roper's control at all times during the run. It should not enter the box until the judge has finished scoring the previous run and is turned, watching the box, and it should then walk quietly into the roping box, turn around, stand quietly but alert, and be ready to leave the box at the roper's cue. A horse that does this should gain points. If the horse refuses to go into the box, this shows a lack of control and should be penalized.

As the horse enters the box and turns around, it may turn in either direction. However, as it turns, it should not rub against either side of the box, and it should turn readily. Although it is legal for the horse to stand anywhere within the box, most ropers will back the horse into the corner opposite the front of the chute. In this case, the horse should stand flat-footed and not be squatting or leaning against the back or sides of the box.

Some contestants want their horses to stand in the box on a loose rein, while others want contact with the horses' mouths. Neither way should be penalized, as long as the horse leaves the box instantly upon being asked by the roper.

Being ready and being so anxious or nervous in the box as to give the roper problems are two different things. A horse should be penalized for moving around excessively in the box, rearing, freezing up so that the roper cannot get it into position, and turning its head at an extreme angle. A horse that has its head turned slightly to one side should not be penalized, as long as it can watch the front of the chute. But a horse that looks straight ahead while sitting in the box certainly should be scored higher on that part of the run than one that did not.

While watching the horse in the box, judges also should take into consideration the behavior of the calf. If the calf is acting up, has turned around, or does anything else that may cause management to delay the run for a few moments, a little movement of the horse may be considered excusable. The roper has the option of asking management to drop the barrier so that he may ride out of the box until the problem has been solved. This action should not incur any penalties, as it is show management's responsibility to have the calf ready when the roper enters the box. But a horse that remains in the box and continues to stand quietly and under control while the calf is being straightened out could score higher on that portion of the run. The roper who remains in the box may want to move his horse up out of the corner and let it relax, as backing into the corner often signals the horse that the roper is ready. On the other hand, if the calf is ready and standing quietly, and the horse is acting up, showing a lack of control, it should be penalized.

Since all calf-roping horses are required to start from behind a barrier, judges should make sure it is working and set correctly for the arena conditions and the cattle. If judges are unsure, they may ask the show management to check it, but judges are responsible for the barrier's placement and legality. The barrier should be set so that the roper has the best opportunity to show his horse. If a barrier is set too long, the calves will have a greater head start and all the ropers are apt to have to run to the end of the arena before they can make their catch. A barrier set too short could have the ropers coming out on top of the calves. Neither condition makes for a smooth run.

Breaking the barrier should be penalized. There are, however, different degrees of a horse breaking the barrier, and judges should consider the conditions of how it was broken when assessing the penalty. If, after the roper has called for the calf, the animal fails to run out of the chute and the horse breaks the barrier due to the roper's misjudgment, that's one thing. But if the horse takes control and runs through or jumps the barrier, that is something else, and that horse should receive a much stiffer penalty.

When evaluating this portion of the run, judges should remember that if a horse that commits some errors in the box is going to be penalized, then the horse that does everything right should receive extra points. A horse that does not want to go into the box, does not enter the box quietly, and does not turn around readily should be penalized from 1 to 2 points, depending on the seriousness of the errors. The same would hold true for the horse that exhibits nervousness in the box, turns its head severely, or squats in the corner. But a horse that refuses to enter the box and does so only after being forced by the rider, then rears up or freezes in the box and refuses to move could be penalized up to 5 points, as these are all serious infractions and show an obvious lack of control.

The horse that is not out of control but breaks the barrier due to the rider starting it early should be penalized 2 points, while one that deliberately runs through or jumps the barrier should receive a 5-point penalty.

The horse that walks calmly into the box, turns around and stands flat-footed, alert and in control until cued by the rider to go, is an above-average horse and should receive 1 or 2 extra points.

When the calf leaves the chute, the horse should break smoothly and evenly, and run to a point directly behind the calf. A horse that lunges out of the box and does not run out smoothly probably was squatting back in the corner, or the roper was holding it, trying to prevent it from breaking the barrier. A horse that is standing up and ready will break smoothly.

After the horse breaks, the ideal position going down the arena is for it to be directly behind the calf, with its head behind the calf's tail. The horse should run to that position and remain there until the roper has thrown his rope. This is called **rating,** and a horse that does not rate should be penalized.

Judges should realize that rating is not when the horse is nearly getting outrun, and the roper is overly kicking to stay in position. A horse that rates well should remain in the proper position without a lot of effort on the part of the roper.

A horse that **scotches** or **sets up** (anticipates the stop and starts to stop on its own) while rating or going to the calf also should be penalized. Some horses will anticipate the roper's throw and will stop just before the roper has released his rope. Even though the roper may be able to go ahead and rope the calf, the entry should be penalized severely. If the horse scotches and then the roper kicks it back up and makes a good run, the horse should be penalized, but not as heavily as the one that stopped completely.

A horse also should be penalized if it is trailing to the right or left of the calf and not directly behind. If the calf is on the fence, however, the horse will not be able to stay directly behind the calf, and judges should take that into consideration.

The horse should follow and rate the calf, regardless of where the animal goes in the arena. Should the calf fade to the right and the horse continues to rate right behind it, the horse can be awarded extra points. This is because the horse will almost always leave the box on the left lead; most ropers are right-handed and have the reins in their left hands; the roper swings the rope on the right side of the horse's head; when the rope comes tight, it occasionally slaps the horse on the right side of his head and neck; the weight of the calf hits the horse on the right side; and when the roper dismounts, it's normally on the right, pushing the horse to the left, thus making it hard to train a horse to trail a calf to the right. When a horse does have to go to the right, it has performed exceptionally and so should receive a higher score on that part of the run, over a horse that only had to run straight down the arena.

Under normal situations, a horse can either gain or lose up to 2 points on the running and rating phase. A horse that runs directly to the correct position, hangs there until the roper throws, and then prepares to stop could be credited with 1 extra point. The horse that continues to trail a calf that goes to the right, as previously described, could receive 2 extra points.

On the other hand, the horse that has trouble maintaining position or is off to one side or the other and not straight behind could be penalized 1 or 2 points, depending on the severity of the infraction.

The horse that scotches but is then kicked back up into position by the roper should be penalized 2 points. The horse that scotches or sets up and stops completely, even though the roper is able to reach to the end of his rope and catch the calf, should be penalized 5 points. That shows a definite lack of control.

One of the most important parts of a run is stopping correctly, and judges should remember that a horse should not stop too hard. The ideal stop would be to jerk the calf down hard enough so that the roper can reach the animal just as it regains its feet and before it has time to run around on the end of the rope.

The horse should begin to stop when the roper pitches his slack. It should drop its rear end into the ground and, as it starts to slide, drop the front end to brace itself. It should never rear up in a stop; a horse that does so should be penalized.

At the end of the stop, the horse should push backward immediately. This might give it the appearance of stopping on its front end, which, in fact, it is not doing. The main thing to watch for is whether the horse's rear end drops into the ground first. If it does, the horse did not stop on its front end. Dropping the front end first, with the rear end up, is an indication that the horse stopped on its front end.

The horse should stop straight. One that quarters off to the left as it stops or ducks off to the left as if to shy away from the rope should be penalized, with the penalty assessed according to the degree of the infraction.

Excessive pulling on the reins as the horse stops and the roper is getting off should be penalized. However, a roper who gets off on the right normally uses his left hand on the saddle horn, and bringing the reins to the saddle horn as he dismounts should not incur a penalty.

Since stopping is a key element, the points should reflect the fact. A horse that doesn't stop well and does so only after the roper has pulled back severely on the reins should be penalized 3 points. A poor stop will affect the remainder of the run. A horse that begins the stop on its front end, rears up when it stops, stops crooked, or ducks off badly should be penalized 3 points. A roper who gets off on his reins, pulling them back behind the saddle horn, should cause his entry to be penalized 1 to 2 points.

By the same token, the horse that stops on its rear end, stays in the stop, and immediately starts to get back—things that help the roper complete the run—should receive an extra 2 to 3 points.

The phase of working-the-rope extends from the time the roper dismounts until he remounts. As the horse completes its stop, it should begin backing and continue to do so until the roper has thrown the calf. If the calf was jerked down, the horse should continue to back until the roper rights the calf and throws it back down. If the calf is moving on the end of the rope, the horse should move back faster, bringing the calf to the roper in as straight a line as possible. It should then keep pressure on the rope, holding the calf's head off the ground until the roper has remounted.

Judges observe whether the horse backs straight; moving laterally gives the impression the horse is working the rope but in reality it is not. The horse that keeps pressure on the rope while backing could chalk up bonus points.

Once the roper has thrown the calf, the horse should stop backing. It should not drag the calf while the roper is trying to complete the tie; to do so would incur a penalty. After the roper has tied the calf and stands up to return to his horse, however, the horse may take a step or two backward, dragging the calf slightly, without being penalized for it.

Slack (looseness) in the rope between the calf and the horse at any time during this phase of the run should be penalized, with the amount depending on the degree of the infraction.

Ideally, the horse should look straight down the rope at the calf while the animal is being tied. If the horse is working the rope well and its head is angled slightly to the side, however, there should be no penalty. A penalty would be imposed if the horse turned its head more than a few degrees to the side, or if it rubbed its head on the rope.

A right-handed roper who runs his rope on the left side of the horse's neck probably does so to prevent the horse from "ducking off" to the left as he stops, and this action should be penalized. If, though, when the roper pitches his slack, it ends up on the left side of the horse, judges should consider whether it was an accident and penalize accordingly. The opposite would apply to a left-handed roper. A horse that sticks its head under the rope while the roper is tying the calf is rubbing the rope and should be penalized.

As the roper returns to his horse following completion of the tie, the horse should not shy away from the roper. If it does, it should be penalized. The calf must stay tied until the roper has remounted his horse and ridden forward to loosen the rope. Failure to do so shall disqualify the entry.

Working the rope is comparable to the stop, and the points deducted or awarded for this phase should reflect that. A horse that does not work the rope makes it hard for the roper to throw the calf and complete the run.

Failure to continue to back while the roper is getting the calf up and flanking it should be penalized from 1 to 3 points, depending on the severity. Failure to continue to work the rope as the roper ties the calf should be penalized as follows: rope lying on the ground, 3 points; slack in the rope, 2 points.

The horse that continues to drag the calf excessively while the roper is trying to tie it should be penalized 1 to 3 points, depending on the distance. Also, the horse that shies away from the roper as he goes back to remount should be penalized from 1 to 3 points.

A horse that turns its head more than a few degrees while the roper is tying the calf should be penalized 1 point. The horse that rubs its head on the rope should receive a 3-point penalty. The right-handed roper who runs his rope on the left side of the horse's neck should be penalized 5 points.

If the roper misses with his first loop and he is not carrying a second, the run is over and he does not receive a score. A roper may throw two loops, but this must be done within two minutes after the calf leaves the chute. He must have his second loop already built and attached to the saddle; he must use this rope for his second loop.

If a contestant uses two loops, the judge should continue to watch the run and score it upon its conclusion. When two runs are equal, a one-loop run will be scored higher than a two-loop run. The two-loop run could, though, be scored higher than a one-loop run in which the horse committed an error.

In youth calf roping, the roper has the choice of carrying a second loop or recoiling and rebuilding the original loop.

The roper may get off his horse on either side during the run, and he may either **flank** the calf or **leg it down.**

The judge should watch the horse and not the roper but must be aware of what is happening with the entire run. Most calf-roping runs are completed in the ten-second range, and the judge must consider all four parts of the run before scoring the entry.

DALLY TEAM ROPING

Dally team roping is actually two classes: heading and heeling. Each is judged and scored separately. Although both classes can be judged at the same time if two judges are used (one judge placing all the headers and the other the heelers), normally two classes are held.

In both classes, the header and the heeler each can use two loops, but there is a two-minute time limit from the time the steer enters the arena until the run is completed. Failure to complete the run in two minutes calls for disqualification. Unlike calf roping, no second loops can be carried, and the ropers must rebuild their loop if they need a second one.

If either the roper or his helper misses with the first loop, the entry competing shall continue to be judged until they complete the run or are eliminated. The run that used two loops on either end should be judged accordingly, and that roper shall not be penalized for having to use a second loop. However, the run that took two loops on one end is not likely to be as smooth and correct as the run that took only one loop.

There are three legal head catches in the heading: around both horns; a **half head,** which is over one horn and around the nose; and around the neck. Any figure-eight catch (when the rope crosses itself) is illegal, as is a catch with a front leg in the loop.

In heeling, a catch is considered legal if it is on one or both hind legs, and figure-eights on the legs are not cause for disqualification. A disqualification occurs if the heeler ropes a front leg while being judged, and the header faces, ending the run. Any catch by the roper *not* being judged is considered legal and acceptable.

LEGAL HEAD CATCHES

ILLEGAL HEAD CATCHES

Before the run is considered complete, both the header and the heeler must dally, taking at least one complete turn with their ropes around their saddle horns. Failure to have a complete dally calls for disqualification. Loss of rope at any time during the run, by either the header or the heeler, even if not being judged, is also a disqualification.

As in calf roping, it is the judges' responsibility to check the equipment of all entries and prohibit the use of bits or equipment he or she considers to be severe. Mechanical hackamores are legal, but any part of the hackamore that runs across the bridge of the nose must be covered. Tie-downs are optional in team roping.

When judging both heading and heeling, judges should be on the left side of the arena (roper's left), about halfway down, from where they can see the horse in the box. It is better, if possible, for judges to be up out of the arena, elevated on the fence or perhaps in one of the first few rows of the grandstand. Wherever they are, they must be able to see all parts of the run.

Sometimes it is difficult for judges to determine whether the roper had a legal catch. When possible, it is helpful to have a mounted flagman in the arena to inform judges on questionable catches.

Team roping is scored on the basis of 0 to 100 points, with 70 denoting an average performance. As in individual calf roping, the roper is judged from the time his number is called and he starts toward the roping box until the run has been completed. Judges should remember that when a horse performs in an exceptional manner, it should be awarded points; and they should be taken away when it commits errors.

HEADING

Walking into the box and breaking the barrier are judged and scored the same as with the calf-roping horse. Judges should remember, when evaluating this portion of the run, that if a horse that commits some errors in the box is penalized, then the horse that does everything right should receive extra points.

As the heading horse leaves the box toward the steer, the move should be one smooth, continuous motion, with the top line of the horse level all the way. Ideally, the horse should leave the box on the left lead because it must turn the steer to the left after the roper makes his catch. Changing leads at this time could affect the rest of the run; if there is hesitation before the head horse can set the steer, then the action of the steer is not as smooth, making it harder for the heeler to rope the legs.

The heading horse should run from the box to a particular position on the steer (its head should be just off the steer's left hip) and wait there until the header ropes the steer and dallies. It should not be directly behind the steer.

Judges should look at how hard the horse runs to the steer, how well it goes to the correct position, and how well it rates the steer, holding its position as long as necessary. The horse should run to the left hip, staying flat and smooth, and not be climbing.

It's also crucial for the horse not to duck off as the header throws his rope. Ducking off by the head horse is a major infraction and should be penalized 3 to 5 points, depending on the situation.

Judges also should consider the amount of effort required by the roper to get his horse into position. If the steer is outrunning the horse, that is one thing. But the horse that gets out late due to the roper's error and then runs to the steer in good shape should not be penalized.

Judges also must take into account how difficult the cattle are. If one or two steers ran much harder than the others in the class, and the horses that drew them did a good job, only a little farther down the arena, those horses could receive 2 to 4 extra points for their runs.

A horse that does not run to the steer or gets outrun by it should be penalized 2 points, as should one that fails to get in the correct position and does not rate.

Setting the steer is one of the most important phases of the heading horse's run. After the header has roped the steer, taken his dally, and picked up on his horse, the heading horse should drop its rear end slightly into the ground, slowing the steer and turning its head to the left. Then the horse should quarter (pivot on its left hind leg), come up out of the set, and lead the steer off to the left.

As the horse comes out of the set, it should have control of the steer, and the header should lead the steer off at a speed that is favorable for the heeler to get a good, quick, controlled throw at the heels.

The heading horse should not stay in the ground when it sets the steer, as a calf-roping horse does. Doing so would cause the steer's rear end to pop around, and the steer will be fishtailing for the first few strides after the set. Such a situation makes it almost impossible for the heeler to get a good shot.

Other difficult circumstances for the heeler are when the heading horse drops its shoulder and ducks off to the left, popping the steer around; when it sets the steer on its front end and then ducks off to the left; or when it completely stops the steer before leading it off. The heading horse should ride its left hind leg around and roll out of the set, bringing the steer with it.

As the horse comes out of the set, it should get its body under the rope and lead the steer off. The header should have control of the steer, and it should determine at what speed and in what direction the team is going.

The heading horse should not change speed after taking control of the steer, unless it's a very gradual increase. If the steer is trotting along, the header should gradually increase its speed so that the steer will begin hopping and give the heeler a better throw. But if the steer is dragging, the header should maintain speed as much as possible so that the heeler has time to plan an already-difficult shot, and not jerk the steer up with a sudden burst of speed, which might cause the heeler to throw behind the steer. Also, the heading horse should be smooth and flat as it is leading the steer off. Any lunging will be penalized.

Ideally, the header should lead the steer in a straight line toward the left fence of the arena; occasionally conditions will not permit that, and judges must take this into consideration. If the steer is roped near the left fence, or if it ducks off to the left immediately after being roped, the header will have to drop back quickly and bring the steer back up the arena.

A heading horse should pull the steer with its body, and a horse that moves sideways, with the weight of the steer on its shoulders, should be penalized. Often this movement causes the steer to arc around, making it difficult for the heeler to get a good throw. The rope, however, should not run straight back over the hip of the heading horse, as that makes it hard for the horse to face. The rope will probably be touching the right hip, or almost so, with the horse on the left lead and quartered slightly to the right.

A horse that quits or refuses to pull the steer should be penalized severely. A disqualification occurs if the horse is not capable of completing the run. If the heading horse quits pulling but the heeler still manages to heel the steer, the header has not maintained control of the steer, and its score should reflect that. This is possibly the most serious fault in a heading horse's run.

In scoring the setting and handling portion of the heading run, judges should first consider whether the horse remained straight as it set the steer and how it rolled out of the set. Severe quartering at the beginning of the set should be penalized from 2 to 3 points. A similar penalty would be assessed a horse that set on its front end. Ducking off, either prior to the set or as a result of setting the steer with the horse's front end, could result in a penalty of 3 to 5 points.

Changing speed as the horse leads the steer off should be penalized 1 point, and a heading horse that lunges as it is taking the steer across the arena should receive a penalty of 1 to 2 points. The horse that pulls the steer with its shoulder should be penalized 1 to 2 points, and the header that refuses to pull the steer should be assessed an 8-point penalty.

The heading horse that sets the steer perfectly and then rolls off to the left, taking the steer in a manner that allows the heeler to get in position and rope quickly, should be awarded an extra 1 to 2 points, as should the horse that performs under adverse conditions, such as when a steer cuts back under its neck to the left.

The final part of the heading horse's run is the **face** (when the header wheels around and faces the heeler). The header should face his horse when the heeler has roped the heels and dallied.

When facing, the heading horse should come around flat, without rearing, and then stay back on the rope. When the face is completed, the heading

*Header sets steer, rolls off to the left, allowing heeler
to position and rope quickly.*

horse should be looking straight down the rope. Both the header's and heeler's ropes should be tight.

Some horses face by pivoting on their front ends, while others pivot on their rear ends. It is preferred and considered more correct for a horse to face by pivoting on its rear end, and this should be considered when evaluating the overall run.

A horse that doesn't quite get around straight should be penalized from 1 to 2 points, depending on the magnitude. Rearing while coming around to face should also be penalized 1 to 2 points.

A horse that makes a quick, smooth, flat face while keeping the rope tight could receive 1 to 2 extra points.

HEELING

The heeling horse, like the heading horse, should enter the box readily and be quiet and under control at all times. Heelers may vary their positions in the box, placing their horse in either corner or in the middle without a penalty being assessed.

In heeling, the heading horse must start from behind a barrier; if that horse breaks the barrier, the heeling horse may be penalized. The barrier is used to keep the heading horse from jumping out on top of the steer and turning it right in front of the roping box. The amount of penalty should vary according to circumstances: If it is obviously a flagrant situation, where the header deliberately charged through the barrier, a 3-point penalty should be assessed. If, in the judge's opinion, breaking the barrier was not deliberate, a 1-point penalty is adequate.

The heeling horse should come out of the box smoothly, moving to the right side and a little to the rear of the steer. After the header has roped the steer and turned it off to the left, the heeling horse should then come to a position just off the steer's left hip and remain there until the heeler releases the rope. When the heeler's rope is released, the horse should drop its rear end into the ground, stop and remain there. It should not bounce or dribble forward, and it should not begin backing immediately.

Occasionally, in heeling, the heading horse may face too soon, causing the heeler to back the horse up a few steps to tighten the rope. Judges should not penalize that move itself, other than when considering the overall smoothness of the run. However, the horse that stops and then immediately sucks backward should be penalized, as this poses a danger to the roper when he attempts to dally. Any movement of the saddle horn caused by the horse dribbling to a stop, rushing back, or shying sideways can cause the heeler to miss his dally and result in a hand injury.

When the heeling horse stops, it should remain in place until the completion of the run. Allowing the heading horse to pull it up out of the stop or shying sideways as the heeler dallies are both faults that should be penalized. The heeling horse that stops on its front feet often will be jerked forward by the heading horse, causing the saddle horn to be lowered; this endangers the heeler while he is dallying.

Also, the heeling horse should stop on its own and not require the roper to move the reins severely. However, if the roper lifts his hand just enough to make contact with the horse's mouth, that should not be penalized.

Timing and position are the two main areas of concern in heeling. When the header turns the steer, he has the animal in a nice, smooth lope, and as the heeling horse comes into position, it should pick up the same stride as the steer. A heeling horse not under complete control could force the heeler to adjust his swing, detracting from the smoothness of the run.

The heeling horse approaches the steer after it has been set in one of two ways: cutting in straight to the hip, or swinging around and approaching the steer from behind. Either is permissible, but the horse that drops its shoulder and ducks straight in to the steer, or one that runs into the steer, should be penalized. In both of these cases it is impossible for the heeling horse to be in rhythm with the steer.

A one-leg catch is as good as a two-leg catch, if everything else in the run is equal. It is the horse being judged, not the roper. However, if there are two otherwise equal runs, a two-leg catch should place over the single-leg catch.

When scoring, judges should notice first how the horse emerges from the box and runs to the steer. Getting out late and failing to reach the steer before the header has roped and turned it should result in a 2-point penalty. This situation will be evident, as the heeler will have to hustle his horse during the entire run.

If the heeler is right with the steer as it goes down the arena and then goes straight to the correct position on the steer's left hip, he could be awarded an extra 2 to 4 points. The heeling horse should never take up a position on the right side of the steer after the header has set the animal; if it does so, it should be penalized 3 to 5 points. An exception to this rule, of course, would be in the case of a left-handed heeler.

The heeling horse that stops on its front end, dribbles to a stop, bounces up out of the stop, or sucks backward out of the stop should be penalized 2 to 4 points, depending on the severity. The horse that shies sideways as the roper dallies should be penalized 3 to 4 points. All of these faults cause the saddle horn to move and pose a danger to the heeler's hand as he dallies.

Riders using excessive force with the reins in stopping the heeling horse should be penalized 3 points. A horse that drops its shoulder and ducks straight in to the steer should be penalized 2 to 3 points. One that runs into the steer should receive a 3- to 4-point penalty.

The horse that stays quiet in the box, runs to the correct position, stops hard on its rear end and remains straight, and does not move after the roper makes his dally should receive from 1 to 3 extra points on each portion of the run.

The object of team roping is for a horse to make the entire run correctly and quickly, but judges should be careful to not let the time of the run affect their judging. The event came from rodeo, where time is the only factor considered, and you should be aware that sometimes judges are influenced by a quick run that was perhaps lacking in control. When two runs are of equal quality, the quickest one should be placed higher, but quickness alone often is used as a substitute for even-handed evaluation, and judges should remember that they are judging the horse, not the roper.

CHAPTER IV

English Performance Classes

WORKING HUNTER

THE ideal working hunter is a horse that has the fitness, athletic ability, and willingness to carry its rider during a day's foxhunt, following the hounds through fields and woods, able to jump over the various obstacles such as hedges, gates, and fences that may block their way. The arena course for working hunters is designed to test these qualities by giving horses an opportunity to show their ability to use their ears, obey the rider's commands, meet each obstacle squarely with sufficient impulsion and at a good takeoff spot driving from behind, jump over them in an arc with the forearms neatly pulled up in front of the chest parallel to (or slightly higher than) the body, and then land in balance, ready to move on to the next fence—all the while maintaining a steady rhythm and pace that are suitable to the course.

The rules specify the penalties for such obvious faults as refusing, running out, and knocking down an obstacle. But judges also have to evaluate other faults when scoring a round, which sometimes leads to misunderstanding. For example, is it worse for a horse to twist over a fence or to hang a leg? Is shifting the hindquarters to the side over a jump worse than jumping inverted with the head in the air? These are not questions of style but of practical importance. That's why I believe, again, that the more dangerous the fault, the more severe should be the penalty. When you understand this event and its criteria, then it's not all that hard to score a working hunter class.

Even though they may not design it themselves, judges should know the requirements of the course and should always check to make sure that it conforms to the rules and is safe. Hunters shouldn't be asked to handle tricky problem fences. They should only have to jump simple, natural obstacles such as might be met in the actual hunt field: gates, brush boxes (simulating hedges), brick or stone walls, chicken coops, banks (simulated by rolltops), and various kinds of fences (rail, log, picket, or ladder). Judges also should verify that all the fences are placed at normal distances that allow the horses to cover the entire course at an even pace, to jump cleanly, calmly, and safely, and to give the rider a smooth ride. As you can see, hunter courses are very different from the jumper division; the latter division requires greater jumping ability over greater heights and widths as well as greater speed, agility, and courage and obedience in order to cope with obstacles set at awkward distances and angles or designed to look strange or spooky.

Hunter fences are far more conservative. They are set at distances conforming to a normal twelve-foot stride in order to enable the horse to produce a flowing pace and jumping arc, which are the most desirable qualities of a hunter. The course diagram is therefore quite simple, usually consisting of two diagonals crossing in the middle of the ring, with another outside line around it—in other words, a figure-eight inside a circle. This gives the horse a good chance to demonstrate its skill in changing direction and changing leads.

The course designer should consider the size of the arena, the location of the ingate and outgate, and the level of competition. A good working hunter championship course would be totally unsuitable for a local amateur class. Also, a course may look great on the diagram, but when it's fitted into an arena that's too small for it, the turns will be too tight and the lines too close together, and the horses will have to shorten their stride and break pace instead of producing the desired flowing round. An unsuitable course makes the class very difficult to judge fairly.

A hunter course is composed of eight jumps. If eight different obstacles are not available, some will have to be jumped twice to make up the required number. If a horse has a knockdown and the jump that has to be taken twice needs to be rebuilt, the horse must interrupt its round and wait till the jump has been reset. If the rider is unaware of the knockdown, the judge will blow a whistle, signaling the rider to stop; the judge will blow it again after the jump has been rebuilt to signal the rider to resume the course. (Obviously, judges should always carry a whistle.)

The most common fences on a working hunter course are simply horizontal rails placed between two upright standards: post-and-rails. The same material can be arranged to build either vertical or horizontal (spread) fences. The verticals may be level, or they may slope slightly away from the approach. The slope must be slight, not to the point of turning into a ramp. Another variation is the in-and-out, with two vertical fences placed twenty-four or thirty-six feet apart, which is the natural distance for making one or two smooth normal strides between them. These rails, incidentally, may be round or octagonal (but always straight), four inches in diameter, with a separation of no more than nine inches. They may be painted white, gray, green, brown, rust, or blue—but not striped or garish (as permitted in jumper classes). Red is taboo, except for the imitation brick wall, because this color is not normally seen in foxhunting terrain. The best obstacles are the most natural looking and rustic, such as birch and cedar rails with the bark left on (if these logs are bowed, the bow should be placed downward); boxes filled with shrubs or fir branches; imitation brick and stone walls; panels simulating gates, ladders, and picket fences. The height of the gate can be increased either by placing a vertical pole on top of it or by placing a box of shrubbery underneath and raising the gate itself.

A good hunter course should start off easy and increase in difficulty as it goes along, with the last line of fences the most challenging. While this is true of all jumping courses, working hunter course designers always should remember that they are not dealing with expert riders and finished horses, but with amateur riders and often green horses. The very last obstacle is usually a spread fence, which should be placed at the end of a line (and not just a few strides after an upright or after a turn, as you see on jumper courses). The spread can be up to three feet wide, measured from the front ("face") of the first element to the back of the second part; and both elements should be in line and parallel. The spreads can be single-unit jumps, like a coop and a rolltop; or they can consist of two verticals placed close together, creating a double-bar spread that is called an oxer, in which case the front element should be three to six inches lower than the second one. Square oxers, with both elements on the same level, are much more difficult for horses to judge, tricky even for open jumpers, and much too risky for working hunters. Safety always should be a prime consideration in designing courses for less highly trained horses.

Likewise, for safety reasons as well as to allow each horse to show to its best advantage, the distances are measured (from the back of one fence to the face of the next) in approximate multiples of twelve feet. This is the average length of stride of a horse, which permits a steady pace at a hand gallop of twelve to fifteen miles per hour. In the hunting field, a horse may have to shorten or lengthen its stride. But in the show ring, the judge is looking for even, flowing strides. For example, if there is a distance of forty-eight feet between two fences, the horse should ideally take off before the first fence at a half-stride distance, land at another half-stride distance, and then take three strides to reach the takeoff point for the next fence. In actual practice, when the riders walk the course and count the strides, they don't count the takeoff and landing half strides, so that a forty-eight-foot distance between two fences is considered to be a three-stride (at a canter); thirty-six feet is a two-stride;

Horse's forearms should be tucked neatly in front of its chest and held parallel (or slightly higher) to its body.

and twenty-four feet, a one-stride. Of course, all horses don't have the same length of natural stride, and a 14.2-hand horse would need to make more strides over fairly long distances than a 16-hand horse. So sometimes riders will have to lengthen or shorten the stride, or add an extra one. If they do so while maintaining an even pace (and if it's not in a one- or two-stride combination), this should not be held against them. However, judges may separate two close competitors who have otherwise performed equally well on the basis of one rider slipping in an extra stride.

Accurately measured distances facilitate rhythm and cadence, which are of prime importance for hunters. They should move with free, long, flowing strides, stretching the forelegs to cover lots of ground, instead of making short, choppy, high strides. And they should maintain the pace as they approach each fence and make the takeoff in stride and in cadence.

Hunter class obstacles should be constructed so as to fall only when they're struck hard, not merely ticked. The rails should be of the same weight and dimensions. In this class it would be unfair to place a very large pole over several thin ones, or to place heavy poles under a flimsy one that would fall at the slightest tick.

Rails and panels are set in cups with pins to fit into holes drilled three inches apart on the upright posts or standards, permitting the fences to be raised or lowered easily. The pins go all the way through the posts and should be inserted on the side from which the horses approach the obstacle. Unused cups should be removed from the posts and from the course; extra poles also should be removed, and never stored under a jump.

Since the purpose of this class is to let the horses and riders demonstrate their abilities and not to set traps for them, all the obstacles should be solid-looking and well defined so they can be seen easily and the required jumping effort easily sized up. "Airy" jumps with no ground line and wide spaces between the rails are very deceptive where depth perception is concerned and should never be used on a hunter course. The construction of other jumps also can promote or hinder safety. For example, the boards in gates, picket fences, and ladders should be spaced either two or eight inches apart; the first spacing is too small for a horse to catch its leg in, and the second is wide enough for a horse that gets caught up in it to slip its leg out again. Although not required by the rules, I like to see wings on either side of the standards, since they delineate the fence and encourage the horses to jump in the middle of it. Ground lines are another safety factor. This can be nothing more than a pole placed on the ground some six inches in front of the fence. Even better is a ground line formed by boxed flowers, shrubbery, or fir branches, which is more solid looking to the horse and more attractive to the spectators.

Hunter course patterns like those seen in the Appendix must be posted at least one hour before the class is scheduled to start. The fences are numbered in the order they have to be jumped, with arrows indicating the direction of travel, and the entrance and exit are marked too. It's helpful if the diagram is drawn on something large, such as a sheet of poster board, and it should be posted high enough to be clearly visible from a distance or from the saddle. Unfortunately, the types of obstacles (except in-and-outs) are never indicated; neither are the distances between them. This information would be helpful to the riders. Riders sometimes are allowed to walk the course before the class, measuring strides between the fences and planning their strategy. A warm-up area with schooling jumps also should be provided.

A good hunter course should look inviting. Having the first jumps relatively simple and rather low gives the horses and riders confidence to complete the rest of the course. It's also good psychology to set the first fence so the horse can approach and jump it heading toward the ingate. Spooky, deceptive obstacles should be excluded, such as a white gate in front of a white arena wall or a dark one in a shadowy area of an indoor arena. Course designers should consider the possibly disastrous effect of light and shade in outdoor rings too, as when adjacent trees or buildings cast dark shadows on a light sandy arena surface, or when an obstacle is placed so that the horse has to jump it into the rising or setting sun.

Before the start of the class, judges should check the course for all of these details. Some of the most common errors I've spotted include sloping verticals inclined in the wrong direction (toward instead of away from the approach); misaligned or square oxers; absent ground lines or improperly set ones (too close to the fence or too far away); and airy, flimsily constructed fences. Judges also should check the footing. It isn't fair to ask a hunter to compete on ground that has been churned up by barrel racers or to run into a wet or muddy spot between jumps, which could cause some horses to shorten stride or else jump over it. Finally, judges must check the height of all the fences and the distances between them and the direction of the fences and wings, making sure that the pins are placed in the standards with the tips emerging on the landing side and that all extra cups and rails have been removed from the arena.

Hunters are scored on a scale of 0 to 100. This gives expert judges a wide range of appreciation for the horses' qualities and enables them to classify the horses accordingly.

The hunter's round begins the minute it enters the ring and is over only when it has passed through the outgate. If the class is held outdoors instead of in an arena, the starting line should be placed about fifty feet before the first fence and the finish line about fifty feet beyond the last one.

Errors should be scored according to how dangerous they are. The worst are refusals, knockdowns, and taking off too far from or too close to an obstacle with the risk of crashing through it. Because of the possible dire consequences, refusals and front knockdowns should be penalized more heavily than hind ones, even to the point of elimination. At the very least, a refusal is a sign of an unwilling, dishonest horse. At worst, it can send the rider to the hospital. For example, if a horse gallops up to an obstacle and then suddenly stops at the takeoff point, the rider, already forward in a two-point position, could be tossed into the fence. Refusals are defined precisely in the rules: When a horse stops in front of an obstacle (not necessarily altering it or knocking it down) and backs up even one little step, it counts as a refusal. If, however, it stops without backing up and immediately jumps the fence, it is not a refusal.

The penalty for a refusal is 8 faults; three refusals (even at different fences) incur elimination. If a rail falls or a fence collapses due to the horse's stopping, it is not scored as a knockdown, but given the greater penalty of a refusal. Unlike jumper classes, in which a horse that refuses a single element of a combination has to rejump the entire combination, hunters are permitted to try again over only the part of the combination they refused.

If the rider, after a refusal, moves the horse up to the obstacle without asking it to jump, he or she will incur an additional 8-fault penalty for "showing an obstacle to the horse." If the rider then circles, asks the horse to jump again, and if the horse again balks or steps back, it counts as a third refusal. Bolting (an evasion of control) and running out (evasion of the jump) are disobediences just as serious as refusals, and are assessed the same penalty of 8 faults, with the third occurrence causing elimination. In fact, the third instance of the above in any combination (refusal, bolting, runout, showing a horse an obstacle) calls for elimination.

Knockdowns occur when an obstacle or any part of it is struck by either the horse or rider, causing a rail to fall, or lowering the top element, even though the dislodged pole may not have fallen to the ground. As mentioned, hunter obstacles, like those found in the hunting field, should be able to withstand a light brush. Faults made by the front legs are penalized more heavily than faults made by the hindquarters or behind the stifle, because the former are more dangerous. The horse that catches its front legs on a fence can flip head over heels and land on top of the rider. For this reason, a front knockdown is given 8 faults and a rear knockdown only half as much (4 faults).

Normally, a light tick by a front foot shouldn't cause a fence to collapse, although judges would note the tick in order to separate very close competitors. If the tick happens to dislodge a pole, judges must penalize the horse 8 faults. If the next horse slides into a jump and crashes through it, almost unseating the rider, it's still the same penalty of 8 faults. But a good judge, all other things being equal, would place the first horse above the second one. In the same way, one horse would get an 8-fault penalty for crashing through a fence chest high and another horse would get the same 8-fault penalty for spooking and running out when a balloon falls into the ring. Obviously, the crash of the first horse was more dangerous than the reaction of the second one, and should result in a lower placing.

The same principle applies to knockdowns. For example, if one entry pulls down two top rails with a couple of light rubs by a hind foot, and another takes down two fences by catching the top rails at its stifle, and if another knocks down an obstacle with its front legs, all of them receive 8 faults. But judges have to decide which errors were more dangerous and place the horses accordingly.

Certain errors lead to automatic elimination whatever the circumstances: jumping an obstacle before it has been reset; bolting from the ring; going off course; jumping an obstacle not included in the course; and fall of horse or rider.

The rules specify all of these penalties. But judges must evaluate other errors and score them accordingly. Inexperienced judges score each round only according to the prescribed penalties for the most obvious errors. But as their eye improves, they will be able to spot more subtle errors, such as incorrect takeoff and landing distances.

Normally, a hunter should take off and land from equidistant spots on each side of the fence: approximately six feet away for obstacles three feet six inches or higher, and about five feet for lower fences. If the horse takes off too far from a jump, it may try to put its feet back down on the near side of the fence and then crash through it. Or it may make an all-out effort to clear the fence anyway, flailing with its front legs in an effort to fly through the air or stretching them as far as it can to dive over the obstacle.

Diving is a serious jumping fault that should preclude any placing in a good hunter class. **Reaching** is a less risky but still dangerous form of diving,

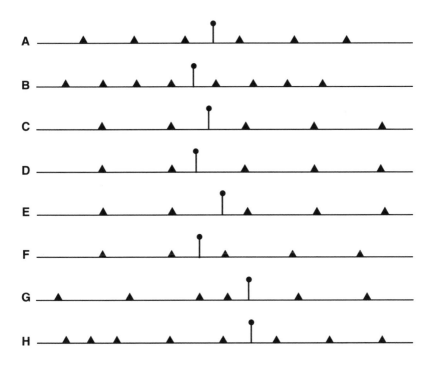

ON APPROACH, A HUNTER MAY BE SEEN
STRIDING AS FOLLOWS:

A, B, and C are correct in approach, with the stride staying the same over the fence.

In D, though the animal stayed in stride, its takeoff point was too close to the fence.

In E, the opposite was true. Its takeoff point was too far away from the fence.

In F, though the animal's stride was correct up to the fence, it took off too close and landed too close.

In G, the approach strides were correct, but the horse threw in a short stride just in front of the fence and took off too close.

In H, either the horse or the rider has a keen eye. They set themselves several strides back and then came on in stride.

The marks on the lines indicate where the horse is hitting the ground in its stride, and the vertical lines are the fences.

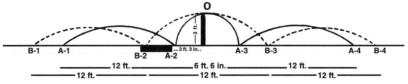

The closest this horse can get to its fence is shown by A-2, which is its point of takeoff. A-3 is its point of landing. The farthest it can stand back and make a good fence would be B-2 to B-3, which is twelve feet six inches. On a three-foot fence, this gives it a leeway of three feet (B-2 to A-2) to make a good fence. This area is called the safe zone. The horse reached the top of arc (O) at the top of the jump, which is as it should be.

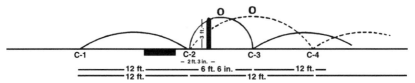

The horse has come in on a twelve-foot stride, taking off one foot closer to the jump at C-2. Both the short parabola at six feet six inches and the twelve-foot parabola put the peak of the parabola O past the jump, and it has come in contact with the jump. The long arc of C-2 to C-4 put the horse hitting the jump rather low and would probably be an unsafe fence with the horse hitting above the knees.

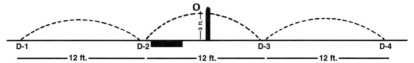

The horse has taken off at D-2, which is outside the safe zone. Reaching its peak at O, it will connect with the jump, coming down either in front or with the hind legs.

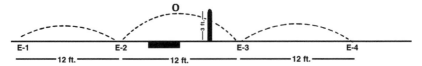

The horse has taken off quite long at E-2. Reaching its peak at O, it could easily spill, catching its front legs on the obstacle. If it is agile enough to clear its front legs, it will probably get a high hind knock-down behind.

O - Peak of Arc
▬▬▬ - Safe Zone JUMPING ARC (PARABOLA, BASCULE)

AN AVERAGE-SIZE HORSE WITH A TWELVE-FOOT STRIDE JUMPING OVER A THREE-FOOT FENCE

To make a clean, safe fence, a horse jumps in an arc or parabola. It should stand back the height of the lowest element on a spread fence, or the height of an up-and-down fence (straight fence), plus two or three inches.
This two to three inches is its margin of clearance.

when a horse that has taken off too far from the jump (but not so far as the diver) unfolds its legs to reach over it. **Cutting down** is when the horse clears the fence all right but immediately drops its front legs on the far side, landing closer than it should to the fence and often catching a rail with the hind legs. This could indicate simply a lack of scope ("scope" in a jumper is analogous to working ability in a cow horse). A more "scopey" (or athletic) horse in the same situation would leave from the longer distance, make a higher arc (more than needed for the height of the jump, but appropriate to the distance), and land on the far side of the fence at the same distance as the takeoff on the other side. If no knockdown occurred in either of these cases, the horse that reached should be penalized more severely than the horse that cut down, because of the increased risk entailed in front-leg faults.

Jumping faults can be caused not only by taking off too far, but also too close, resulting in propping and chipping in. Propping usually happens when the horse approaches an obstacle too fast and seems to be pushing away or setting back from the fence at the takeoff point, with its hind legs well under the body and the front legs well extended, not unlike a cow horse making a quick stop. A scopey horse usually can compensate for taking off from a close or deep spot and still make a good jump by instinctively collecting itself, bringing the hocks well up under the body at the takeoff, and then rocking slightly backward, so that its legs clear the rails. Chipping is an extreme form of propping. It happens when the horse arrives at the takeoff spot off stride and, in an attempt to adjust, throws in an extra short stride, which often makes it take off on only one hind leg instead of both.

Hanging a leg means that the horse drops or partially unfolds its legs from the elbow down. Hanging a leg in front of a fence is a dangerous fault, almost as bad as a knockdown or a refusal, because it too can result in serious injury. In the hunt field, a horse that hangs a leg and hits a fence is very apt to fall. Most often a horse will hang its legs when it comes in too close to an obstacle without folding them to avoid a knockdown. A similar fault is dropping the shoulders, in which the horse's shoulders and forearms are lowered toward the ground, past the center point of the horse, even though the forearm, knee, and cannon bone may be correctly folded.

The smooth rhythm that is one of the desirable qualities of a hunter is often a matter of temperament. High-strung, hot horses tend to get quick, patting the ground just before the takeoff. They should be penalized for this and for any other signs of anxiety and nervousness. Green or sluggish horses, on the other hand, may "dwell off the ground" or in the air. "Dwelling off the ground" can be caused by lack of momentum at the takeoff, when the horse hasn't approached the fence with an easy, free-flowing stride. But it also can occur with green horses that have arrived at the obstacle in stride and in form but are hesitant to jump due to inexperience, lack of leg by the rider, fear of taking off or landing, or fear of jumping into the rider's hands.

Dwelling in the air is something like the way a ball tossed high hangs at the apex of its arc for a split second. Like the ball, the horse seems to hover over the fence for a moment. This can be the result of jumping quickly with insufficient impulsion or of too slow a pace and a powerful takeoff. In any case, it is undesirable.

Hunters should approach the fence in a straight line and jump over the center in a smooth arc, without wavering or drifting to one side or the other. During the jump, they should be attentive and relaxed, with neck and back rounded. An inverted or flat top line simply may be an individual jumping style, or it can denote a lack of scope. **Drifting** describes the horse that takes off headed for the center of the fence and then drifts to one side or the other. It may be a lateral evasion of the rider's aids, a sign of poor training, or the horse's reaction to the rider's bad habit of leaning to one side or placing more weight in one stirrup than in the other. In any case, it can result in injury if the rider's leg gets caught on a standard. Less serious, but still subject to penalty, is the horse that jumps straight but off center. However, jumping straight but at an angle is permissible if its purpose is to insure the flowing continuity of the course.

Overjumping is when the horse clears a fence higher or longer than necessary. Again, this may be the sign of a green horse, a nervous or anxious one, or simply an exuberant animal.

The hunter should clear the fences with its body absolutely vertical, that is, without **laying on its side.** The latter can put the rider in a perilous position by throwing him or her off balance to the lowside; also, the horse may not be able to land safely on its feet. **Twisting,** when the upright horse shifts its fore- or hindquarters to the side in order to clear an obstacle, is less risky but still a fault that should be penalized.

A horse that doesn't fold its legs tightly is said to show loose form. This is not as serious a fault as hanging a leg from the elbow or shoulder, but, all else being equal, such a horse still should be placed lower than an athletic one that moves well and folds properly.

Other faults of form include moving with the legs so close together that the hooves cross or moving with the legs so far apart that they extend beyond the horse's chest. These faults aren't dangerous, but they're still enough to rank a horse below another one that displays proper form.

Form can influence manners and way of going. Good manners and good moving don't guarantee good form, but bad ones can make good form practically impossible. A hunter should be able to be ridden in hand, with the rider guiding its placement and stride by light, sensitive, almost invisible actions. This is very different from the exaggerated kind of hand riding where the horse is constantly under restraint, held tightly in a frame, never allowed to move freely but "set up" by the rider at every jump, which is entirely unsuitable in a hunter class. The question of degree also arises concerning use of a crop. It may be marginally permissible for urging forward a horse that needs encouragement, but any excessive use should be severely penalized.

All performance horses should know how to make changes of lead on command. Working hunters should be able to make them when clearing a jump or coming into a turn. For example, if a horse on the right lead comes around a turn into a jump that is followed by a left turn, it should respond to the rider's aids for changing to a left lead while in the air, and land on the left lead; or else it should be able to make a flying change of lead before entering into the left turn. Judges prefer a horse that makes flying changes at the right places to one that picks up the correct lead in front and then changes behind. I'd place a horse lower down that cross-canters (moving with front and hind legs on opposite leads), because this disunited action poses great risk to horse and rider and therefore merits a significant penalty.

As you see, there's a lot more to judging a working hunter class than simply counting ticks and knockdowns. The general policy should be to penalize unsafe and bad jumping form, whether the fences are touched, and to pick the horses the judges themselves would like to ride in the hunt field. In order to do this fairly, judges have to have a clear idea of what is unsafe or dangerous.

Let's say that one horse in a hunter class had a good round except for one fence, which it approached too fast, really having to scramble to avoid a wreck. The next horse performed a good, even round but had a light rub with a hind leg that brought a rail down. Because of the all-important danger factor, the second horse should be placed ahead of the first one.

So many different things can happen from beginning to end of a working hunter round that it is absolutely necessary for judges to devise some kind of accurate bookkeeping system in order to keep score of the contestants. The system should be so detailed that the judges can refer to the records many years later and see exactly how each horse in the class negotiated each obstacle. This approach also enables judges to explain their final placings to the exhibitors, who have the right to question judges—but not to contest their decision, which is final.

The working hunter scorecard includes a section with a numbered box for each obstacle on the course and another section for grading the overall performance. It's a good idea to identify each obstacle (gate, oxer, brush, etc.) as a memory aid when comparing close rounds or responding to questions from disgruntled exhibitors. Each box contains a record of how the horse handled that particular fence: whether it took the brush box in good form or chipped in at the gate, knocked down the post-and-rail, or refused the wall and then ran through the oxer. In order to note all these things, judges need a quick and accurate shorthand system.

Novice hunter judges haven't yet acquired the eye to spot every detail at every fence, so they can use relatively few symbols to record the major faults. But as they gain skill and experience, they'll spot more subtle errors and they'll need a wider range of symbols to record them. After each round, which judges record fence by fence, they should turn to the second section of the scorecard, where they make additional comments and rate the horse's general impression, way of going, and jumping form with a numerical score.

A good mover, well mannered, well balanced, jumping well and in cadence, should score in the 90s (the equivalent of an A). A horse that performs reasonably well, with nothing outstanding but nothing bad either, should get a score of 80 to 89 (a B). An average horse, only a fair mover, should be given 70 to 79 points (a C). Below that, the scores take a nosedive: in the 60s for poor performances by bad movers or clumsy horses who have made minor mistakes; in the 50s for major faults such as a knockdown, refusal, or breaking into a trot; in the 40s for two or more major faults; and 0 for failing to complete the course or being eliminated.

The best viewpoint for evaluating this class, especially the finer points, is for judges to be seated outside of the arena in an elevated position, where they see the horses in profile over most of the fences. Incidentally, as the class proceeds, it is useful and time-saving to keep a running tally of the high-score rounds, especially in very large classes. While judges have an objective standard to go by, when it's time to award the ribbons, they have to measure each entry in comparison with all the others. Before arriving at the final decision, they often have to separate close competitors. If they think a round deserves a score of 84, they should compare it with any others they have already marked 84; if this one was slightly better or slightly inferior, it should receive an 85 or an 83.

Certain standards of performance are so firmly established that a horse that is only a fair mover can never hope to score in the 90s, even though it jumps the course cleanly; and a bad mover, even with a faultless performance, can never hope to make it into the 80s. In order to get a top score, an A, the horse has to be a good mover, jump every fence in good form at an even hunting pace, and do it all with style.

HUNTER UNDER SADDLE

Horses competing in the hunter under saddle class are judged on performance, including way of going, manners, and soundness. In other words, they are supposed to display the athletic proficiency necessary for a horse that has to carry its rider during a day of foxhunting. The show ring competition attempts to simulate the conditions found in the hunting field, and the judges rate the aptitudes and performances of the contestants as compared to those of an ideal hunter.

The class requirements consist of performing at a walk, trot, and canter, both ways of the ring. Except for green classes, the horses also may be required to gallop at least one way of the ring in a group of no more than twelve at a time.

The purpose of this event is to demonstrate the basic qualities of a field hunter. Until fairly recently, people used to hack to a hunt meet; therefore, the most desirable horse was one with a long, low, ground-covering stride, to enable the rider to arrive on time for the meet with a mount that had expended little energy and had plenty left for a four- or five-hour foxhunt. Thus the quality of the gaits is most important in this class, although the quality of the riding also plays a part.

The rider should maintain a light contact with the horse's mouth; in other words, the rein contact should not be loose and slack but have a certain tension. This light contact is what pulls the horse together and is sometimes described as "holding the horse between the rider's legs and hands." The rider should move the horse forward with his or her legs (impulsion), pushing it into the bridle and reins while exerting a slight tension on the bit (collection). The horse should have a head position somewhat forward (certainly not downward, which would weigh down the forehand), with its head and neck slightly leaning on the bit, and with the poll flexed. It should not, however, be flexed to the extent of dressage horses, with the horse's profile perpendicular to the ground.

The required gaits are evaluated according to certain ideal standards.

The **walk** should be animated and ground-covering, without turning into an extended walk like that of the dressage horse. It should seem natural and effortless.

The **trot** should be ground-covering too, with low strides close to the ground—what foxhunters describe as "mowing the grass." This is the gait the horse can maintain over the greatest distance at a fair speed with the least effort. A good trot also should be reasonably comfortable and untiring for the rider.

The **canter** should be even more ground-covering, with long, low strides that are not too fast. However, it is a very bad mistake to canter so slowly—in an effort to show off the horse's calm and quiet good manners—that it appears to be a four-beat canter.

The **hand gallop** should be a controlled lengthening of stride from the canter, with the horse responding willingly and immediately when asked to move on. This also should be a ground-covering gait, more forward reaching, but still under control so that the horse immediately and obediently can come back and halt at the rider's command.

The most important feature of the horse's gaits in this class is their efficiency, in other words, the best result for the least output of energy. A horse that lifts its legs high instead of stretching them forward is wasting energy. Another important point is the horse's ability to increase or decrease speed willingly on demand, since this is often necessary during an actual foxhunt,

Horse should not have its head and neck down,
being heavy on the forehand.

where it may be in the company of ten to eighty other horses. When a fox is sighted and the hounds start to run, the entire field moves at once. And if the fox and hounds change track all of a sudden, the field has to stop abruptly and move in the new direction just as fast.

Needless to say, good manners—and especially good "company manners"—are very important in a field hunter. They're even more important in a youth or amateur class. But the single most important standard of judgment in under saddle classes is the way the horse moves.

AS I SEE IT

In hunter under saddle classes, let the horse tell you how it needs to be shown, and at what pace and frame it is comfortable. A horse's head should be slightly in front of the vertical and the poll should be above the withers. How far above the withers depends on the particular horse's conformation.

At the walk, the horse should move out naturally; you should not restrict or hold it back. Don't be afraid to pass other horses if your horse happens to have a longer stride. Constantly holding a horse back to form an elephant brigade (head to tail) on the rail is not going to impress the judge; at least it shouldn't.

When showing at the trot, it should be a working trot, one that is neither

*Trot should be long-strided, low, and ground-covering—
"mowing the grass," so to speak.*

too fast nor too slow. If an extended trot is asked for, it should be different from the working trot.

Some horses canter more slowly than others, but if you canter too slowly, your horse will fall out of gear behind. The canter of most hunters under saddle shown today is still mechanical, like a Western pleasure type of canter. But hunters should not be shown that way. Riders need to allow the horse to reach up under itself with its hind legs, to elevate at the canter and go forward. The horse also needs to be balanced and have a level top line (that portion of the back from the withers to the croup where the rider sits). The top line should be as level or smooth as a horse's conformation allows at any gait.

After the horses have worked the rail and are called to the center for the lineup, riders should prepare their horses for the backup. The hunter under saddle should back readily and smoothly. It doesn't need to back fast or very far, but it should show the judge that it is responsive to the bit and flexible at the poll and can step backward quietly. A horse that throws its head and is unresponsive to a rider's invitation to back will be marked down. I often use the backup to separate two horses that are equal on the rail.

A hunter has to be able to lift its head up if it is going to jump. Even if the horse is never going to jump, it still should be able to carry its head where it is comfortable. The rider should maintain light contact with the horse's mouth through the reins. A loop in the reins in the hunter under saddle class is incorrect, as is a horse that overflexes or is behind the vertical.

THE COURSE

In both hunter and jumper events, the course designer is an active participant in the final outcome. The designer's knowledge or lack thereof directly affects the competitors' performance. Many problems are created or solved by the course itself. Very subtle changes can cause an accurately measured course on a twelve-foot stride to become "uneven" in the amount of effort it takes to cover these set distances. For example, all things being equal, three lines of five strides (that is, seventy-two feet), each measured accurately, should ideally ride equally, but this is not always the case in practice.

If the class in question is held early in the show, for example, the greener or more apprehensive horse may have a problem. It might be "backed off" (not willingly going forward), which subtracts from its natural stride, making it shorter. Often a new arena, new jumps—in short, anything unfamiliar— makes a horse look at everything and lose concentration on the job at hand. It may then become hesitant, losing forward motion. Even if it doesn't stop or have a refusal, it may become distracted enough to need an extra stride.

Good course designers take everything into consideration and will modify a course to suit the competition. Modifications such as shortening the first line going away from the ingate by a couple of feet, making the first fence jump toward the ingate, or lowering the first jump and simplifying it are simple tricks of the course designer's trade. Later in a show, such concessions can be removed and stricter demands placed on the horses according to the quality of the competition.

MOTION

Everybody who shows a horse desires a good mover. The subject of motion is a part of every backgate discussion, even though it differs with each class. Everyone talks about it, most see it, some cultivate it, but few can describe it. Why? Because what we want keeps changing. As soon as we define a particu- lar way of going, up jumps a horse with a little different style or "athletic ability" and our whole direction changes. We constantly hear such well-worn clichés as scopey, mows the grass, daisy cutter, folds well, soft, level, smooth, trappy, thrashy, pounds—describing good and bad. Western pleasure emphasizes movement. Hunters are scored on their way of going, using symbols to depict motion: GM stands for good mover; FM, fair mover; BM, bad mover; and one of my own favorites, FAS, which means find another sport.

Desired motion is not only different in every class but in every breed with the same class title. Nowhere have we seen a greater change in movement than in the pleasure division, both English and Western. Horses in these classes bear little resemblance to those of a few years ago.

With all this commotion about pleasure or under saddle horses today, we're seeing some changes come about in what we refer to as good movers. There seem to be a lot of people who don't fully understand what ingredients make up a horse's movement or why horses go as they are designed to go. I say this because the mechanics of how a horse moves are really quite simple. Most people think of motion as only leg movement. (A fallacy, at best.) That's why we see weighted shoes, unnatural hoof angles, rubber bands, shackles, developers, exercisers, running-Ws, chains, rattles, hock hobbles, and in many instances irritants, all with the sole purpose of changing leg movement. Let's look at what really makes the horse move.

Motion in the horse comes from several sources and mostly from a combination of sources. If we compare a horse to an automobile, the hind-quarters are the horse's motor, the back is the transmission, and the forelegs constitute the suspension system. Contrary to some beliefs, the forelegs have *no* necessary function in moving the horse forward. The horse is propelled forward from behind, and its back (spine) governs the type of movement its legs will make.

Taken as a whole, the spine (from poll to tail) is a many-jointed and therefore flexible part of the horse's body. The shapes of the articular surfaces between the individual vertebrae in the back determine the movements that each portion of the back can make and the positions each can maintain. The joints between the neck vertebrae permit free movement in any plane.

The largest muscle in the horse's body lies along either side of the spine. Many people mistakenly believe it's there to hold up the spine, but the horse's back is not held up by any muscle. The back functions like a cantilever bridge. Muscles work by contracting, not when they are stretched. Normally when a muscle is stretched, it's relaxed. Ligaments are just the opposite. They work like cables, only when they are stretched. The horse's back is held up by the dorsal, the animal's single longest ligament. It runs in sections from the poll to the withers; the withers to the middle of the synsacrum (front of the croup about at the hip), the middle of the synsacrum to the tip of the tail, and the middle of the synsacrum in another branch reaching to the hock.

Angles are the key to a horse's motion. Angles in shoulders, quarters, and pasterns greatly determine the horse's action and freedom of motion. If the shoulder is too steep, it puts the horse's front legs too far under, cramping its stride and making it restricted in reach. A good horse should be able to reach out well past its nose with its front feet. How many classes do we see today where the horses can't or won't do this? A horse with a long sloping shoulder has more room for a better length of muscle. A horse with an upright shoulder and similar angle in the quarters is cramped in leg action, and its gaits lack elasticity. The horse moves up and down, virtually in one place.

The way a horse moves and its ability to move in balance are a direct result of the angles. If they are the same or similar, the horse will move with more rhythm. The steeper they are, a more up-and-down, less ground-covering type of motion will result. The more sloping the angles, the more level, reaching, and ground-covering the gait will be. Mismatched angles create conflicting movement and a tendency toward mixed gaitedness or inability to maintain form for any length of time.

The conformation of the humerus (upper arm) of the foreleg is critical to the presence of natural high motion. Technically speaking, motion is the product of three components: (1) rotation of the scapula (shoulder blade); (2) unfolding at the scapulo-humeral joint (where upper arm and shoulder connect); and (3) folding at the elbow and carpus (knee).

Longer scapulas are capable of a greater arc of rotation. Sloping scapulas will spend most of that arc going up. A lever system is needed to increase the range through which the carpus can be moved. The humerus is that lever. Therefore, horses with the longest, steepest humeri will have the highest natural motion. If a horse has a long, sloping shoulder but a short, horizontal humerus, it can be taught to fold tightly at the elbow and carpus but will be unable to raise the carpus above the level of the elbow.

In short, the horse with the longest humerus has the most scope. It follows that you can predict the style of movement a horse will have just by looking at its bony conformation. For example, horses with long, steep humeri have spectacular motion that is both scopey and high. Horses with short, steep humeri have high motion also, but it is short and choppy. Horses with long, horizontal humeri have a mow-the-grass type of action.

Most Arabians have a moderately to very steep humerus. Hackney horse and ponies, however, have the longest, steepest humeri of any breed. Only a few Quarter Horses possess a humerus proportionally as long as the average Thoroughbred or American Saddlebred.

So, even when the functional back is truly short, some Quarter Horses seem to stand over too much ground. It's because the short humeri place the elbow and thus the rest of the foreleg too far forward. This is why Quarter Horse classes should look different from Saddlebred classes. Most Saddlebreds have a different type of scope and can fold higher and tighter, instead of longer and flatter.

Horses that are able to extend—use their motion and good sloping angles to their advantage (be fluid)—actually lengthen their stride, not just go faster in an up-and-down restricted manner. Desired motion will change over the years as we find more athletic horses. Those horses that are closest to the style considered to be in at the moment in any given class will be called "good movers."

Desired motion for any class should be that which allows the horse to be balanced at any gait. Remember, collection plus impulsion equals balance.

Motion or athletic movement is a direct result of form to function, or ability to move more naturally. Horses go as they are designed to go.

HUNTER HACK

A hunter hack horse should move in the same style as a working hunter, so most of what was said in that section would be applicable to hunter hack. The one added element in this class is rail work, which combines jumping ability with under saddle characteristics. While only two fences must be jumped, the jumping portion constitutes 70 percent of the judging. The hacking or rail work accounts for the other 30 percent. Thus, jumping ability and style predominate and are evaluated just as if a full course of fences were taken.

Horses must have good jumping form and style, not simply struggle over the fences without knocking them down or refusing. To win a working hunter class, a horse must have an even hunting pace plus all the other ingredients.

While counting strides to determine a horse's athletic ability to jump from a set distance (with only two fences) is not the only criterion for the judge, strides do take on an additional importance. If the fences are set in a straight line, jumping away from the ingate is more difficult than jumping toward it. Broken lines are more difficult than straight lines. The easiest of courses is one fence on each side of the arena with no set distance between.

Some riders make a courtesy circle before jumping and others do not. Both are perfectly acceptable options for the rider, just as in the working hunter class.

The rail portion is performed just the same as in a hunter under saddle class. The horse should be a pleasure to ride on the flat: well moving, with good manners and good cadence. If every horse went like that, judging would be nice and easy.

In reality, judges often find horses that jump very well but crossfire, get on the wrong lead, or won't hand gallop or stop properly, which creates a dilemma even before the rail work begins. Added to this is the fact that some horses perform very well individually but move like thrashing machines on the flat.

Juggle and struggle is the judge's motto. Sorting out the what-ifs seems to be the norm at many shows. The 70/30 ratio is definitely a help, but where does the hand gallop come into play? If judges always keep in mind the basis of the class, judging becomes somewhat easier.

The hunter hack dates back to the days before trucks and trailers when people wanting to hunt needed to ride their horses to the starting point, sometimes involving miles of hacking before the fox chase actually began. Hence they wanted a well-mannered, easy-to-ride horse that had plenty left for the hunt and didn't wear the rider out before the horn blew. Then, once at the meet, they used a couple of fences as warm-ups before heading out.

Because of time constraints and class size, today we do the jumping first and then hack. By using the exact scoring system and penalties as for the working hunter, giving a numerical score to the fence and hand gallop portion becomes easier. Most judges could place the class comfortably at the end of that portion.

Where we get into difficulty is trying to analyze the rail work in conjunction with the jumps. In effect, we should score each part separately, add the two scores together, and end up with the placings using the 70/30 scale. Some judges place the class over fences and use the rail to separate horses that are close in points but require a bit more analysis to maintain the proper relationship. This works most of the time, depending on the confidence level of the judge.

The most important thing about hunter hack is that the class has filled a gap for both horse and rider, being a halfway point for both to start over fences. Many riders want to start their horses over fences. However, jumping eight three-foot fences seems to deter them, whereas two small fences seem more manageable and within the grasp of most riders. The availability of classes such as hunter hack in the English division has resulted in growth and is a positive indication that they are here to stay.

JUMPERS

Although show jumping probably evolved in European countries from exercises or sport for cavalry regiments, it was the beginning of the twentieth century before show jumping was recognized in Europe as a competitive sport.

In the absence of established historical facts, one can only speculate on the origin of American show jumping. Most likely, an evolution from point-to-point to hunter trial to jumping competition is involved, because the first American jumpers were surely foxhunters.

Though high-jumping competitions were unquestionably the glamour event in the early days, the hunting-field origin of the jumper is reflected in the fact that, for many years, it was a common practice to cross-enter between the hunter and jumper classes.

In the "old days," when I grew up, you didn't need a course designer because the jumps usually were set up where they were dropped off the truck. The course consisted of four fences, jumped twice around the outside. The jumps themselves were not the precision-made variety we see today, but crude standards with poles resting on blocks or pins. Some were single-poled, topping five feet with lots of air underneath (prohibited by present rules). There were no changes of direction and no variations, of course. In fact, making a change in direction was unheard of. But change did come about, as happens everywhere. Now we have many different levels of jumping classes with course requirements and judging standards.

If you think, as many people do, that judging a jumper class involves no more than adding up the scores, then think again. Even though it's only performance that counts, no matter how unstylish, these classes still require judges to arrive at many different, sometimes difficult decisions.

In order to make good ones, jumper judges have to have acquired a lot of knowledge. They should be accurate scorekeepers as well as accurate timekeepers, because they have to signal the riders to start their round. They have to know a lot about jumper course designing, because they have to inspect the course before the start of the class to make sure it conforms to the rules. And they should know the rules practically by heart, because they'll have to make rapid and fair judgment calls. To do their job well, they need the eye of an eagle and the judgment of Solomon. They even need to be a good psychologist when particularly difficult decisions have to be made.

The jumper's round begins when horse and rider pass through the starting line, placed at least twelve feet ahead of the first obstacle; and it ends when the horse and rider cross the finish line, at least twenty-four feet beyond the last obstacle, in the prescribed direction. Both of these lines should be clearly marked with flags on each side, set at least twelve feet apart.

Time is a factor even before crossing the starting line. When the contestant's number is called at the ingate, he or she must enter the ring within one minute. The rider is then given one minute to cross the starting line after an audible signal (by bell, gong, horn, whistle, or buzzer) has announced the start of the round. Failure to observe these one-minute time limits incurs elimination—by the management, if the entry hasn't entered the ring on time, or by the judge, if the starting time limit is exceeded.

In timed classes, the timing starts the moment the horse's chest reaches the starting line and stops when it has crossed the finish. Time is interrupted whenever a jump needs to be reset after a refusal, stopping at the instant of refusal and resuming when the signal is given for the rider to continue the course. If any knocked-down element prevents the horse from jumping the next obstacle, the time taken to remove it is deducted from the time score. Since a timed jumper competition can be won or lost by a fraction of a second, when no electronic timing device is provided, the show committee should appoint at least two timekeepers equipped with reliable digital stopwatches that measure to one hundredth of a second. In case there's a glitch with the electronic timing equipment, someone taking the time manually with a stopwatch should provide backup.

It's very important for riders to wait for the starting signal, indicating that the judges and timekeepers are ready and the course is set up. Once riders have entered the ring, they should immediately obey any audible signals judges may give for such things as:

- Starting the round.
- Stopping because of some incident (during which time is not counted against the rider).

- Retaking an obstacle that has been knocked down by a refusal.
- Continuing the round after an interruption (from which moment timing is resumed). Note: It's the rider's responsibility to be ready to resume the course when this signal is given.
- Leaving the ring upon elimination, signaled by a long, repeated ringing.

Everything in a jumper competition is carefully prescribed. The general jump requirements are that:

1. When bars are used on obstacles, they shall be at least four inches in diameter.
2. The only device permitted for holding all poles, rails, or like elements shall be cups, preferably metal. Devices working on a principle of tension or friction are prohibited.
3. Brush jumps shall have a clearly visible bar resting or placed above or beyond same.
4. Double crossed poles (two pairs of crossed poles, with a spread between them) shall not be used, and care should be exercised in constructing single crossed poles to prevent any abnormal difficulties.
5. All suspended components (gates, panels, etc.) must be hung not more than four inches from their top edge.
6. There must be a minimum of eight jumps—twelve jumps maximum—and at least three jumps in a course of eight shall be of the spread type.

Jumpers are scored on a mathematical basis. The scoring in general is as follows:

1. Penalty faults, which include disobediences, falls, and knockdowns, shall be incurred between the starting line and the finishing line.
2. When a horse makes two or more faults at an obstacle, only the major fault counts; in the case of equal faults, only one will count, except in the case of a disobedience, which counts in addition.
3. When an obstacle is composed of several elements in the same vertical plane, a fault at the top element is the only one penalized.
4. When an obstacle to be taken in one jump is composed of several elements not in the same vertical plane (oxer, triple bar, etc.), faults at several elements are penalized as one fault.
5. When an obstacle requires two or more jumps (in-and-out), the faults committed at each obstacle are considered separately. (Note: In case of a refusal or run-out at the second or third element of a combination, the entry must rejump the previous as well as the following elements, upon notification that the obstacle has been reset, if necessary.)

6.   Should a rider disregard a signal to leave the ring, the entry may be disqualified from future classes at the show.

7.   In cases of broken equipment or loss of shoe, the rider may either continue without penalty or be eliminated.

Disobediences include refusals, run-outs, loss of gait, and circles.

Refusal means stopping in front of an obstacle to be jumped, whether the horse knocks it down or displaces it or not. The term is defined within the following parameters:

I.   Stopping at an obstacle without knocking it down and without backing followed *immediately* by a standing jump is not penalized.

2.   If halt continues, or if the horse backs even a single step voluntarily or not, or retakes course, a refusal is incurred.

3.   Knocking down an obstacle in stopping or sliding constitutes a refusal, whether the horse goes through it or not. The obstacle must be retaken or the horse is eliminated.

4.   The action of showing an obstacle to a horse after a refusal and before immediately retaking course is cause for elimination. The same penalty is inflicted when a rider shows the horse any of the obstacles before jumping them.

A run-out consists of evading or passing the obstacle to be jumped or jumping an obstacle outside its limiting markers.

After a run-out or refusal the horse must, before proceeding on course, rejump the obstacle at which the disobedience occurred or be *eliminated*. If the standard, wing, or obstacle has not been reset when the horse is ready to jump, the horse must await the signal to start or be *eliminated*.

Halting or stepping backward by the horse after crossing the starting line unless due to a refusal, run-out, or on order from a judge due to unforeseen circumstances (such as a fence being blown down) is considered a **loss of gait.**

Any form of **circle** or circles, whereby the horse crosses its original track between two consecutive obstacles anywhere on the course, except to retake an obstacle after a refusal or run-out, is a disobedience. (Note: Coming sideways, zigzagging, or turning brusquely toward an object in jumping does not constitute a disobedience unless the horse passes the obstacle or turns back to the next obstacle or finish line.)

An obstacle is considered **knocked down** when a horse or rider, by contact: lowers any part thereof that establishes the height of the obstacle or the height of any element of a spread obstacle, even when the falling part is arrested in its fall by any portion of the obstacle; or moves any part that establishes the height of the obstacle as described so that it rests on a different support from the one on which it was originally placed.

Should a pole resting in a cup come to rest on the lip of the cup or on the bracket, if the bracket is an integral part of the cup, it is not considered a knockdown. Narrowing the width of a spread obstacle without altering the height of any element as just defined is not considered a knockdown. If an obstacle falls after a horse leaves the ring, it shall not be considered a knockdown.

A horse is considered off course when it deviates from the course and takes an obstacle prior to rectifying the deviation. To rectify the deviation, the horse must resume the course from the spot where the error was committed. Any disobedience that may be committed while rectifying the deviation must be scored.

The following scoring guidelines will go a long way toward distinguishing winners from losers:

1. Knockdown of obstacle, standard or wing with any portion of horse, rider, or equipment — 4 faults
2. Knockdown of automatic starter equipment or other designated markers on starting or finishing line with any part of horse, rider, or equipment during the round — 4 faults
3. First disobedience (anywhere on course) — 3 faults
4. Second cumulative disobedience (anywhere on course) — 6 faults
5. Third cumulative disobedience (anywhere on course) — Elimination
6. Fall of horse and/or rider — Elimination
7. Jumping obstacle before it is reset or without waiting for signal to proceed — Elimination
8. Starting before judge's audible signal to proceed; jumping obstacle before starting or after crossing the finish line, whether forming part of course or not; jumping obstacle out of order; off course — Elimination
9. Failure to enter ring within one minute of being called — Elimination
10. Failure to cross the starting line within one minute after judge's audible signal to proceed — Elimination
11. Jumping any obstacle before crossing starting line unless said obstacle is designated as a practice jump — Elimination
12. Failure to jump in designated order — Elimination

If more than one horse has a clean round (that is, does not incur any faults, by knockdown or otherwise), there will be a jump-off. The jump-off course usually contains fewer jumps than the original. While the jumps must be taken in the proper order and direction, the course designer may leave several options or "shortcuts" open for the rider to take in an effort to deliver the best time. This is what makes the jump-off the most exciting event in jumper competition. Furthermore, it may give an edge to athletic Quarter Horses whose ability to turn on a dime often can shave a precious second off the time, making the difference between first place and runner-up.

PLEASURE DRIVING

The name pleasure driving actually describes this event in two ways, because driving a harnessed horse from a vehicle nowadays is almost always for pleasure rather than a means of transportation, as it once was. For this reason, the horses competing in the class really should appear to be a pleasure to drive.

Horses in this class are shown in light harness, hitched to a suitable two-wheeled cart, and in three different gaits. Entering the arena at a park gait, they also perform a road gait and a walk. After demonstrating these gaits around the ring in both directions, they are asked to line up in the center, where they demonstrate their ability to back and to stand quietly, which are both very important abilities for a driving horse.

As always, proper head position is critical in controlling the horse's balance. The proper head position in harness is achieved by the bridle and overcheck instead of only by the aids, as in riding classes. It's vital to hitch the head correctly, neither too high nor too low, in order to permit the horse to move in balance. Taking time to experiment to find the best way to hitch each individual horse is time well spent. A horse that's improperly hitched can be beaten before it starts in this class.

A pleasure driving horse should possess good manners and a calm temperament. Judges are also favorably impressed by a horse that seems to be enjoying its work. Obviously, disobedient, unwilling, or nervous individuals haven't got a chance in this class. The top horses are sensible, reliable, capable, and consistent. The horse's conformation also can influence the final decision, because judges look for harmony and symmetry of action that adds up to an attractive overall picture.

With pleasure the criterion, the demands of this class should not be too strenuous or require extreme speed or exaggerated action. The driver should give the impression of effortless ease, and the horse should carry itself in a proud, alert, collected manner.

The park gait should be smart and stylish, but still easy, with no straining on the bit or pulling on the driver's arms. The horse should be able to make a smooth transition into the road gait, which is a more extended trot. The point of this transition is not to see how fast the horse can trot, but rather to show how willingly and precisely it responds to the driver's signal to move into a more animated gait.

In the same way, the horse should respond immediately to the demand to slow down to an animated, ground-covering, flat-footed walk. If the horse has been properly bitted and the head-check properly adjusted, it should be able to perform the walk smoothly, without twisting, turning, or bobbing its head, all of which are faults.

When the horses have lined up in the center of the ring, judges should give all competitors, even those who haven't got a chance of winning, the same careful attention. When asked to back, drivers should first make sure their horse is lined up straight, and not so close to the horses on either side that a judge has trouble walking through between them. Horses hitched to a cart aren't expected to run backward, only to take three or four normal walking steps in that direction.

The rules concerning driving equipment should be obeyed to the letter. The prescribed driving harness consists of a bridle with blinkers, overcheck (with a separate overcheck bit) and/or sidecheck, a martingale, cavesson, and a straight or jointed snaffle bit. Since some of these items are safety features, none should be omitted. For example:

- Blinkers keep the horse's eyes looking ahead and prevent distractions from behind or on either side.
- The overcheck prevents the horse from dropping its head, perhaps in preparation for kicking back at the driver or cart and causing physical injury or costly damage.
- The martingale keeps the horse straight and prevents it from tossing its head up preparatory to running off.
- A properly adjusted cavesson keeps the horse's mouth closed and permits the snaffle to function. Too low, it pinches the horse's mouth. In case of a runaway, the cavesson may also help prevent the bit from being pulled through the horse's mouth.

Each element of the harness should be carefully fitted. The blinkers shouldn't press against the horse's eyes, which would cause it to turn its head to the side to avoid the irritation. The cavesson should be placed under the overcheck. Correctly used, the overcheck bit helps keep the head straight and permits the snaffle to function as it should. The saddle portion of the harness should be well fitted too, so as not to interfere with the horse's shoulder movements and limit the length of stride. The breast collar should fit just above the point of the shoulder. Finally, a horse that has been properly hitched should have enough leg room to make free strides without hitting either the shafts or the front of the cart.

Performance is important in this class, but so is quality. Judges should be looking for ease, style, alertness, willingness, and confidence.

Drivers can show their horse to best advantage by using foresight in trying to stay on the rail instead of continually crossing the ring or passing other slower contestants. Not only does crossing or passing interfere with the other drivers' rounds, it also prevents a horse from performing smoothly. Too fast a pace is just as harmful as one that is too slow, forcing the other horses to pass.

While circling around the ring, drivers should always bear in mind that a change of direction may be ordered at any moment. They'll usually make it by crossing to the opposite wall of the ring. But before doing so, the drivers must make sure that the way across they have chosen is clear and that they will end up on the other side in a good position on the rail.

Because each horse's natural speed depends on its size and length of stride, a small horse that tries to keep up with a big one that has a longer stride will simply lose form. In this class, drivers should constantly try to create a pretty picture of a horse moving easily with its hocks well underneath it to maintain speed and elevation. Driving horses should maintain a certain degree of collection in all three gaits. It's a mistake to think that greater speed will improve your chances if it's at the expense of collection. Speed and animation are desirable, but consistent good form is even more important.

One of the most frequent errors I see in driving classes is overchecking, which makes the horse stick its nose out and lose cadence behind. Quarter Horses aren't built like Saddlebreds, with the neck rising straight out of the withers. Their necks are placed somewhat lower. Overchecking can cause them great discomfort, and to avoid it they will hollow their backs, toss or swing their heads, and come apart in the hindquarters. If you notice that a driving horse is hitching behind, its head probably is checked too high. If the head is hitched too low, you'll see it leaning on the harness and pulling with the front instead of the hindquarters. This is contrary to the whole purpose of the overcheck, which is to teach the horse to raise its front and drive from the hindquarters, with the hocks well underneath its body.

Horses at liberty carry 65 percent of their body weight on the forehand. This is why we teach them collection, to lighten the forehand and create forward impulsion from behind in order to produce a light, elastic action with good front extension and elevation. The overcheck is a useful aid in achieving this result.

A lot of things can go wrong during a driving class, most often due to the inexperience of horse or driver or both. Judges should carefully watch the way each horse enters the arena, and the ringmaster should cooperate in observing how the horses move into the extended gaits. If a horse risks disrupting the class by constantly breaking into a canter, by acting unruly, or if it seems to be out of control, judges should excuse it from the ring and bring the class back to a more orderly gait. An even greater risk to the smooth progress of the class is the horse that refuses to move forward; refusal can be the warning signal that it's going to rear and perhaps flip over into the cart.

Safety should be one of the judges' prime considerations when there is a large group of driving horses in the ring. The danger escalates if the ring is

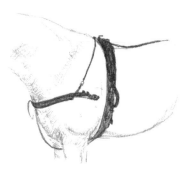

Harness saddle set too far back.   *The proper position.*

Breast collar shown too low.   *Too high.*

Correct.

FITTING THE HARNESS

Too high.   *Too low.*   *Just the right angle.*

THE SHAFTS SHOULD BE AT ABOUT THE SAME HEIGHT
AS THE BREAST COLLAR

*The point of the shafts should not be too far forward but should come
to just about the point of the shoulder.*

*The wrap straps should hang straight
and in line with the harness saddle
and belly band, as shown.*

*The wrap strap is shown
too far back.*

*A crupper strap adjusted too tight
against the horse's tail and dock
will cause pain and discomfort.*

*The correct adjustment should allow
one finger width of space between
the tail and strap.*

FITTING THE HARNESS

too small, or if the shape and footing are unsuitable. Small arenas can accommodate only small classes. When there are too many entries for the size of the ring, judges should divide the class into sections, with a final round between the leaders, instead of inviting disaster by crowding too many horses and carts into too small a space.

Another danger signal that should alert judges is the horse that sets its jaw while the rider tugs on the reins to no avail. The best move is to return the entire class to a walk. When the runaway horse has given up, judges should have the ringmaster lead it until it has calmed down enough to resume the forward movement.

Reversing direction in the ring, as required in this class, is another tricky moment. When there are only a few entries in the class, judges can simply ask the drivers to reverse (always at a walk). But if many horses and carts are in the ring, it's advisable for judges to ask the ringmaster to have them reverse their direction one at a time, on the diagonal of the arena.

As soon as the horses have all lined up, headers (grooms or assistants) should be allowed into the arena to help hold them steady and under control. Taking every possible safety precaution is one of the duties of everyone concerned in a driving class, judges and contestants alike.

CHAPTER V

Equitation / Horsemanship

HUNT SEAT EQUITATION

ALTHOUGH a suitable, well-trained horse is the basic ingredient of every horse show competition, the hunt seat equitation class is a test of the rider rather than the horse. He or she is judged on the basic position while working on the flat and performing various individual tests, and then during a jumping phase. Judges are looking for riders who are flexible and versatile and able to hack a horse, hunt cross-country, and show a hunter or jumper.

Such a rider should give an appearance of competence and control, being supple and light and in a position to cope with any situation that might arise. This riding position can best be described by dividing the rider's body into three parts: the leg, the base, and the upper body.

The rider's **leg** is considered the part from the knee down (not from the hip down). The stirrups that support the leg should be adjusted at a moderate length, neither too long nor too short, for the security of the rider and the freedom of the horse. The rider should place the ball of the foot firmly in the stirrup, instead of pushing the foot "all the way home," which makes it difficult to keep the heel down and to flex the ankle, both of which contribute to the rider's security. The heel should be just behind the girth. If it is properly flexed, it acts as a shock absorber for the horse's hoofbeats at its gaits and when landing over a jump.

The calf and inner knee bone should maintain contact with the horse's sides. This is one of the most important means of communication the rider has with the horse. Pinching with the knees simply forces the lower calf away from the horse's sides and results in a loss of communication. At the other extreme, riders who grip with the lower leg or calf and no knee at all are using as a support what really should be a driving aid. For smooth communication, the contact should be evenly distributed between the calf and the inner knee bone.

The rider's thighs and seat are the principal **base** of support. The thighs should be placed flat, and the seat bones should be in contact with the horse's back through the saddle. From this basic position, the rider can shift easily between two different kinds of seat: two-point contact and three-point contact. In the three-point contact, the rider's seat and both legs are in close contact with the horse. Two-point contact is used when galloping

Stirrup hangs parallel with girth.

GOOD LEG POSITION

Leg too far back, tipping rider forward, out of balance.

Leg too far forward, rider out of balance, behind motion.

IMPROPER LEG POSITIONS

CORRECT

*Ball of foot placed
correctly in stirrup.*

INCORRECT

*Heel up, all weight
placed on toe.*

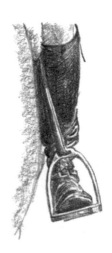

CORRECT

*Heel that is flexed
in and down acts as
a shock absorber.*

*Contact with the
calf and inner
knee bone.*

INCORRECT

*Pinching with just
the knee forces the
lower calf away from
the horse; incorrect use
of the leg aid.*

POSITION OF FOOT IN STIRRUPS

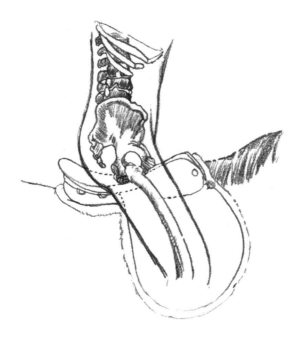

CORRECT POSITION IN THE SADDLE

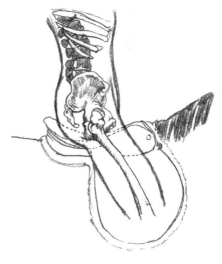

PELVIS TILTED TOO FAR FORWARD

Allowing leg to swing back to counterbalance.

PELVIS TILTED BACK

Placing weight on tailbone, makes leg swing forward (out of balance).

THE BASE

*A correct hand position: halfway between
the horizontal and the vertical.*

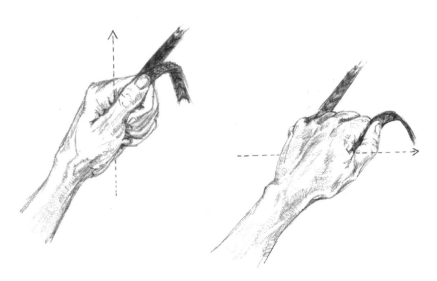

A straight up-and-down hand.   *A flat hand.*

POSITION OF HANDS

or jumping, when the rider maintains contact with the legs but places no weight at all in the saddle. Nevertheless, the rider should be able to remain in control in both positions.

The **upper body** consists of the rider's chest, arms, and hands. The arms should form a straight line from the elbow to the horse's mouth. They should be held above and in front of the withers, a few inches apart, with the thumbs held halfway between the horizontal (a flat hand) and the vertical (a straight up-and-down-hand). This is the softest, most flexible form of contact with the horse's mouth, which is a vital communication point. The elbows should rest at the rider's sides, and his or her chest should be held high, a posture that also strengthens the back and increases the rider's control.

Some people believe that riding is done only with the hands and legs, not realizing that the back (and particularly the small of the back) plays a great role. It should follow the horse's every movement, relaxed and supple. When you have the chance to watch a really good rider, notice how the small of her back moves in harmony with the horse's movements. It's not something that can be forced, but it is the natural consequence of a good position and one of the marks of a good rider.

The same good rider would hold her head erect and straight, her shoulders back, her chest high, her entire bearing unforced, elegant, and graceful. You'd never see her slouching, hunching her back, or caving in her chest.

The rider's eye should be focused straight ahead, anticipating the next moves. The rider should be able to *feel* what the horse is doing at every moment and

PINCHED IN	OUT	NATURAL
Pressed downward from shoulder, stiffens entire back, neck, and shoulders.	*Causes balance to come from arms, stiffens shoulder, neck, and hands brace on horse's mouth.*	*Relaxed, comfortable, resting easily at rider's side.*

POSITION OF ELBOWS

see what has to be done next; he or she should never look down to see what the horse is doing now. In fact, judges would penalize a rider who is always looking down to confirm a lead or a diagonal instead of feeling it, and rightly so.

The position of the upper body should be adapted to the horse's gait: absolutely upright at the halt; slightly in front of the vertical at the walk; a bit more forward at a slow sitting trot; and inclined even farther forward at a posting trot, in order to follow the horse's movement smoothly. At the canter, the upper body should return to the same position as the slow sitting trot. The position at a hand gallop is the same as at the posting trot, although the rider maintains a steady two-point contact instead of posting. In these positions, the rider adjusts the forward inclination of his or her body to the speed of the gaits and remains in balance, following the horse's movement instead of being ahead or behind it.

You might visualize the rider shifting his or her weight forward, by leaning forward, to keep it always over the horse's center of gravity, which moves farther forward as the horse increases its pace. For a horse and rider to remain in balance, both of their centers of gravity should always coincide.

The flat class routine of hunt seat equitation closely follows that of Western

Correct position at the halt.

HUNT SEAT RIDER

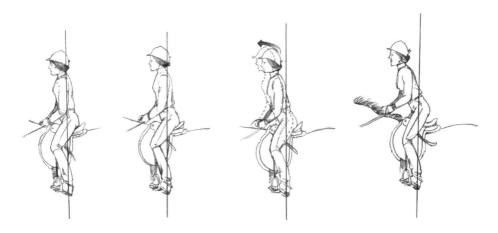

Upper body positions as they vary with the different gaits.

horsemanship. It consists of two phases: an individual test and work on the rail. An individual test is any combination of maneuvers that the judge deems necessary to determine the equitation ability of the rider. Any of the following maneuvers may be required:

- Back.
- Gallop and pull up.
- Figure-eight at a trot, demonstrating change of diagonals. At left diagonal, the rider should be sitting the saddle when the left front leg is on the ground; at right diagonal, the rider should be sitting the saddle when the right front leg is on the ground. When circling clockwise at a trot, the rider should be on the left diagonal; when circling counterclockwise, the rider should be on the right diagonal.
- Figure-eight at a canter on correct lead demonstrating simple change of lead. (This is a change whereby the horse is brought back into a walk or trot and restarted into a canter on the opposite lead.) Figure-eights are to be commenced in center of two circles so that one change of lead is shown.
- Ride without stirrups.
- Dismount and mount.
- Figure-eight at a canter on correct lead, demonstrating flying change of lead.
- Change leads down center of ring, demonstrating simple change of lead.
- Execute serpentine at trot and/or canter on correct lead, demonstrating simple or flying changes of lead. A series of left and right half circles off center of an imaginary line where the correct diagonal or lead change must be shown.

- Canter on the counter lead.
- Half turn on forehand and/or half turn on haunches.

In short, the hunt seat equitation class is designed to demonstrate the rider's ability to ride a horse over a typical hunter course with smoothness, accuracy, and control; to cope with any problems that may arise; and to do it with style and good form. Above all, the rider should show understanding and consideration for his or her horse.

OVER FENCES

Riding on the flat in the correct basic positions is the foundation of equitation, but not all of it. Riding over fences deals with more complicated methods and techniques.

During the approach to a jump, the rider should have the same sensation of being with the horse's movement that he or she gets when posting at the trot, neither behind nor ahead of it. In both cases, the horse's center of gravity has shifted forward, so the rider has to incline the upper body forward too, rising out of the saddle, in order to keep his or her own center of gravity over that of the horse. The rider's heels should be flexed downward to absorb the shock of landing after the jump, just as they are flexed during the trot to absorb the shock of the horse's hoofbeats. In jumping, the rider's weight is carried by the heels, thighs, and inner seat bones rather than by the buttocks.

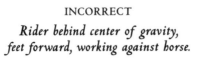

INCORRECT
Rider behind center of gravity,
feet forward, working against horse.

CORRECT
Rider in balance—
correct center of gravity.

The first thing judges notice is whether the rider is in balance, leaning forward, and accompanying the horse's motion throughout the jump.

The beginner's mistake I see most often and soonest is in the release, which simply means giving the horse the freedom of its head to stretch forward and make an arc over the jump. The first release the novice rider learns may be to grab the horse's mane halfway up the crest. This gives added support. But if the release is made below the crest, it can result in loss of balance, a collapse on landing, and even a fall.

The next important point is the rider's eyes, which always should be looking ahead to anticipate the next turn. In other words, when a corner has to be turned coming into a jump, the rider's eyes should have turned the corner before the horse has reached it and already be looking ahead to the next turn or jump. When approaching a fence, the rider's eyes should be focused on a point about thirty or forty feet beyond it, and not on the obstacle itself. "Eye work," as it's called—getting, holding, and stopping on a line—is an absolutely essential technique for the rider to learn.

Heel control is just as important. When the rider's ankles and heels are flexed properly, they act as shock absorbers, as I've already mentioned. Instead of being jarred and jolted halfway out of the saddle on landing, the rider will feel no violent upheaval because the impact has been absorbed by his or her ankles and heels. The heels are also a security factor in acting as a brace or vice when gripped against a horse that's pulling. The rider has a much

THREE-POINT CONTACT
*Inclined slightly
forward.*

TWO-POINT CONTACT
*Upper body inclined
more forward.*

better chance of controlling a puller by driving his or her heels down than by letting them slip up and fly back against the horse's ribs.

These are all basic jumping techniques: moving with the horse's motion, the release, eyes controlling the line, and heels.

Another important technique is seat contact. As we've seen, this can be either two-point or three-point. For hunter and equitation jumping, most often the rider has to be in a two-point contact, out of the saddle, in order to accompany the horse's movements over the fences without getting left behind. When secure in this position, the rider can give the horse the freedom to arc its body over the fence. First, the horse should close its stride and gather itself, then close its upper body angulations. Riders always should let the horse do the jumping and not imagine that they can do it for their horse by throwing their own body forward over the fence.

With three-point contact, the rider sits deep in the saddle with a vertical upper body. This is the best position for riding green and hesitant horses, balkers, and open jumpers. When trotting up to a fence, the rider shouldn't give the signal to jump by anticipating it in his or her body movement, but

Rider's head is up, inclined forward (two-point contact),
and in balance with the motion of the horse.

GOOD POSITION

rather should use the legs, a cluck, or a release at the chosen takeoff point. Normally the horse will respond at once by jumping the fence. Throwing the upper body forward in an exaggerated way to get the horse to leave the ground is a fault of equitation.

Judges usually have the opportunity to inspect the course before the class begins. If not, they should consult the course designer, because checking the fences and the distances between them is one of every judge's responsibilities. It's best to keep the distances in in-and-outs at twenty-four feet, which is a normal one-stride distance. Anything less would be too tight; anything over forty-eight feet (a normal three-stride distance) would be too long. More pace is needed to handle long distances; less pace for short ones. Judging the pace correctly in relation to the distance is especially important with combinations. The only way to jump them smoothly is to determine the pace that creates the right length of stride for negotiating them accurately.

Combinations are a series of fences separated by distances of one, two, or three strides—in other words, twenty-four-, thirty-six-, or forty-eight-feet distances. Anything longer would not be considered a combination. In hunt seat equitation classes, if a horse refuses at one element of a combination, it is required to try again at that element only (although it can rejump the entire combination if the rider so chooses). In judging combinations, it's important to know the distances.

Turns are another critical point for judges to observe and score. They look at how the rider uses the upper body, either in the deep-seated three-point contact or in the lighter forward two-point. They should know that the rider's upper body has to open up slightly and then straighten a bit when taking a turn, because of the balance and collection needed. If the rider's body has been just in front of the vertical on the straight line, it should be on the vertical during the turn. And if it was inclined forward on the straight line, it should be just in front of the vertical for the turn.

When entering the arena and before starting the equitation course, the rider always should execute a circle. This makes a good first impression. The rider can do it any way he or she likes, but it should display accuracy, discipline, and control. This is the means for establishing the pace well before arriving at the first fence.

Riders who are ready to compete in these classes shouldn't have to think about things like heels, hands, upper body position, and other technical details while riding a course. They should concentrate on pace and lines of direction, measuring and focusing their eyes on the lines and turns, controlling the pace along each line and during each turn.

In order to avoid the risk of run-outs or refusals, riders should use a combination of rein and leg aids when angling fences or jumping narrow or spooky obstacles. For example, if the horse is thinking about running out to the left, a right rein aid and left leg (shoulder to hip) should be used to correct the deviation. Equitation judges always take into account the way a rider handles such adversities.

Judges always should bear in mind the difference between a hunter and a jumper. As I've said, a light forward two-point position shows off the hunter to best advantage and gives a flexible, fluid, unified picture. For jumpers as well as green horses, the three-point position, deeper, more controlled, and balanced more toward the rear, is more appropriate. Very green horses, almost too green to be shown, can be ridden in a very deep seat. But in equitation classes over fences, where smoothness is a plus point, the two-point contact is best.

Hunt seat equitation tests are designed to show that the rider is able to perform over a hunter course with smoothness, accuracy, and control, producing a fluid, balanced ride. Pace is also a factor. It should be considerably slower for green horses than for seasoned hunters.

The rider is expected to display style and form as well as consideration for the horse. He or she must never act in a rough or inconsistent manner. If necessary, the rider should demonstrate an ability to handle any emergency that might arise. In short, he or she should be a workmanlike yet elegant example of a fine horseman or -woman. Judges take all of these things into account when selecting the top winners.

What are the mistakes they look for? Show ring beginners seem to think judges are scoring faults only. And it's true that beginners often make obvious mistakes that are almost sure to keep them out of the ribbons. The hunt seat equitation course over fences, with eight obstacles, and lines and turns between them, offers plenty of chance for error. However, nearly all the judges I know, myself included, follow the same general policy: Pick the best rider with the best qualities, not the one who's made the fewest mistakes.

Of course, we've all got our favorite concerns and give more or less weight to different errors. One of my pet peeves is what I note on my scoresheet as "HON," standing for "hands on neck," which I penalize severely. I expect a rider who hopes to win a class under me to be capable of riding the horse off the ground and give it the support it needs when it needs it; not gallop down to a fence in cadence and then, three strides away, throw the reins, grab a handful of mane, and hope for the best. I like to see the equitation rider "feeling" the horse all the time, letting it jump out of his or her hand, giving with it as it arcs over the jump, remaining in balance at both the takeoff and landing. I like to see a smooth, subtle release in cadence, not some desperate last-minute move. Experienced equitation riders maintain a fluid motion with their hands, never jerking, grabbing, or rating back and then spurring forward; in short, there is constant communication with the horse, which judges are bound to observe and appreciate.

A common beginner's error is looking down or to one side when the horse leaves the ground. Doing so looks as if the rider is about to dismount in midair and destroys the impression of good balance, even if the horse jumps perfectly. The only place the rider needs to look after leaving the ground is straight ahead between the horse's ears, preparing for the next fence. Besides, putting the head to one side or the other places more weight on that side and is detrimental to balance. Experienced riders always look to the next fence, lining it up in advance, and plan how to get there. By doing their looking in advance, they don't need to look anywhere but where they're going.

Another fault I often notice in novices is lack of flexibility. The rider makes such an effort to keep his or her head straight that it gives an undesirable impression of stiffness and rigidity. You don't have to be artificially posed or robotlike to see where you're going without leaning on the horse's neck. Winning riders have the flexibility to adjust as necessary in order to jump in a smooth, attractive manner. Judges can easily spot the riders who are flexible and able to cope with any situation, in contrast with those who brace themselves against the horse either leaning forward with stiff legs or a rigid back, or with unyielding arms and hands, when clearing a jump.

A lesser fault, but by no means minor, although it's less visible to the layman, is the rider's failure to remain in motion with the horse, instead being either way in front or way behind it. Many riders, after performing pretty well over most of the course, will roll out at a fence—in other words, chase the horse off the ground instead of waiting for it. This usually upsets the balance and causes the horse to "chip in" (get in too close before it jumps). At the other extreme, a rider can get too far behind the motion and find him- or herself in the rumble seat when the horse leaves the ground, especially if it has stood off and jumped before the rider was ready.

Of course, all of these common mistakes should still be related to the overall performance. I find bad leg position and function to be especially common faults. For example, far too many riders in equitation classes simply let their legs hang loose, with no contact at all. Another example of faulty equitation is when the rider tries to keep a secure leg but, feeling that the horse is backing off on the approach to a fence, tries to influence it by making continual pumping, twisting, or wiggling movements of the torso to drive it forward—at the same time, of course, destroying the seat contact. These are obviously riding faults that judges must penalize.

Many errors are committed after the landing. Some riders anticipate the landing by sitting up too early and then leaning backward, only to find themselves so far out of balance that they drop forward again when the horse has landed. Other riders brace themselves against the landing with their feet "in the dashboard," giving an unattractive picture of rigid stiffness. Good form, meaning balance and harmony between the horse and rider, should be maintained throughout the entire jumping process: approach, takeoff, arc, landing, and moving on.

It's surprising how many mistakes are made the moment a rider enters the arena. If a rider is unsure of the course, the direction to circle, even whether

*Rider's head is down, body hunched
with hands on the neck.*

*Rider is ducking badly to
the left and looking down.*

*Rider's hands are tucked into
waist because reins are too long,
causing elbows to bow out.*

*Rider has fairly good position but
has opened fingers, which may cause loss
of rein, a minor, quite common fault.*

COMMON EQUITATION FAULTS

*Rider is balancing
on the horse's mouth,
stiff and rigid.*

*Rider is ahead of the horse,
lower leg is loose and too
far back, gripping only
with the knee;
all control has been lost.*

*Rider has been left
totally behind the motion,
feet pushed into the
dashboard, hanging onto
reins for support.*

COMMON EQUITATION FAULTS

to circle at all, judges will note the indecision and mark it down as lack of preparation. What the rider should do first is know the course, enter the ring with confidence and good form, circle in the correct direction, on the proper lead, and without cross-cantering.

The horse should be on the proper lead not only during the circle but also around the corners of the course and whenever a change of direction is called for. If a rider gallops around a turn on the wrong lead and then tries to adjust at the last moment to make a proper takeoff in front of a fence, judges won't give him or her a good mark at that fence. And if a rider cross-canters around the turn and meets a fence too unbalanced to make a good, graceful jump, you can be sure that judges won't give him or her a good score at that one either.

Wrong leads aren't the only mistakes that can be made between the fences of an equitation course. As I mentioned, in this division it's not the horse that is judged but the rider. So judges try to determine which rider is best of all, which one second best, and so forth. Judges study the riders from the moment they enter the ring until the moment they have left it. The horse is merely the vehicle by which a rider demonstrates his or her ability to negotiate a course of fences in form and balance. Even though it's not the horse that is being judged, it helps a lot to have a fairly good one or at least a compatible animal. If riders have to fight their horses to get them around a turn, they won't have much of a chance to demonstrate their best riding skill.

As I've said, judges should look for qualities as well as errors, and then weigh the different qualities and errors of the different competitors according to their importance. Some slight mistake made by rider or horse often can be offset in a judge's reckoning if the mistake was corrected immediately in a calm and effective manner.

What does it take to win a hunt seat equitation class? I'd say that the top-winning equitation riders are the ones who have a well-balanced attitude: aggressive but not overeager, confident but not conceited, self-disciplined and knowledgeable. Of course, a major mistake would exclude even such a good rider from the winner's circle, unless all of the other competitors had committed errors that were just as bad or worse. The final decision is up to the judge, who takes everything—including his or her own personal taste— into consideration.

STYLE OR UNSTYLE

What needs to live on is a tradition and a respect for the art of the system that has made our Olympic riders the most functional, natural, and competitive riders in the world. The foundation for all of these riders has come from the American jumping system—in other words, hunt seat equitation.

Hunt seat equitation is based on a few cornerstones. The first has to do with a **correct position**—how a rider should sit, ride, and communicate with a horse.

The second has to do with riders having their **basic training** over fences originating on **hunter-type tracts** and preferably riding these courses on an American Quarter Horse. Riding a sensitive animal forward, evenly, quietly, and imperceptibly, is what it is all about.

When the basics have been learned, the rider is then ready to negotiate **equitation-type tracts** and then finally to ride and analyze **jumper-type courses,** which will include higher fences, a faster pace, and more difficult lines and distances.

Style changes to accommodate the horse you are riding, the present fad, the winningest rider, or the loudest, most popular guru of the day. That is why I consider myself an advocate of the **unstyle.** As examples, the crest release is now out and the flat saddle is no longer the only correct type to have. Dressage is no longer just another French word, and stirrups have changed lengths as often as women's hemlines.

There is no one style, no one way that is better than all others, unless you confuse basic position with riding style. Everyone must have the same fundamental or basic position, depending on the type of saddle. But style is something that must be developed for yourself. It's your personality that shows. There are as many styles as there are riders; each style is individual.

When a rider walks into the ring, that rider tells me right away whether she is actually riding or whether she is simply sitting on a wonderful horse following a program she has practiced by rote. When the rider makes his first circle, I can tell whether my score belongs in the 60s, 70s, 80s, or even 90s. The rest of the course usually verifies my first impression.

A rider's performance is subsequently scored by the worst thing he or she does on course. When scoring numerically, if a rider misses a distance, the score could be anywhere from a 72 to 78, depending on which range the rider was in on the first impression. I picked this fault because it is the most common. A really bad miss is in the high 60s.

To get an 80 on my card, you need to "find" the eight (or so) distances, get the proper number of strides for your horse, have all clean lead changes in the corners, and maintain the proper pace.

In my opinion, the three most common faults that reveal poor rider education and demonstrate a slipping of standards today are riders who:

1. Do not ride to the proper takeoff distance.
2. Abandon their horse's mouth by either setting their hands on the neck and/or by not releasing in a straight line to the horse's mouth in the advanced equitation classes.
3. Let their legs swing forward or backward, loosely in the air.

It is vitally important that all judges seriously think about their priority system and not rely on the trend at the time. The look is important, but if equitation is a means to the end of developing good jumper riders, we have to concentrate and base our teaching and judging on sound principles.

By the choices they make, judges are directly responsible for the type of riders that are produced. To understand the elements that make up a good equitation round, such as the appropriate step, track, take off distance, and body position between fences and in the air, judges have to be aware of the philosophical priorities of the class they are judging.

Riders should start out riding hunters and learn their basics in courses that encourage a forward, even ride done in mostly a half seat (two-point contact). This course is traditionally over a figure-eight course using natural-type rails and obstacles. In hunter-type equitation, the emphasis is on a forward, even ride and a half-seat position wherever designated by the specific course or horse that is being ridden.

As riders become more sophisticated, they are ready for the equitation-type course. These courses present jumper-type problems over smaller fences without any more time being taken to negotiate the course. This prepares a rider to deal effectively with jumper-type fences, distances, combinations, turns, and pace variance. At this level, we have more stringent criteria to separate riders with. A robotlike rider will not make it at this degree of competition.

As judges we need to remember that different riders and horses are never going to look the same because of variations in the way they are built. We should concentrate on finding the best rider, one who could go on to higher competition, not someone who looks stamped out by a cookie cutter.

TESTS

The equitation division is unlike any other because it is the rider who is judged rather than the horse. Many horsemen or -women active in training, teaching, and showing think of riding as much more than a sport. For them it is also a science and an art. It follows that such a special kind of competition requires judges with special qualifications as well as carefully planned tests.

I have to agree with the many people who think the current types of tests don't always bring to the fore the best riders. All too often, equitation division classes seem to reward good coaching instead of good riding. Obedience to the advice of trainers given at home, in the warm-up area, and even from the ringside seems to be more important than thinking for oneself and developing good communications with the horse, which is what the art of riding is all about. A good rider also should be a good horseman or woman who understands how horses work mechanically and mentally. Equitation classes should require riders to demonstrate this understanding under the pressure of competition, not simply to put on a robotlike rehearsed or teleguided public performance.

The equitation judge should give a test that includes the basics of riding and offers riders a chance to show that they know how to make the most of their horse. To do so, riders must understand certain fundamental principles, such as that going from the walk to the trot, and from the trot to the lope or the walk to the canter are transitions that require increased impulsion; conversely, that going from a canter or lope to a walk or from the lope into a trot are recessive or softening movements requiring reduced impulsion. A good equitation test should demonstrate riders' abilities to make these transitions by using aids (leg for impulsion, hand for softening) in a way that's almost invisible to the spectators, but evident to a good judge.

Another basic thing riders should know and be able to demonstrate is that collection plus impulsion equals balance and that the proportion of collection to impulsion varies according to the different gaits.

Most important of all is a good seat and good hands. A good seat involves more than sitting in the saddle close to the horse, which is the most elementary stage of riding. At a more advanced degree, it involves the engagement of the seat bones (not the leg) first to produce impulsion, with the leg then acting as an aid to urge the horse into forward movement.

A simple test will show judges that a rider understands this process: loping or cantering forward from a standstill, which obliges the rider to engage the seat and leg. To take up the left lead, the rider should feel it through the seat that the horse is stretching or tightening its right back muscle; if the rider doesn't, he or she knows that the horse is not in position to pick up a left lead. The lope (or canter) requires impulsion. Exactly how much depends on the individual horse, its conformation and responsiveness.

When stopping after a lope or canter, it's the hand that acts to retard the horse's movement, while the seat continues to maintain a certain impulsion. The two aids work together, although the hand action is the dominant one in this instance. It should always be sympathetic, asking for the transition while maintaining balance.

Equitation tests should give riders an opportunity to show they are able to "feel" their horse, in other words, to sense its needs even before the horse does, instead of making necessary adjustments only after they have become urgent and evident. Riders should be able to anticipate what the horse is going to do by feeling it through the seat bones and hands, as the horse's muscles expand and contract.

The horse's mouth is another telltale point of communication that reveals what the rest of its body is doing. For example, when the horse backs up, if the hindquarters start to drift to one side or another, the rider should be able to feel the direction of drift through the hands and seat. He or she then can engage the proper aid to straighten the horse and allow it to move back straight and easy. The rider also can demonstrate control and riding ability during simple turns, when the horse must be maneuvered through the simultaneous use of hand, seat, and leg.

Whatever test judges require, they should have good reasons for choosing it. Every part should provide a means of demonstrating some phase of riding technique and ability, and the contestants should know what it is.

Useless tests are those that only show that a rider knows how to count strides and follow the trainer's instructions to "canter six strides, stop, back four, stop, walk five, stop" and so on.

A good test needn't take more than thirty or forty seconds. In stock seat equitation, for example, you don't have to give a test that amounts to an entire reining or stock horse pattern. And a hunt seat rider shouldn't have to make a series of maneuvers that are totally unrelated to the work of jumping over fences. Most of all, the judges should have respect for equitation or horsemanship as a true art, and recognize talent when they see it. Otherwise the tests don't mean a thing.

All of the tests I give have a definite purpose behind them. I believe that simple tests are more revealing of the rider's ability than the memory-linked, rehearsable kind. I work them out well in advance, taking into account the layout of the arena, the level of competition, and the type of class, such as amateur or youth. Since I have been carded to judge most all-breed and open (AHSA) shows, I vary my basic tests according to the event. But the standard pattern is as follows.

In the lineup, I ask each rider to back until I tell him or her to stop; lope or canter forward to the rail on a specified lead (left or right, depending on how hard I want to make it); stop and stand facing the rail. What could be simpler? Well, you'd be surprised how this helps me to separate the contestants. While the backup is a simple maneuver that any rider of any age or experience should be able to accomplish, it permits me to spot immediately the light hands and "feel" of the horse's mouth that I'm looking for. By asking riders to back until I tell them to stop, I can see if they really understand the horse's mouth. Any decently trained horse will back up the first three or four steps. But for more than that, a feel of the horse's mouth is necessary, and some adjustment probably will have to be made because the mouth has been pulled on and dulled. At this point many horses either hang up (stop) or begin to back crookedly, requiring an adjustment of the leg aid as well as the rein. Good riders can make this adjustment imperceptibly; and good judges who are also good horsemen will see and give them credit for it.

I next ask the riders to lope or canter forward on the left lead. I tell riders to stop backing up when the horse is in position to canter forward on the left lead, or I can stop riders out of position, which would require an adjustment in order to take a left lead, and make everything more difficult. The same is true when I ask for a right lead when the horse is not in position for it. In this test, I want riders to show me that they know that loping or cantering forward from a standstill requires their aid in creating impulsion. Judges should know that if the horse is to lope or canter on the left lead, the first muscle to be engaged is the right back muscle. Riders should show that they know this too, by engaging their seat bones to cue the movement. Rising out of the saddle is a major fault.

Impulsion is the key to all of the horse's movements, but the amount of impulsion needed to produce a lope or canter depends on the individual horse. Good riders should be able to feel how much impulsion the horse they are riding needs.

The next degree of difficulty depends on where I choose to stand to judge in relation to the other horses in the line. If I stand a considerable distance away, the space between me and the next horse is wide and thus easier to pass through. If I stand close, however, the opening narrows and a steadier, more controlled ride would be necessary to pass through smoothly.

Another trouble spot occurs after riders have gotten onto the proper lead. If they then are content simply to coast along, they may well find the horse quitting or backing off when it has to pass the other horses in line. Then, approaching the rail, the horse will tend to focus on the activity there and back off again, requiring riders to maintain impulsion all the way to the end of the test.

In the tests I use, riders cannot coast through or rely on coaching. The rider who truly understands how the horse functions and who is able to execute the different maneuvers with soft, invisible aids usually ends up on top. As I've said, every equitation test should have a purpose, which both judge and rider should know. And all of the different requirements should be a means of letting riders demonstrate their ability as horsemen.

THE RIGHT PROPORTIONS

The equitation division is divided into two distinct sections: Western horsemanship and hunt seat equitation. In equitation classes, judges must remember that only the rider is being judged; therefore, any horse that is suitable for a particular style of riding and is capable of performing the required routine is acceptable. Judges cannot afford the luxury of their own preference as to color, type, or age, as long as the horse is suitable to the rider.

Using Western horsemanship (rail only portion) as an example and realizing that it is to be judged on seat and hands as the basics (with equal emphasis on each), we can then break this system down further on a relative value basis.

The seat should be close to the saddle, which is impossible if a rider is not communicating with the horse using the aids. The hands, of equal value with the seat, must be the "telegraph line" between the rider's desires and the horse's mouth. Let's say that hands coupled with seat equal 100 percent.

Riders are judged on the rail at the walk, jog trot, and lope both ways of the ring. A rider's body should appear relaxed, comfortable, and flexible, which is the ideal, or 100 percent, of that phase.

I always advocate a positive system of judging, that is, finding the best rider in the class and not the least lousy. From that standpoint, starting at the walk, let's examine the rail portion of a class and its perspectives, using the idea of percentages to establish value.

Although the walk should be a relatively easy gait to perform, too often judges overlook it and use it only as a means to get from one gait to another. The walk has special emphasis in its relationship to the jog and the lope, and should receive 30 percent of the total score. For example, if a rider can execute the walk by being relaxed and comfortable in motion with the horse, he or she achieves the full assigned value. But on the other hand, if a rider constantly must check back, or drop behind the motion, or wiggle the legs back and forth to make the horse move, he or she receives less than 30 percent.

Judges must take into consideration what a rider does to get a horse to walk properly. If a horse breaks for a step or two and the rider does what is needed to get it to resume the walk, he or she would not be penalized. If this action became excessive or frequent, however, the rider would be heavily penalized because of lack of control.

The jog trot comes next and must be judged during the transition period as well. In fact, the most important part of the jog is when the rider gives the aid—too much, too little, or just right—adding up to 20 percent of the total judging picture. Horsemen know the jog is the easiest gait to perform after this transition, so the major percentage should be assigned to the transition and not to the rider's form as he or she jogs around.

The lope, like the walk, has special emphasis, and it should get the largest share, or 40 percent of the score. The emphasis is on getting into the lope on the correct lead, then maintaining the lope in position, along with speed of gait and control.

Thus, in rail work, the walk should account for a possible 30 percent, the jog-trot, 20 percent, and the lope, 40 percent, with the percentages demonstrating the relative difficulty of performing each gait. The remaining 10 percent is for the rider's attire. This adds up to 100 percent if all is perfect in an equitation class performed on the rail only.

The degree of difficulty is the basis for the relative values no matter what judges ask for. If individual tests are called for, their value relative to the rest of the work should be established at the outset.

For instance, in classes where riders work the rail and perform an individual routine, the rail work would account for 40 percent and the individual portion for 60 percent of the score. You could take the rule book and list the tests and assign a percentage of difficulty to each one and relate it to the overall judging practice, thus eliminating the chance of the whole class being judged on one item. The total should be 60 percent.

In rail work, the walk makes up 12 percent of the score, the jog, 7 percent, the lope, 18 percent, and the rider's attire, 3 percent. The total is 40 percent of the entire judging picture, or a ratio of 60 percent individual performance to 40 percent group performance. This is the proper difficulty factor ratio in this type of class.

Classes judged entirely on individual performance can be adjusted more easily because, for example, each fence jumped in hunt seat equitation over fences is a separate item and can be viewed as such.

There is a narrow line, though, between judging in proportion and getting into the predicament of "not seeing the forest for the trees." I am not advocating that judges keep a running numerical total on each phase the rider performs. Rather, judges, trainers, parents, and exhibitors should place the same emphasis on the same parts of the class, using the overall picture to determine the winner.

We all need to look at a performance with the same perspective. But how can we do that until we establish what that perspective is and agree to follow it?

SHOWMANSHIP

Showmanship, as easy as it may look to some, requires a perception of many subtleties that separate good showmen from those whose knowledge of their horse is limited. Judges understand that exhibitors must show their horse to its best advantage, not just be mechanical and move from side to side without a reason.

You don't need a horse with great athletic ability or ideal conformation to do well in showmanship. What is necessary to succeed is a systematic approach and attention to detail. This begins at home by working out a program that includes being on the alert for errors and correcting them subtly when they happen. The competitor should have the ability to work patiently and carefully toward a performance that's as flawless as possible.

Over the years I've seen showmen or handlers who show themselves far more than they show the horse. They wiggle and grin a phony smile, overdo eye contact by always looking at the judge (no matter what the horse is doing), are stiff and rigid with painted-on clothes, and give the appearance, as they jump or sashay back and forth, of trying to dance with the judge (or horse).

Meanwhile, the judge walks around the horse trying to avoid this horizontal "jumping jack," only to find the horse standing out of position with its ears back and looking dull. Sometimes handlers actually turn their heads all the way around, owllike, to keep looking at the judge, and run into the horse in front of them.

Eye contact is fine when used properly. However, use of the eyes also includes looking where one is going, not where one has been. The basic idea of a showmanship class is to show the *horse* to its best advantage, whatever that advantage may be. You should know and understand your horse's good points and its weaknesses, then be able to accentuate the finer points and camouflage the weaker ones.

Promptness is a must, and a positive attitude is a big plus in your favor. Just being a robot—smile, walk up, stop, smile, point a toe at a foot, smile again, a "Yes, sir," and trot back to the line—is not going to win an award.

Even though the horse is merely a prop to show the ability of the showman, the class is judged on the aptness to fit and show in a halter class. The horse's appearance—condition, grooming, hair, coat, mane and tail, hooves and trimming—are all taken into consideration. The tack should be neat, clean, and in good repair. The exhibitor's attire should be neat, clean, and suitable to the horse being shown.

The horse should be led at an alert walk with the handler on the left side holding the shank in the right hand near the halter. (How near depends on the particular horse being shown.) The rest of the shank should be held in the left hand safe and neat (not tightly coiled), and the horse should lead readily at the walk or trot.

Judges should inspect each horse individually; handlers should be sure judges get a clear view of the horse's action by allowing sufficient lead for the horse to move freely and in a straight line.

Straightness, or lack of straightness, is the cause of most showmanship problems. If the horse isn't straight from head through shoulders through hips, this will manifest itself down the line, resulting in poor turns, crooked tracking, stopping at the wrong places, and lining up at an angle.

Straightness problems can begin with your equipment. The halter is a key part of the control mechanism, so it has to fit well. Several options are available for shank attachment and length, among others, depending on handler preference.

When posing the horse, stand toward the front, facing the horse, but not directly in front of it. Safety is a must. Even if the rules did not describe the danger zones, it is important to be aware of them. As one judge told me, "The reason my front teeth are false is that I stood right where some of the youths stand—directly in front—but it only took once, and a large dental bill, to know that was enough."

Keep an eye on the judge, know where he is, but don't overdo it. Show the horse, not yourself. Don't crowd other exhibitors when side by side or head to tail. Be natural, don't overshow or fuss at your horse; be courteous, spontaneous, and, by all means, keep showing your horse until the entire class has been placed. Be prepared in the warm-up area, don't be late, don't forget your number or any of those other small items so clearly seen by the judge.

When posing the horse, stand toward the front, facing the horse, but not directly in front of it.

While the only requirement regarding attire is that it be "suitable," you must understand what this means. Chaps and spurs are pieces of riding equipment, not halter-showing equipment; they therefore have no place in showmanship classes.

You must remember to keep your horse's attention during the class. The length of time a horse stands has a bearing on how easily it will be led, especially if it's allowed to go to sleep while others are being shown. More than likely it will "hang up" when asked to move out. The key is to pay attention and prepare ahead; in other words, *act* and not react.

I'd like to share a couple of principles from a judging standpoint:

- Think about your horse *all the time;* constantly ask yourself if you're doing what your horse needs you to do with *your* body so it can do whatever is asked of it with *its* body.
- Show your horse to *its level of training;* don't push it to give more. Ask only for what it's capable of doing. You'll both keep a lot calmer and your chances of placing will increase rather than leaving you with no ribbon at all.

These basic principles need to become part of your thinking. It's not enough to be concerned only with your part of the performance. You have to think about what your horse needs you to do with *your* body in preparation

A judge's assessment begins at the ingate—the handler should make sure the horse is straight from poll to tail so its first stride is forward into the arena.

Then, when the horse begins the turn with its right foreleg to walk around the arena, its body will be straight and balanced. (The handler should be between the horse's head and shoulders.)

ENTERING THE ARENA CORRECTLY

As the turn is completed, the horse should be ahead of the handler.

ENTERING THE ARENA CORRECTLY

for each movement you want it to do with *its.* The position of your shoulders, rigidity of your arms, and timing of your movements make its job easier, harder, or next to impossible.

Your horse can't give you more than its training level allows. Just about any horse *can* do well at showmanship, but only with lots of time and practice. If your horse is green and doesn't lead up promptly, be patient and work at *its* pace. You'll do a lot better if you take your time, stay in position, and keep it as straight as you can than if you hurry it and it goes crooked or tosses its head.

Horses come in all sizes. A smaller horse that's short-coupled, short-backed, shorter everything usually is easier to keep straight. There's more of an art to making a bigger, taller, longer-backed horse travel as tight and look as straight as a smaller one. But don't let that scare you. It simply means you'll need to spend more time at home getting to know what "straight" looks and feels like and put more emphasis on departures and stops.

Keep in mind that showmanship isn't a class where you want to call attention to your horse's size; the main objective is to impress the judge with unity or how well the horse and handler go together. The better matched you are in size, of course, the easier that impression is to create.

Judges' assessments of you begin before you enter the arena, when they nod to you at the ingate, signaling you to lead your horse in. They take into

*By omitting a straight stride forward before turning right,
the handler will be facing the horse instead of straight ahead.
Both horse and handler are out of position.*

*This results in a poorly executed turn—the horse's elevated head
and awkward-looking legs show it's lost its balance.*

ERRORS IN TURNING

consideration how well you lead, maneuver corners, line up, stop, set up, and turn around while executing the prescribed pattern.

The days of a standard showmanship pattern are long gone. Today's judges are permitted and encouraged to devise patterns (depending on the level of the show) that truly test the handler's ability. Although it is impossible to cite every pattern you might encounter, I'll take you through Pattern One and give you tips that can lead to a winning performance.

In many ways, Pattern One resembles the old standard showmanship pattern: You enter the arena counterclockwise, line up side by side, and lead your horse out to the judge for the individual work. This contains three elements, however, that make it harder than it appears on paper.

The first is the requirement to trot, rather than walk, out of the lineup toward the judge. The trot requires more impulsion than the walk, but if you try to get that impulsion by taking off at a trotting pace and pulling on your horse's head, you'll lose points for making excess contact with the lead shank. The best way to handle the situation is to wake up your horse while the previous horse is working, then take one step at the walk before asking for the trot.

The next item of difficulty in this pattern is the 360-degree pivot to be executed before the setup. Most people are used to setting up as soon as they reach the judge, so you need to rehearse the pattern thoroughly in your mind in order to avoid a memory error—an error that I often see when this pattern is called for.

Then, because you'll be making the 360-degree turn right in front of the judge, with the setup to follow, there will be no room for error when making the pivot. If the horse shifts its pivot foot to the right in an attempt to stay balanced through the maneuver, its hindquarters will be too far to the right and off to one side of the judge once it's completed. To correct this, don't aim your horse for the middle of the judge. Instead, aim at the judge's right leg (which will be on your left as you approach). This will compensate for being off center.

The final tricky part of this pattern occurs after making the 180-degree turn to walk back through the lineup. If you aren't careful, you may find yourself on "autopilot" and taking off at a trot; or, once your horse has been to a few shows, find that it's anticipated trotting back to the lineup before you did. To prevent this, remind yourself to make a split-second pause after closing the pivot, take a relaxing breath, and tell yourself "walk." By putting the walk message into your own mental computer, you'll translate the slow-down message, via your own body language, to your horse.

To be a winner, practice the following patterns—one, two, three, and four—at home with a partner acting as judge and pay careful attention to the kinds of details just mentioned.

Arriving in the lineup, the handler should face forward until all four of the horse's feet have stopped, then quietly step back to get into position.

When the setup is completed, the handler should step back and slide the hand a few inches down the shank.

To make a smooth turn into the lineup, the handler should first angle the horse slightly toward the rail for one stride (keeping head and shoulders straight).

IN AND OUT OF THE LINEUP

While turning, the handler should press the right hand forward to maintain momentum and stay in position between the horse's head and shoulders. These subtle moves will enable the horse to follow through with a smooth, rounded turn.

When leaving the lineup, the handler should face forward, cluck, and push the right hand forward.

This enables horse and handler to step off together.

IN AND OUT OF THE LINEUP

THE QUARTER METHOD

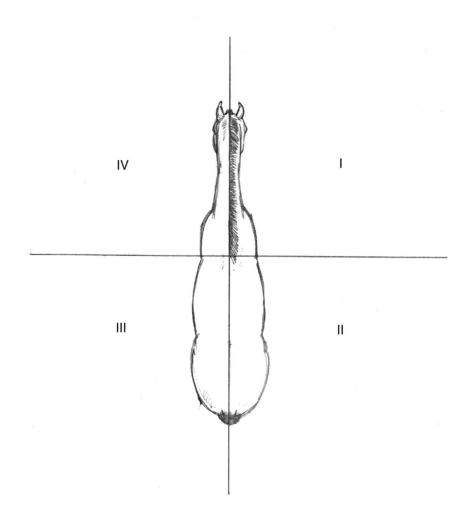

THE QUARTER METHOD:

The following suggested guidelines are meant to serve as an illustration of movement around the horse while showing in Showmanship at Halter and are for the exhibitor's information. Imaginary lines bisect the horse into four equal parts. (Note: The quadrants will be numbered I, II, III, IV for ease of identification.) One line runs across the horse just behind the withers. The other imaginary line runs from head to tail. When the judge is in I, the handler should be in IV. As the judge moves to II, handler should move to I. When the judge moves to III, the handler moves to IV. As the judge moves up the horse to IV, the handler returns once more to I. This method is based on safety as the handler can keep the horse's hindquarters from swinging toward the judge should the horse become fractious.

PATTERN ONE

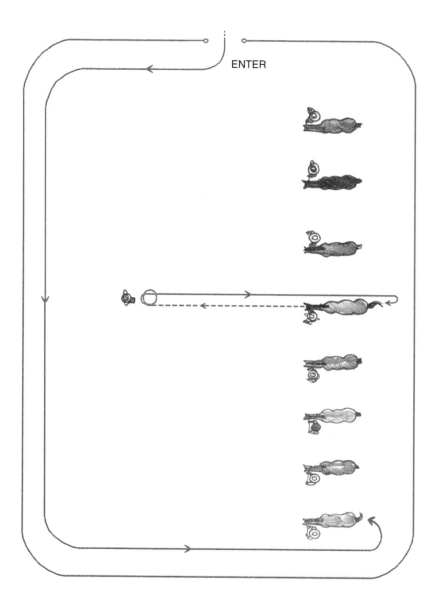

ENTER

1. Enter arena counterclockwise and line up side by side.
2. Trot out of line to judge.
3. Do 360-degree pivot.
4. Set up for inspection.
5. D0 180-degree pivot and walk back through line.
6. Do 180-degree pivot and set horse up in original position.

PATTERN TWO

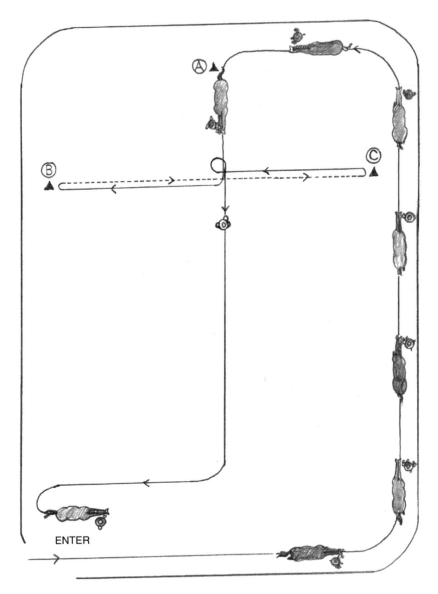

1. Enter arena counterclockwise and line up head to tail on the rail.
2. Begin from halt at Cone A; walk halfway to judge and do 90-degree pivot to face Cone B.
3. Walk to Cone B; do 180-degree pivot to face Cone C.
4. Trot to Cone C; do 180-degree pivot to again face Cone B.
5. Walk halfway between Cones B and C; do 270-degree pivot (three-quarter turn) to face judge.
6. Walk to judge and set up for inspection.
7. Line up side by side on opposite side of arena.

PATTERN THREE

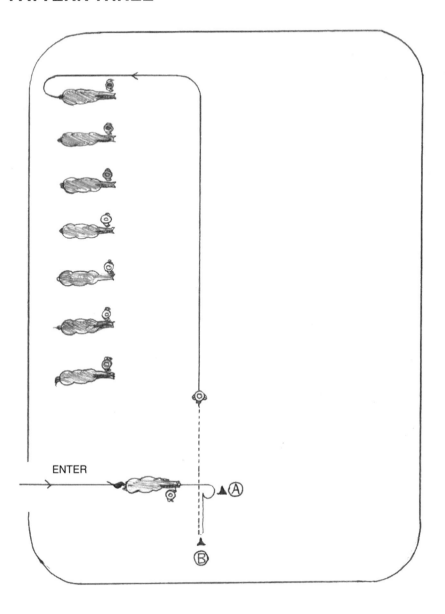

ENTER

1. Enter from arena gate at judge's signal.
2. Walk to Cone A; do 270-degree pivot (three-quarter turn) to face judge.
3. Back horse to Cone B.
4. Trot to judge.
5. Set up for inspection.
6. Take position in lineup.

PATTERN FOUR

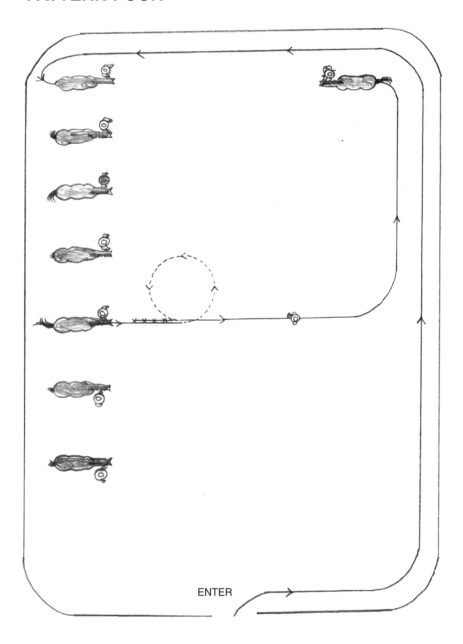

ENTER

1. Enter from arena counterclockwise and line up side by side.
2. Walk out of line halfway to judge.
3. At halfway point, trot a circle to the left.
4. Close the circle, halt, and back four steps.
5. Walk remaining distance to judge; set up for inspection.
6. When excused, form new line on opposite side of arena.

WESTERN HORSEMANSHIP

Horsemanship or equitation is an advanced form of communication. At the competitive level it means showing the judges which riders are capable of having their horses perform any task requested using invisible aids. It sounds simple, but even on the basis of limited criteria, Western horsemanship can be a controversial subject. The rule book says Western horsemanship is to be judged as follows: "Riders will be judged on seat, hands, ability to control and show horse, appointments of horse and rider, and suitability of horse to rider. Results as shown by the performance of the horse are NOT to be considered more important than the method used in obtaining them."

Even though the basics are the same, there are as many different styles of riding as there are trainers and teachers. Style seems to vary with the part of the country in which you happen to be competing. It is *style,* then, that leads to controversy, not horsemanship.

Several years ago, horsemanship or equitation was based on sending riders into the arena on push-button horses. They were told to remain in one position; not to move or do anything but stay on the rail, walk, jog, lope, and if they made all the leads, they would come out on top. This is not equitation today, however. What judges look for now is the best rider with the best

A rider should never look stiff, but should be straight, square, and graceful, presenting a composite picture to the judge.

(most suitable) horse, working together as one. "Most suitable horse" means the one that fits the rider best, making him or her look good, not the best halter or conformation horse. While the horse is not being judged per se, it is the vehicle used to show off the rider's talents, whatever they may be.

As riders enter the ring, they present a composite picture to the judge, coordinating all body parts to make a free, natural, quiet picture. Riders should never look stiff but should be straight, square, and graceful.

Certain basic positions must be adhered to.

HEAD

The rider's head should be alert, lifted in line and in balance with the body. It should never be carried, turned, or tipped down. Eyes should focus in front and thirty to forty feet ahead of the horse with the freedom to look around. Some eye contact with the judge is acceptable.

SHOULDERS

Shoulders should be square, with one hand holding the reins over the horn. There is a decided tendency to carry the shoulder (holding the reins) forward, but this can be eliminated by a slight turn at the waist to line up the shoulders. Shoulders should never be carried back or hunched.

ARMS

The upper arms should fall freely down the shoulders toward the hip bones. Never let arms be tight against the body or allow them to fly with the horse's motion. The forearm, holding the reins, should be parallel to the ground. All handling should be done with hand and wrist and by bending the elbow. The bend in the elbow is of paramount importance, as this provides a cushion for the horse's mouth. The off forearm should be bent to conform with the angle of the upper body and thigh.

HANDS

There are two ways of holding the reins depending on whether split or romal reins are used. Split reins are held running across the palm of the hand from the index finger to the little finger. One finger may be between the reins. The ends of the reins are left hanging on the near side of the horse. If the finger is not between the reins, the rein end must be on the off side. The position of the hand not holding the reins is optional. With romal reins, the hand is carried in a loose fist, with the reins running from the little finger out over the thumb. The second knuckles of the fingers are pointed toward the horse's ears with the thumb up and folded on the knuckles. The reins then run across the body and are gripped by the off hand, which is held on the thigh. Reins should be carried immediately above or slightly in front of the saddle horn.

There are two ways of holding the reins.

ROMAL REINS   SPLIT REINS

Avoid holding the free   *Good position for*   *Carrying the free hand*
hand stiffly in a fist.   *the free hand.*   *down tends to throw the*
shoulders out of balance.

Even though the position of the hand not holding the reins is optional,
some positions are better than others.

| Hand is too high. | This is a fairly good hand position except the thumb is pointing down and the hand should be raised slightly. | Hand is too low and casual for horsemanship. |

| CORRECT | INCORRECT | INCORRECT |
| Hand forms a straight line with the arm, thumb level. | Wrist cocked up, looking unnatural and tense. | Wrist cocked down, looking loose and casual. |

Hand should remain above horn as much as possible; appear light, relaxed, and quiet.

HAND POSITIONS

BACK

The back should be straight, not stiff, and preferably with no arch or slump.

HIPS

The hips should be directly under the shoulders, and the hipbone should be tilted slightly forward. The hip motion should never be from side to side. This kind of motion, which is found at the jog, causes the saddle to move on the horse's back and can produce soreness in the horse's loin area.

SEAT

The seat should be deep and always in the center of the saddle. The rider should never sit on his or her tail bone. The rider's spine always should be in line with the horse's spine.

THIGHS

The thighs should be kept firmly against the saddle with relaxed contact, but no rolling or rigid gripping. The thigh angle should be more downward than forward.

LOWER LEGS

The lower leg placement is extremely important to the balance of the entire body. The legs should hang down straight below the knee from a side view. From a front view, they should hang naturally away from the horse. The lower leg should never dangle, be spraddled wide or thrust forward. Too great of an effort to hold legs too close to the horse results in faulty turned ankles, incorrectly placed foot pressure, loss of knee contact, and looseness of thighs.

FEET

The ball of the foot should make contact with the stirrup for the entire width of the boot sole. Pressure should not be put on the ball of the foot but on the heel, so the heel will be down. Feet should be held naturally, neither extremely turned in or out.

RIDER'S MOTION AND POSITION AT GAITS

The walk may be the most important gait executed during a class. Remember, first impressions are important when entering a show ring. Any motion or equitation fault evident at the walk will be much more pronounced at any of the faster gaits. At the jog trot, keep a slight up-and-down motion to overcome the side-to-side tendency produced by the diagonal two-beat gait. When loping, a rider must deal with the problem of the thrust from the horse's hindquarters. The body must be kept with the

Rider in center of saddle with rider's and horses's spines in alignment.

CORRECT POSITION

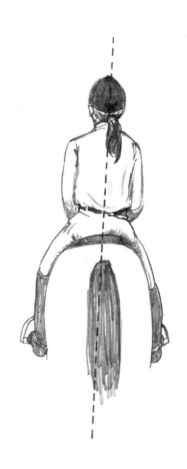

Crooked back, out of balance with horse.

RIDER LEANING OFF CENTER

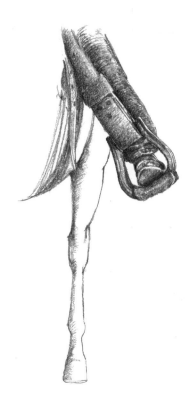

The ball of the foot should make contact with the stirrup with the entire width of the boot sole . . .

As opposed to putting more weight on the inside of the stirrup.

horse's motion. If not, the rider's upper body will tend to bump back and forth. There is a natural tendency for the inside leg to drift forward and put the rider off center in the saddle.

USE OF AIDS

The proper use of aids (hands, body, legs, and feet) cannot be over-emphasized. Each aid must be used subtly but effectively. The hands must be quiet, with no jerky motions, yet must be solid and flexible. The hands should remain above the horn as much as possible. The hands should always appear light, relaxed, and quiet. The only leg motion should be to apply slight calf pressure, when necessary, to promote impulsion. The feet should be used behind the cinch only. Keeping the leg no farther forward than the cinch shortens the distance the foot must travel to apply pressure to the horse. The heel should not be raised when using the foot as an aid. The body weight should be distributed properly to be in balance with the horse. Weight distribution should be adjusted gracefully and lightly.

These basic principles are all fairly well and uniformly accepted, but *style* is something else. Each rider is different and each horse equally individual, and therefore they must be treated differently. A six-foot-tall, slender rider will not be mounted in exactly the same position as a four-foot, chubby rider, and they in turn will not be in the same exact position on different horses. In horsemanship, the basics must be combined in a way that makes rider and horse one symmetrical unit. This is what judges look for as each rider enters the arena. It's a style or an unstyle (as previously stated) that works for the individual rider being judged.

Judges silently address each rider as he or she enters the ring. Does the rider look presentable? Does the saddle fit? Is the attire correct and fitted? Are horse and rider a unit? If yes, these things will be conspicuous at first glance; by the same token, the sloppy dressed, overtacked, under- or overmounted rider will elicit negative answers.

When it comes to show ring attire, think about the whole picture, with neatness and simplicity being basic. Fit is mandatory for clothes, but don't confuse fit with cost; a dart, tuck, or letting out can do wonders. Chaps should fit properly and be neither too long nor too short. The hat should be shaped and kept nice. Boots should fit and be polished. Riders also should know the proper way to wear or carry their accoutrements.

Fit is not limited to clothes. The bridle should fit the horse and the bit should fit in the mouth and be adjusted properly. The saddle should fit the rider and the horse and be cleaned regularly. All of these simple, often neglected items separate the ne'er-do-well from the true showman. It's difficult for judges to award a blue ribbon to someone who has had his or her hat on backward for the whole class; or spurs on upside down; or rope or riata wadded up like a clothesline; or number whittled down in size so it's illegible; or no number at all. If the rider takes the time to coordinate the attire and tack to flatter the horse and not overshadow it, judges will take note.

After judges have given the riders the once-over, they will be asked to work individually, performing any of the maneuvers the judges feel are necessary to determine the riders' horsemanship ability. Any of the following may make up the test:

- Walk, jog trot, lope or gallop in a straight line, curve or circle.
- Stop.
- Back.
- Turn on the haunches, spin and rollback, turn on the forehand.
- Side pass.
- Simple change of lead through the trot, walk, or halt, in a straight line, figure-eight or any other pattern.
- Flying change of lead in a straight line, figure-eight, or any other pattern.
- Countercanter.
- Dismount and mount.
- Ride without stirrups.

While performing the individual maneuvers, judges should reward riders for precision and position. A horse should work with some speed, but the rider always must give the impression of being in complete control. Showing in this phase of equitation should be accomplished with promptness, dispatch, and a true knowledge of how the horse reacts and what is necessary to get it to perform. The object is to have the horse do the routine perfectly while the rider looks good doing it; along with a few other ingredients such as self-discipline, confidence, determination, and poise, these make up the winning recipe.

Judges will use these individual tests to determine the top riders to be called back for the final phase, which is working on the rail.

After all riders have entered the arena for the rail work, usually at the walk, normally they proceed into the jog. This transition period, the period between any two gaits, is the most important period of showing. We'll assume the appearance is perfect, the horse is turned out just as well as any of the others, and the judges really took notice of the overall picture. This transition period is where riders must show their abilities. If they overaid the horse, such as too much leg or spur, or if they don't aid enough, it all comes to light during the transition periods.

After the horse is into the jog, then it's easy for riders to get back into the basic position. But during the change from the walk to the jog, the real test of how the rider and horse work together becomes apparent. The horse also either helps or hinders effectiveness. If it tends to fight the rider, it looks rough; if it cooperates with the rider, it looks smooth.

Another question judges ask themselves as the class proceeds around the ring: Are the riders in front of the motion, behind it, or right with it? To be in balance with the horse, a rider should be in motion with it. As I said before, all horses do not go alike, and judges must take this into consideration. A heavy-going horse with its hea.d down can't be ridden the same as a high-headed, wandering type of horse. The rider must find the balance point of any given horse and ride the horse accordingly, maintaining that horse's particular motion or balance.

Getting into or keeping out of trouble also shows up during the transition period. Judges must take into consideration a rider's ability to adjust his position in the ring if he is in a crowd. Does he get out of the crowd? If he's by himself, does he stay there?

The next transition will be into the lope or back to the walk and then into the lope. Whichever, it is a transition nevertheless, and good points and bad are again put to test.

There is one other very important ingredient of the successful horseman-ship or equitation rider, and that is attitude. After everything else is taken care of, this single attribute will be the deciding factor. Attitude is that indefinable quality, both good and bad, that surfaces as the rider performs. The right attitude is the basic ingredient of a champion. There is a big difference between being knowledgeable about a sport and winning in that sport.

CHAPTER VI

Miscellaneous Events

BARREL RACING

THERE'S a lot more to barrel racing than running around three barrels in a cloverleaf pattern. It's far more difficult than most people think. Speed event horses have more style now, and besides speed, they have to be able to turn handily. Yes, barrel racing has changed, and undoubtedly it will continue to do so.

No longer is there the image of the pig-tailed girl kicking and charging her horse around three barrels in an arena, being referred to, almost jokingly, as a "can chaser." Barrel racers now make money—lots of it. And this event is not just for women anymore, as men are becoming more involved and openly competing.

This speed event is a big draw on the rodeo circuit as well as at horse shows. It takes a highly trained horse to maneuver around each barrel without knocking it down and then be able to turn on the speed to cross the finish line. Scores are within fractions of a second from one another, and any slight deviation from the pattern can be costly to a rider.

The key is having the horse broke. Notice this horse and rider are in balance—the rider is not leaning into the barrel.

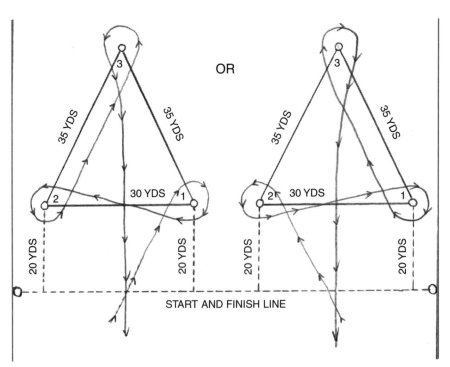

BARREL RACING PATTERN

The arena must be measured accurately for the barrel course, including the start and finish line. At a signal from the starter, the contestant will run to barrel number I, pass to the left of it, and complete an approximately 360-degree turn around it; then run to barrel number 2, pass to the right of it, and complete a slightly more than 360-degree turn around it; then run to barrel number 3, pass to the right of it, and do another approximately 360-degree turn around it; then sprint to the finish line, passing between barrel number I and 2.

The barrel course also may be run to the left, taking barrel number 2 first (passing on the right), then barrel number I (passing on the left), then barrel number 3 (passing on the left), followed by the final sprint to the finish line. Knocking a barrel down carries a five-second penalty, and failure to follow the course is cause for disqualification. A hat or helmet must be worn while the exhibitor is in the arena or a five-second penalty will be assessed.

Successful barrel racers need well-trained horses that enjoy the event. Everybody wants to see how fast a horse can run the pattern, but speed is the biggest mistake in training. The horse needs to be broke and learn to handle first. Speed is the last thing that is added once the horse is doing things correctly.

Some people will take a horse straight from the racetrack and go right to the barrels. The unbroke colt doesn't have the foundation from which to work. If trainers use force and intimidation on horses, they may end up with thirty-day wonders, but those horses will never reach the goals that their physical and mental abilities are capable of.

The key is having the horse broke prior to going to the barrels, followed by quality time on the barrels. The result is a barrel horse that can react in the middle of any competition, regardless of arena size or ground conditions, one that will respond to a rider's commands and react without compromising its athletic potential. The horse should then last a lifetime.

POLE BENDING

"Bending" back and forth through a line of six upright poles set twenty-one feet apart, at top speed, is an excellent test of a horse's speed and maneuverability. The first end turn after the run-down is the most critical and establishes the rhythm for the rest of the run.

The judging of speed events is done primarily by timers, either electronic or by hand. If the timing is done by hand, at least two watches must be used and the average of the watches is the official time. Even though time is the deciding factor, an official judge must preside over these classes to see that there are no rule infractions.

Pole bending has a prescribed pattern that consists of six poles set in a straight line and a start and finish line. The contestant must run to the far end,

The first end turn after the run-down is the most critical. The horse must plant a pivot foot deep and sharply turn around the pole. This gives it the impulsion (forward) to run through the poles.

around the pole, serpentine back through the six poles, circle the sixth pole, zigzag back again to the first pole and around it, and then head for the finish line pronto. A horse has the option of starting either to the left or right of the first pole and then run the remainder of the pattern accordingly.

Similar penalties apply to barrels and poles: Knocking over a pole carries a five-second penalty, and failure to follow the course is cause for disqualification. Also, not wearing a hat or helmet while in the arena results in a five-second penalty.

Pole bending isn't reining. To make a good run, you have to use your body, hips, and legs and move with the horse. You don't rein the horse through the pattern. Think of it in this manner: Poles are set in a straight line, and the two ends are points. The shortest distance between two points is a straight line. The straighter the horse is maneuvered through the sequence of poles, the quicker the time will be. By shifting your hips and using leg pressure to move its body, the horse will try to avoid the poles on its own. The straighter the horse threads through the poles, the quicker the run. This is where speed is gained and why control is important.

Probably one of the most vital aspects of being successful in any speed event is knowing your horse. That's why it's essential to spend a lot of time just riding

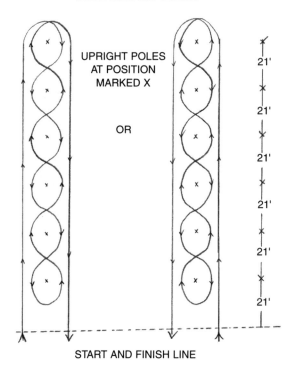

POLE-BENDING PATTERN

the horse. Learn its rhythm and how it reacts to certain situations. The bottom line is that the horse needs to be broke before being taken to a show. If the horse is physically capable of the maneuvers, after working a long time at home, and is technically correct on the pattern, then pole bending is fairly simple.

CUTTER AND CHARIOT RACING

Mention cutter and chariot racing and the first image that often comes to mind is of wild chariot races during the days of ancient Rome as depicted in the movie *Ben Hur*. However, modern American chariot racing had its beginning in the Rocky Mountain valleys of Colorado, Utah, Idaho, Wyoming, and Montana during the late 1920s and early 1930s as an offshoot of sled races.

The small farming communities were the hotbeds of cutter racing, with farmers and cowboys pitting their feed and hay wagon teams of draft horses against one another. Much of the country was mountainous and wooded, and the streets were the only straight and flat land around. The streets also provided saloons for the farmers and cowboys, places where they could stay warm, have a drink, and challenge another team.

*Two Quarter Horses harnessed together and running at more than
forty miles per hour are exciting to watch.*

There are usually two headers, one for each horse, when the gates open.

Eventually they traded their heavy sleds and draft horses for lightweight cutters and fast Quarter Horses. Wheels have replaced the cutters, and fast tracks equipped with starting gates have replaced the valley roads. Two Quarter Horses harnessed together and running at more than forty miles per hour are exciting, to say the least.

The sport is growing rapidly, both in interest and as a means of training a prospective runner. Many people use the chariot as the first step in training young horses for flat racing. To some cutters (participants) or charioteers, cutter racing is merely a hobby, something to do in the winter. To others, it's a profession.

Chariot teams compete over a 440-yard distance, commencing from a starting gate and ending when the nose of the leading horse of a team crosses the finish line. There are usually two headers—one for each horse—when the gates open. The headers make sure the horses are set and are standing straight. Officials for the race consist of a presiding steward and two associate stewards, a starter, a clerk of the scales, and three timers. If electronic timers are used, there must still be two hand timers. Safety requires that each driver keep the team in its lane of the track. If he or she doesn't, the driver can be penalized or disqualified.

Chariots are made of fiberglass and lightweight metal, and weigh approximately fifty to sixty pounds. The rules state that the weight of the cutter or chariot, harnesses, bridles, and driver must not be less than 275 pounds, or weight will be added. The chariot is equipped with bicyclelike tires, a long slender pole called the tongue, and doubletrees, which are the bars located in front.

To do well in chariot racing, it is necessary to have a good working knowledge of horses. Racing requires a lot of strength and control, and the training is very specialized.

The racing chariot is made of fiberglass and lightweight metal. The long slender pole is the tongue and the doubletrees are the white bars in front.

The hole man (bottom) has closed the gap between the pen and the fence; the wing man (far right) has positioned himself just off the wing of the pen; and the pusher (top) has begun to bunch and drive the cattle toward the pen.

The hole and wing men are funneling cattle toward the opening, while the pusher drives them in.

The pusher has driven the cattle into the pen, positioned himself at the opening of the pen, and called for time, stopping the run.

THE ACTUAL PENNING PROCESS

TEAM PENNING

Team penning traces its origins to ranch and feedlot work that cowboys have been performing on horseback for a century or more. It wasn't until after World War II, however, that it became a competitive event. Since the rules became more standardized across the country, most competitions require three riders to cut three head of cattle from a herd of around thirty and pen them in less than two minutes.

Each team penning differs slightly because there is no standard arena size, but all have the same basic layout. (See course design.) At one end is the cattle grouping area, where the herd is bunched. At the opposite end, about three-quarters of the distance down the arena, a pen is constructed. While the pen can be set up either on the left or right side of the arena, it must be sixteen feet away from the fence. A starting and foul line is drawn across the arena. Two flagmen are situated just outside the arena, one on the starting and foul line, and the other even with the opening of the pen.

After a team rides into the arena, the flagman at the starting line calls out when the cattle are bunched and the arena is ready. At this time, the riders begin to move toward the cattle. As the first horse's nose crosses the starting line, the flagman waves for time to begin and the team's designated number is called. This number, from 0 to 9, will be marked on three head of cattle that the team must cut out.

One, two, or all three riders will enter the herd and begin searching for their (numbered) cattle. Once they are found, they are quickly cut away from the herd and driven toward the pen at the opposite end of the arena. After the correct three cattle have been isolated, the riders, in some form or fashion, should drive them into the pen.

Once the cattle are safely penned, one rider raises a hand to call for time. At this instant, the flagman drops the flag, stopping the clock, then checks the cattle in the pen. The team may call for time with only one or two designated cattle. However, times with three correctly penned cattle will place above times on one or two. If undesignated cattle are penned, the team receives a no-time. Also, when time is called, all undesignated cattle must be on the cattle side of the foul line; if not, the team receives no-time. Finally, no more than four cattle can ever cross the foul line at one time. If this happens, the team will receive a no-time.

That's team penning, in a nutshell. In theory, it sounds simple enough, but with three riders, normally riding at high speeds, trying to cut three head of cattle from a herd of around thirty animals, all under the pressure of the stopwatch, things can get a little tricky. Therefore, it helps to develop a strategy before the run, using a little cowboy logic on the cattle, horses, and the run itself.

Team penning requires a horse that possesses both speed and intelligence,

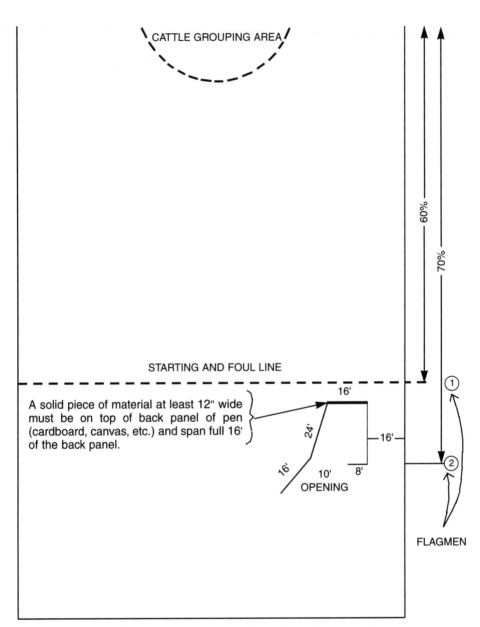

(Note: Pen can be placed on either side of arena)

COURSE DESIGN FOR TEAM PENNING

two characteristics that are trademarks of the Quarter Horse. It also calls upon its superb cattle-handling skills. Like polo, this is an event for people who enjoy riding, but world-class horsemanship isn't necessary. It has the excitement and "cowboy romance" of a cattle event, but expert cutting or roping skills are also unnecessary.

Team penning does take practice to get good at it, but even the most skilled, experienced team penners can get beaten by three novices with a little luck. The sole measure of success is a stopwatch. Eighty-year-old grandfathers have done it and so have five-year-old granddaughters.

But above all, it's fun! And that alone probably explains why team penning is one of the fastest-growing horse events in the country.

Appendix

TERMINOLOGY

Broodmare. Female horse kept for breeding.

Colors. Bay—reddish shades from tan to dark mahogany, with black mane and tail; Gray; Brown—various shades; Chestnut—shades from golden yellow to dark, reddish brown, with mane and tail the same color or lighter than the body; and Black.

Colt. Young male horse that is either sexually immature or has not yet reached the age of four.

Dam. Female parent of horse.

Filly. Young female horse under four years old.

Foal. Young animal that is still nursing.

Gelding. Castrated male horse.

Get. The entire progeny of a stallion.

Markings. Most common include stars, strips, or blaze faces, snip noses, and a white foot or more, or white stockings.

Prepotent. The unusual ability of an individual or strain to transmit its outstanding characteristics to offspring because of genetic strength for numerous traits.

Produce. The entire progeny of a mare.

Progeny. Offspring or descendants of a horse.

Sire. Male parent of a horse.

Stallion. Mature male horse kept for breeding.

Stud. A stallion used for breeding purposes.

Stud fees. Fees that the owner of a stallion collects when his stallion is bred with a mare.

Type. Strong and clearly marked similarity so that each is typical of the group.

Weanling. A young horse recently taken from its mother; takes food other than by nursing.

GLOSSARY OF STANDARD TERMS
DESCRIBING HUNTERS

Airy. An obstacle with large open spaces. Hunter fences should be made with plenty of material so they don't appear airy, as they can be quite deceptive to both horses and riders. "Airy" may also refer to the horse itself. If it overjumps and there is a lot of air and space between it and the obstacle.

Bascule. Good form; rounding the back while in arc over fence.

Chipping in. Taking off from a point too close to the fence; also called "too short."

Course pattern. A diagram that shows the arrangement of obstacles on a course, with arrows indicating direction travel and each obstacle numbered in the order in which it is to be taken. Although riders are not compelled to follow compulsory track, each obstacle must be jumped in the direction shown by arrows. The distances between fences, measured from the back of one obstacle to the front of the next, are figured on strides of approximately twelve feet. Patterns for each class must be posted at least one hour prior to the class.

Courtesy circle. A circle taken by exhibitors prior to beginning the course to establish hunting gait and pace, and again upon completion of the course, to demonstrate soundness at the trot on a loose rein. In order to save time, a judge may restrict the circle to a mandatory line, in which case a dotted line must be included in the diagram and announced one hour prior to the class, and a marker showing where the circle is to begin and end must be provided in the arena.

Cutting down. Landing closer on the far side of the fence than the takeoff point on the near side.

Dangling. Having one or more legs hanging down, rather than correctly folded, while jumping an obstacle.

Diving. Stretching the front legs far forward in an effort to clear the rails. Usually the result of taking off too far from the fence or with too much speed, diving is a severe, and potentially dangerous, form of reaching.

Drifting. Moving to either side of the obstacle, away from the center, when jumping.

Dropping a leg. Not keeping both front or both back legs up and evenly together.

Dwelling in the air. Something of an illusion; it is akin to throwing a ball in the air and watching it hang for a split second at the apex. When a horse dwells in the air, he seems to hang momentarily over the fence, the result of greenness, jumping quick but with no forward impulsion, a fear of taking off or landing, or lack of help from the rider.

Dwelling off the ground. Caused by a lack of momentum before takeoff, when the horse doesn't continue to the jump with an easy, free-flowing stride.

Element. One of the parts or components of a jump or obstacle. For instance, the top rail of an obstacle is also known as the top element.

Folds correctly. Forearms parallel to ground, or higher, with front legs flexed at knee, front feet close to elbows, and hindquarters neatly flexed and folded at hocks.

Flat back. Top line straight, rather than rounded; the horse doesn't use its back, head, neck, or shoulders.

Good arc. Takeoff and landing at points equidistant from the fence.

Ground line. A pole or rail placed on the ground approximately six inches in front of a jump. By further delineating the jump, a ground line helps the horse and rider judge the amount of effort required to clear the obstacle. Fillers such as brush boxes filled with shrubs or flowers are often used in lieu of a ground line.

Hand ridden; ridden in hand. Placed by rider's hands and legs, with stride and pace guided by subtle and sensitive aids from the rider.

Hard rub. Hitting a fence or standard with either the front- or hindquarters, and causing a loud knock or thud.

Head out. Carrying head to the outside and shoulder to the inside, instead of bending in the direction of travel.

Hunter pace. Usually twelve to fifteen miles per hour, but depends on size of course.

Impulsion. Thrust; related to collection and vertical motion, impulsion is created by the rider's legs asking the horse to go forward while his hands restrict the horse's speed.

In-and-out. A combination of two fences placed twenty-four to thirty-six feet apart, to be taken in either one or two strides. The first and second elements of an in-and-out are judged as two separate obstacles.

Inverted. A fault of jumping form, in which the back is hollowed, rather than rounded, and the head and hindquarters are higher than the back.

Iron. The term for stirrup.

Knockdown. Rail or top element of obstacle is displaced from original position, resulting in change of height or width of obstacle.

Lands in a heap. Instead of landing and going away from the fence in a smooth, flowing motion while maintaining cadence and gait, the horse stalls, literally plops down, and breaks up the rhythm upon landing.

Laying on side. Tilting of the body while in midflight over a fence, such that one side is inclined upward.

Line. Two or more fences placed in a row so as to be jumped consecutively without changing direction.

Loose form. Not folding legs tightly, but instead having more open legs while jumping, though not to the point of hanging or dangling.

Loss of forward movement. Failing to maintain a hand gallop or canter after beginning the course.

Overflexed. Breaks at withers or middle of neck, with head and neck below horizontal, and/or the face behind the vertical.

Overjumping. Jumping higher than necessary over an obstacle.

Oxer. A spread fence not exceeding three feet in width and usually consisting of rail fences placed together, one behind the other. Oxers in working hunter classes consist of two elements, and are measured from the front of the first element to the back of the second. Oxers must ascend, with the front element three to six inches lower than the back. Square oxers, those with elements of the same height, are prohibited in hunter classes, and are used only for jumpers.

Propping. An appearance by the horse of pushing back from the fence at takeoff. Though it's often a result of taking off from a point too close to the obstacle, horses may prop from any distance. A scopey horse may compensate for a takeoff point too close to the jump, but it also may become habit in horses that are allowed to slow down when approaching a fence.

Quick.   Coming off the ground quickly on takeoff, or a short, rapid stride or strides immediately before takeoff.

Reaching.   Front legs extended to clear the fence. Usually caused by taking off too far away from obstacle.

Refusal. Stopping in front of an obstacle, and then taking at least one step backward.

Runout. Evading or passing by an obstacle to be jumped; jumping an obstacle outside the limiting markers; horse or rider knocking down a flag, standard, wing, or other limiting marker without jumping the obstacle.

Safe jump. Horse jumps clean and in stride, with good arc and legs folded correctly.

Scope. The athletic ability required for jumping. The word is used similar to the term "cow," or cow sense, in cutting horses, though scope relates to physical ability, while cow is more a matter of mental ability.

Showing the horse an obstacle. Riding a horse up to an obstacle, without jumping it, in order to show the obstacle to the horse.

Skimming. Insufficient elevation. Also called "low belly," it is often associated with fast, flat jumps, or jumping with little effort.

Soft. The rider is able to ease off on the reins before a fence and at the finish; related to hand-ridden. Soft may also refer to an easy, or "soft," spot for takeoff.

Splitting. A horse having one leg forward and one back while jumping.

Strides. Theoretically based on twelve-foot increments. Strides are counted as the distance between jumps. (For example, sixty feet counts four strides, as in "1, 2, 3, 4, jump.")

Gate

Oxer

Ladder

Brick Wall

Vertical Post
and Rail

Picket

Coop

Riviera

Rolltop

Brush

In-and-Out

(One or two strides, 24 or 36 feet)

COMMON NAMES OF JUMPS

WORKING HUNTER — Basic Course

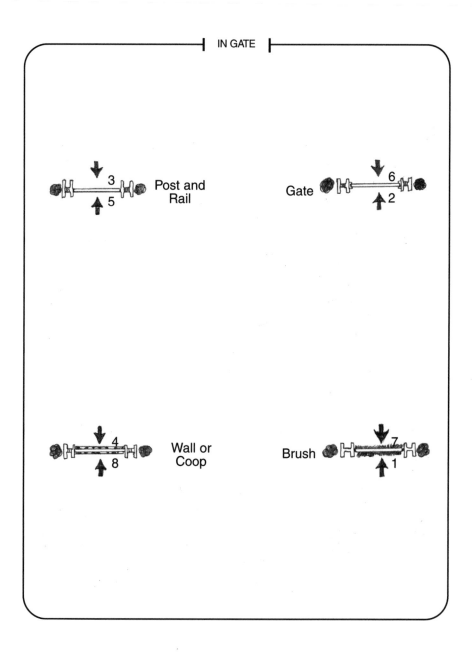

WORKING HUNTER — Modified Basic Course

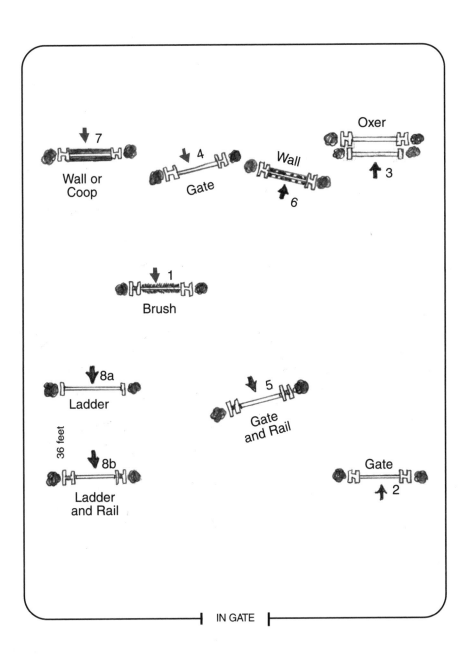

Takeoff box. A box with small shrubs or flowers that is placed on the ground in front of a jump, and used as part of a ground line.

Twisting. Body not traveling straight while going over fence, but instead twisting to either side in order for its legs to clear the obstacle.

Unsafe jump. A style or form of jumping that could result in a fall.

ROPING GLOSSARY

Barrier. Two pieces of cotton rope stretched end to end in front of the calf roping and heading horses, and tied together with string. This is used to ensure the calf or steer a head start. The barrier may be hand-pulled, or it may be released by the calf or steer as the animal reaches a certain point out of the chute. If the horse "breaks" the barrier, it is the piece of string holding the two ropes together that is broken.

Some shows may use an electronic barrier, where two "wands" are used across the front of the box instead of the rope. The calf or steer electrically trips the barrier, allowing the horse to come out of the box without "breaking the barrier."

Bow off. A horse that runs up to a calf and then begins to rate is said to have "bowed off."

Box; roping box. The part of the roping chute where the horse stands at the beginning of the run. The calf roping and the heeling boxes are the same, and are to the calf's or steer's right. The heading box is on the steer's left.

Climbing. A horse that is not rating, but is being held in position by the roper, often has his front end elevated and is reaching with his front legs, giving the impression of climbing.

Dally. In the team roping, both the header and the heeler must dally before the run is completed. That is, the roper must take at least one complete turn with his rope around his saddle horn.

Daylight. In calf roping, if the calf was jerked down, and is still down when the roper reaches it, the roper must get the animal up, or daylight it, before he can begin the tie.

Double-hock, single-hock. A steer with both hind legs roped is double-hocked; one leg is a single-hock.

Duck off. A heading horse sometimes anticipates the move to the left before the steer is set, and ducks off before the roper is ready to turn him.

Face. At the completion of the team roping run, the heading horse turns to the steer and the heeler. This is known as facing.

Figure-eight catch. An illegal head catch in the team roping. Any time the rope crosses itself on the steer's head, it is said to have figure-eighted, and that disqualifies the contestant in the heading.

Flank. In calf roping, most ropers go to the calf's left side, reach across the animal with their right hand, and catching the calf in its flank, lift it and throw it to the ground. This is known as flanking the calf.

Get out late. When the roper sits in the box too long and gives the calf or steer too much of a head start, he is said to have gotten out late or left late.

Half head. One of three legal catches in the team roping. The rope must be around one horn and then over the nose or around the neck of the steer.

Jerk line. Usually a piece of cotton rope with one end fastened to the bit, and the other end run through a pulley on the saddle horn, and then tucked into the belt of the roper. This is sometimes used in calf roping to make the horse back up as the roper is going to the calf. It is illegal in horse shows.

Keeper. Usually a small loop fastened to the noseband of the tie-down, through which the lariat rope is run. This may be used in addition to the neck rope, but not in place of, and it can be fastened only to the tie-down—never to the bridle or the bit.

Leg down. A roper that goes to the calf's right side, lifts the calf's right front leg, and pushes him over is said to have legged the animal down.

Neck catch. In heading, when the rope goes over the steer's head and draws up around its neck, that is known as a neck catch. One or more front legs in the loop is illegal.

Neck rope. A piece of rope tied around the horse's neck, through which the lariat rope used is run. This is a safety measure to prevent the horse from running off and dragging the calf after the roper has left the horse.

Piggin string. A short piece of rope or cord used to tie the calf's legs.

Quarter. A slight turn in either direction by the horse. When the heading horse sets the steer, he then quarters to the left.

Rate; rating. When a horse is traveling at the same speed as the calf or steer, and maintaining a particular position on that animal, he is said to be rating.

Score; scored. A horse is said to have scored well if his manners in the box are good. The head start the calf or steer is allowed is also known as the score.

Scotch. A horse scotches when he anticipates the rider's moves and attempts to stop before he is cued to do so. This is the same as set up.

Set. When the heading horse goes into the ground with his rear end, slowing the steer and turning its head to the left, the horse is said to have set the steer.

Set up. A horse sets up when he anticipates the rider's moves and attempts to stop before he is cued to do so. This is the same as scotch.

Slack. In calf roping, after the roper has roped the calf, he pulls his slack, which is the excess rope, and then he may pitch that slack toward the calf.

Tack collar. A breast collar with sharp protrusions on the underside. This is illegal in all roping events.

Tie-down. An abbreviated headstall usually made up of a noseband and a piece over the poll, with a strap from the noseband fastened to either the breast collar or the cinch under the horse's heart girth. This is used to keep the horse from raising his head excessively.

Index